Sayings Traditions in the *Apocryphon of James*

HARVARD THEOLOGICAL STUDIES
34

CAMBRIDGE, MASSACHUSETTS

Sayings Traditions in the *Apocryphon of James*

Ron Cameron

DISTRIBUTED BY
HARVARD UNIVERSITY PRESS
FOR
HARVARD THEOLOGICAL STUDIES
HARVARD DIVINITY SCHOOL

Sayings Traditions
in the
Apocryphon of James

Harvard Theological Studies 34

Second printing, 2004

Cover design: Gene McGarry
Cover art: First leaf of the *Apocryphon of James*, reproduced with permission of the Institute for Antiquity and Christianity, Claremont, California.

Library of Congress Cataloging in Publication Data

Cameron, Ron
Sayings traditions in the Apocryphon of James

(Harvard theological studies; no. 34)
Abstract of thesis (PhD.)—Harvard University, 1983
Bibliography: p.
Includes indexes.
1. Apocryphon of James—Criticism, Form.
2. Jesus Christ—Words. I. Title. II. Series.
BT1390.C29 1984 229′.806 84–45189
ISBN 0–6740–1789–7

This book is printed on acid-free paper

For Peggy

CONTENTS

PREFACE

The present volume is a slightly revised version of a doctoral dissertation presented to The Committee on the Study of Religion at Harvard University in September 1983. It is the product of several years of work inspired by lectures and guided by seminars in early Christian literature at Harvard Divinity School. My initial probing into the *Apocryphon of James* was supported by a generous grant from the Deutscher Akademischer Austauschdienst, which enabled me to use the facilities of the Orientalisches Seminar and the Institutum Judaicum at the University of Tübingen in the summer of 1978.

I would like to thank my dissertation advisors, Helmut Koester, George MacRae, and Albert Henrichs, for their continued support and constructive criticism. Dieter Georgi and John Strugnell read various drafts of this manuscript with their customary erudition and insight. This project would have been impoverished without them. Steve Skiles was always available to discuss problems of text, translation, and interpretation. Gary Bisbee and Joe Snowden deserve special credit for the exceptional care with which they prepared, at different stages, the final version of the manuscript. I am indebted to the staffs of the Andover-Harvard Theological Library and the Olin Memorial Library, Wesleyan University, for their untiring assistance. I am also grateful to the members of the Department of Religion at Wesleyan University for their encouragement during the past two years.

Unless otherwise noted, all translations of ancient texts and modern discussions are my own. References to the *Gospel of Thomas* are given in accordance with the conventional numbering of the saying(s) as well as by the page and line number(s) of the Coptic text. Thus, for example, *Gos. Thom.* 9: 34.3–13 would refer to saying no. 9, which is found on p. 34, lines 3–13 of the codex. Whenever the Coptic (Subachmimic) text of the *Apocryphon of James* is given, the numerous orthographic inconsistencies in the transcription are not standardized.

Finally, let me thank the editors of Harvard Theological Studies and Fortress Press for accepting this monograph as part of their series. And let me express a word of dedication and gratitude to Peggy Hutaff, who listened to my frustrations and exhilarations with equal good cheer. I would not have wanted to complete this project without her help.

Ron Cameron

Wesleyan University
Middletown, Connecticut
January 1984

ABBREVIATIONS

Abbreviations used in this volume for sources and literature from antiquity are the same as those used in Gerhard Kittel, ed., *Theological Dictionary of the New Testament*, vol. 1 (Grand Rapids: Eerdmans, 1964) xvi–xl. Some abbreviations are adapted from that list and can be easily identified. In addition, the following abbreviations have been used:

AB	Anchor Bible
Acts Pet. 12 Apost.	*Acts of Peter and the Twelve Apostles*
Acts Pil.	*Acts of Pilate*
Add Esth	The Additions to the Book of Esther
Ap. Jas.	*Apocryphon of James*
Ap. John	*Apocryphon of John*
1 Apoc. Jas.	*First Apocalypse of James*
Apoc. Paul	*Apocalypse of Paul*
Apoc. Pet.	*Apocalypse of Peter*
ASNU	Acta seminarii neotestamentici Upsaliensis
B	Bohairic
BAC	Biblioteca de autores cristianos
BAG	Walter Bauer, *A Greek-English Lexicon of the New Testament and Other Early Christian Literature* (2d ed.; rev. Frederick W. Danker; trans. William F. Arndt and F. Wilbur Gingrich; Chicago/London: University of Chicago Press, 1979).
BASP	*Bulletin of the American Society of Papyrologists*
BBB	Bonner biblische Beiträge
b. Ber.	*Babylonian Talmud, Berakot*
BDF	Friedrich Blass and Albert Debrunner, *A Greek Grammar of the New Testament and Other Early Christian Literature*, trans. and rev. Robert W. Funk (Chicago: University of Chicago Press, 1961).

BG (Codex) Berolinensis Gnosticus
BHTh Beiträge zur historischen Theologie
BJRL *Bulletin of the John Rylands University Library of Manchester*
BLE *Bulletin de littérature ecclésiastique*
b. Sanh. *Babylonian Talmud, Sanhedrin*
BZ *Biblische Zeitschrift*
BZNW Beihefte zur *Zeitschrift für die neutestamentliche Wissenschaft*
CChr Corpus Christianorum
1 Clem. *1 Clement*
2 Clem. *2 Clement*
CMC *Cologne Mani Codex*
Crum W. E. Crum, *A Coptic Dictionary* (Oxford: Clarendon, 1939).
CSCO Corpus scriptorum christianorum orientalium
CSEL Corpus scriptorum ecclesiasticorum latinorum
Cyprian
Testim. ad Quir. *Testimoniorum libri tres ad Quirinium*
Dial. Sav. *Dialogue of the Savior*
Dion. Hal. Dionysius of Halicarnassus
De Thuc. *De Thucydide*
DJD Discoveries in the Judaean Desert
ed. pr. *editio princeps*
Ep. Apost. *Epistula Apostolorum*
Ep. Pet. Phil. *Letter of Peter to Philip*
Epiph. Epiphanius
Pan. *Panarion*
Ancor. *Ancoratus*
EThL *Ephemerides theologicae lovaniensis*
F Fayyumic
frg. fragment
FRLANT Forschungen zur Religion und Literatur des Alten und Neuen Testaments
GCS Die griechischen christlichen Schriftsteller der ersten drei Jahrhunderte
Gen. Rab. *Genesis Rabbah*
Gos. Eg. *Gospel of the Egyptians*
Gos. Heb. *Gospel of the Hebrews*
Gos. Mary *Gospel of Mary*

Gos. Naz.	*Gospel of the Nazoreans*
Gos. Pet.	*Gospel of Peter*
Gos. Phil.	*Gospel of Philip*
Gos. Thom.	*Gospel of Thomas*
Gos. Truth	*Gospel of Truth*
Great Pow.	*Concept of our Great Power*
HDR	Harvard Dissertations in Religion
Herm.	*Hermas*
Mand.	*Mandate*
Sim.	*Similitude*
Vis.	*Vision*
HNT	Handbuch zum Neuen Testament
HTCNT	Herder's Theological Commentary on the New Testament
HTR	*Harvard Theological Review*
Hyp. Arch.	*Hypostasis of the Archons*
IDBSup	Keith Crim, ed., *Interpreter's Dictionary of the Bible*, Supplementary Volume (Nashville: Abingdon, 1976).
Iren.	Irenaeus
Adv. haer.	*Adversus haereses*
JAC	Jahrbuch für Antike und Christentum
JBL	*Journal of Biblical Literature*
Jerome	
Adv. Pelag.	*Adversus Pelagianos*
Comm. in Isa.	*Commentariorum in Isaiam*
De vir. inl.	*De viris inlustribus*
Epist. ad Hedyb.	*Epistula ad Hedybiam*
JTC	*Journal for Theology and the Church*
JTS	*Journal of Theological Studies*
LCL	Loeb Classical Library
LSJ	Henry George Liddell and Robert Scott, *A Greek-English Lexicon*, rev. Henry Stuart Jones (Oxford: Clarendon, 1940).
LThK	*Lexikon für Theologie und Kirche*
Luc.	Lucian
Hist. conscr.	*Quomodo historia conscribenda sit*
Man. Ps.	*Manichaean Psalm-Book*
Melito	
Pass. Hom.	*Passover Homily*
MeyerK	H. A. W. Meyer, Kritisch-exegetischer Kommentar über das Neue Testament

NedThTs	*Nederlandse theologisch tijdschrift*
NHC	Nag Hammadi Codex
NHLE	*The Nag Hammadi Library in English*
NHS	Nag Hammadi Studies
NovT	*Novum Testamentum*
NovTSup	Novum Testamentum, Supplements
NS	Neue Serie
NTApo	Edgar Hennecke, ed., Wilhelm Schneemelcher, rev., R. McL. Wilson, trans. ed., *New Testament Apocrypha* (2 vols.; Philadelphia: Westminster, 1963–65).
NTS	*New Testament Studies*
NumenSup	Numen, Supplements
OLZ	*Orientalische Literaturzeitung*
Orig. World	*On the Origin of the World*
PG	J. Migne, *Patrologia graeca*
PL	J. Migne, *Patrologia latina*
Pol. *Phil.*	Polycarp, *Epistle to the Philippians*
Pref.	*Prefatio*
Prot. Jas.	*Protevangelium of James*
Ps.-Clem.	*Pseudo-Clementines*
Hom.	*Homilies*
Recog.	*Recognitions*
PVTG	Pseudepigrapha veteris testamenti Graece
PW	Pauly-Wissowa, *Real-Encyclopädie der classischen Altertumswissenschaft*
11QPs[a] Plea	(Qumran) *Psalms Scroll, Plea for Deliverance*
RechSR	*Recherches de science religieuse*
RGG	*Die Religion in Geschichte und Gegenwart*
S	Sahidic
SAQ	Sammlung ausgewählter kirchen- und dogmengeschichtlicher Quellenschriften
SBL	Society of Biblical Literature
SBLDS	SBL Dissertation Series
SBLMS	SBL Monograph Series
SBLTT	SBL Texts and Translations
SC	Sources chrétiennes
SPAW	Sitzungsberichte der königlich preussischen Akademie der Wissenschaften
StPatr	*Studia Patristica*
SUNT	Studien zur Umwelt des Neuen Testaments
s. v.	*sub voce*

TDNT	Gerhard Kittel, ed., *Theological Dictionary of the New Testament* (10 vols.; Grand Rapids: Eerdmans, 1964–76).
Tertullian	
Res. carn.	*De resurrectione carnis*
Thom. Cont.	*Book of Thomas the Contender*
ThR	*Theologische Rundschau*
ThStK	*Theologische Studien und Kritiken*
T. Levi	*Testament of Levi*
Treat. Res.	*Treatise on Resurrection*
TS	*Theological Studies*
TU	Texte und Untersuchungen
VC	*Vigiliae christianae*
WMANT	Wissenschaftliche Monographien zum Alten und Neuen Testament
ZKTh	*Zeitschrift für katholische Theologie*
ZNW	*Zeitschrift für die neutestamentliche Wissenschaft und die Kunde der älteren Kirche*
ZThK	*Zeitschrift für Theologie und Kirche*

SHORT TITLES

Information appears here for frequently used works which are cited by short title. A few short titles do not appear in this list, but in each instance full bibliography is given on the page(s) preceding such references.

Bammel, "Papias"
E. Bammel, "Papias," *RGG* 5 (3d ed.; 1961) 47–48.

Bauer, *Orthodoxy and Heresy*
Walter Bauer, *Orthodoxy and Heresy in Earliest Christianity* (Philadelphia: Fortress, 1971).

Beyschlag, "Papiasfragmente"
K. Beyschlag, "Herkunft und Eigenart der Papiasfragmente," *StPatr 4* (TU 79; Berlin: Akademie-Verlag, 1961) 268–80.

Bornkamm, "πρέσβυς"
Günther Bornkamm, "πρέσβυς," *TDNT* 6 (1968) 651–83.

Brown, *John (i–xii)* and *(xiii–xxi)*
Raymond E. Brown, *The Gospel according to John* (2 vols.; AB 29/29A; Garden City: Doubleday, 1966–1970).

S. Brown, "James"
Scott Kent Brown, "James: A religio-historical study of the relations between Jewish, Gnostic, and Catholic Christianity in the early period through an investigation of the traditions about James the Lord's brother" (Ph.D. diss., Brown University, 1972).

Bultmann, *History*
Rudolf Bultmann, *The History of the Synoptic Tradition* (2d ed.; New York: Harper & Row, 1963).

Bultmann, *John*
Rudolf Bultmann, *The Gospel of John: A Commentary* (Philadelphia: Westminster, 1971).

Cameron, "Apocryphon of James"
: Ron Cameron, "The Apocryphon of James," in idem, *Other Gospels*, 55–64.

Cameron, *Other Gospels*
: Ron Cameron, *The Other Gospels: Non-Canonical Gospel Texts* (Philadelphia: Westminster, 1982).

von Campenhausen, *Ecclesiastical Authority*
: Hans von Campenhausen, *Ecclesiastical Authority and Spiritual Power in the Church of the First Three Centuries* (Stanford: Stanford University Press, 1969).

von Campenhausen, *Formation*
: Hans von Campenhausen, *The Formation of the Christian Bible* (Philadelphia: Fortress, 1972).

Dibelius, *Tradition*
: Martin Dibelius, *From Tradition to Gospel* (New York: Scribner's, 1934).

Dodd, *Historical Tradition*
: C. H. Dodd, *Historical Tradition in the Fourth Gospel* (Cambridge: Cambridge University Press, 1963).

Epistula Iacobi Apocrypha
: Michel Malinine, Henri-Charles Puech, Gilles Quispel, Walter Till, Rodolphe Kasser, R. McL. Wilson, and Jan Zandee, *Epistula Iacobi Apocrypha* (Zurich/Stuttgart: Rascher, 1968).

Grant, *Earliest Lives*
: R. M. Grant, *The Earliest Lives of Jesus* (London: SPCK, 1961).

Haenchen, *Acts*
: Ernst Haenchen, *The Acts of the Apostles: A Commentary* (Philadelphia: Westminster, 1971).

Hahn, *Hoheitstitel*
: Ferdinand Hahn, *Christologische Hoheitstitel: Ihre Geschichte im frühen Christentum* (FRLANT 83; 3d ed.; Göttingen: Vandenhoeck & Ruprecht, 1966).

Hedrick, "Kingdom Sayings and Parables of Jesus"
: Charles W. Hedrick, "Kingdom Sayings and Parables of Jesus in *The Apocryphon of James*: Tradition and Redaction," *NTS* 29 (1983) 1–24.

Jeremias, *Parables*
: Joachim Jeremias, *The Parables of Jesus* (2d ed.; New York: Scribner's, 1972).

Jeremias, *Theology*
: Joachim Jeremias, *New Testament Theology* (New York: Scribner's, 1971).

Jesus and Man's Hope
David G. Buttrick, ed., *Jesus and Man's Hope* (2 vols.; Perspective; Pittsburgh: Pittsburgh Theological Seminary, 1970-71).

Kee, *Community*
Howard Clark Kee, *Community of the New Age: Studies in Mark's Gospel* (Philadelphia: Westminster, 1977).

Kennedy, "Source Criticism"
George Kennedy, "Classical and Christian Source Criticism," in *Relationships Among the Gospels*, 125–55.

Kipgen, "Gnosticism in Early Christianity"
Kaikhohen Kipgen, "Gnosticism in Early Christianity: A Study of the Epistula Iacobi Apocrypha with Particular Reference to Salvation" (Ph.D. diss., Oxford University, 1975).

Kirchner, "Epistula"
Dankwart Kirchner, "Epistula Jacobi Apocrypha: Die erste Schrift aus Nag-Hammadi-Codex I (Codex Jung)" (Th.D. diss., The Humboldt University of Berlin, 1977).

Koester, *Introduction*
Helmut Koester, *Introduction to the New Testament* (2 vols.; Foundations and Facets; Philadelphia: Fortress, 1982; Berlin/New York: De Gruyter, 1983).

Koester, *Überlieferung*
Helmut Koester, *Synoptische Überlieferung bei den apostolischen Vätern* (TU 65; Berlin: Akademie-Verlag, 1957).

Kürzinger, "Papiaszeugnis"
Josef Kürzinger, "Das Papiaszeugnis und die Erstgestalt des Matthäusevangeliums," *BZ*, NS, 4 (1960) 19–38.

Kuhn, *Ältere Sammlungen*
Heinz-Wolfgang Kuhn, *Ältere Sammlungen im Markusevangelium* (SUNT 8; Göttingen: Vandenhoeck & Ruprecht, 1971).

Lawlor, "Papias"
H. J. Lawlor, "Eusebius on Papias," *Hermathena* 43 (1922) 167–222.

Lührmann, *Logienquelle*
Dieter Lührmann, *Die Redaktion der Logienquelle* (WMANT 33; Neukirchen: Neukirchener Verlag, 1969).

MacRae, *Invitation to John*
George W. MacRae, *Invitation to John* (Garden City: Doubleday, 1978).

Manson, "Life of Jesus"
T. W. Manson, "The Life of Jesus: A Survey of the Available Material. (4) The Gospel According to St. Matthew," *BJRL* 29 (1945/46) 392–428.

Meeks, "Hypomnēmata"
Wayne A. Meeks, "Hypomnēmata from an Untamed Sceptic: A Response to George Kennedy," in *Relationships Among the Gospels*, 157–72.

Meeks, "Man from Heaven"
Wayne A. Meeks, "The Man from Heaven in Johannine Sectarianism," *JBL* 91 (1972) 44–72.

Munck, "Presbyters and Disciples"
Johannes Munck, "Presbyters and Disciples of the Lord in Papias: Exegetic Comments on Eusebius, Ecclesiastical History, III, 39," *HTR* 52 (1959) 223–43.

Perkins, *Gnostic Dialogue*
Pheme Perkins, *The Gnostic Dialogue* (New York: Paulist, 1980).

Puech, "Gnostic Gospels and Related Documents"
Henri-Charles Puech, "Gnostic Gospels and Related Documents," in *NTApo*, 1. 231–362.

Relationships Among the Gospels
William O. Walker, Jr., ed., *The Relationships Among the Gospels: An Interdisciplinary Dialogue* (Trinity University Monograph Series in Religion 5; San Antonio: Trinity University Press, 1978).

Robinson, "Gnosticism and the New Testament"
James M. Robinson, "Gnosticism and the New Testament," in Barbara Aland, ed., *Gnosis: Festschrift für Hans Jonas* (Göttingen: Vandenhoeck & Ruprecht, 1978) 125–43.

Robinson, "LOGOI SOPHON"
James M. Robinson, "LOGOI SOPHON: On the Gattung of Q," in *Trajectories*, 71–113.

Schoedel, *Fragments*
William R. Schoedel, *Polycarp, Martyrdom of Polycarp, Fragments of Papias*, in Robert M. Grant, ed., *The Apostolic Fathers: A New Translation and Commentary*, vol. 5 (London/Camden/Toronto: Nelson, 1967).

Smith, *Clement*
Morton Smith, *Clement of Alexandria and a Secret Gospel of Mark* (Cambridge: Harvard University Press, 1973).

Streeter, *Four Gospels*
Burnett Hillman Streeter, *The Four Gospels: A Study of Origins* (New York: Macmillan, 1925).

Swanson, "Christian Prophetic Speech"
Donald N. Swanson, "Basic Forms of Christian Prophetic Speech" (Th.D. diss., Harvard University, 1981).

Trajectories
James M. Robinson and Helmut Koester, *Trajectories through Early Christianity* (Philadelphia: Fortress, 1971).

Vielhauer, *Geschichte*
Philipp Vielhauer, *Geschichte der urchristlichen Literatur* (Berlin/New York: De Gruyter, 1975).

Wallert, *Palmen*
Ingrid Wallert, *Die Palmen im Alten Ägypten* (Münchner ägyptologische Studien 1; Berlin: Hessling, 1962).

Zahn, *Introduction*
Theodor Zahn, *Introduction to the New Testament*, vol. 2 (3 vols.; Edinburgh: T. & T. Clark, 1909).

INTRODUCTION

In early Christianity, the memory of Jesus was alive in the traditions of worshiping communities which produced and preserved sayings in Jesus' name and stories attributed to him. Scholars past and present have relied almost exclusively on the Synoptic Gospels of the NT as primary sources of the sayings of and stories about Jesus. The Gospel of John is rarely considered in discussions of the earliest stages of the Jesus tradition, and even then mainly for the purposes of elucidating the Synoptic Gospels. And noncanonical gospels have been routinely regarded as secondary traditions, assumed to be dependent on or influenced by the Synoptics. The assessment of Wilhelm Schneemelcher is representative of this consensus of scholarship:

> The use of the canonical Gospels in most works of this character [noncanonical or "apocryphal" gospels] can be clearly shown. These "gospels" are then works which have connections with the canonical writings, develop them further and do not leave the given form of the gospel unaltered.[1]

However, recent discoveries have given us reason to call this consensus into question. These are making it possible for us to examine more fully the history of the literature in which Jesus traditions were transmitted, since substantial noncanonical texts can now be used as primary sources to clarify the developments of gospel traditions. One of these texts is the *Apocryphon of James* (*Ap. Jas.*).

The *Ap. Jas.* is a Coptic translation of an originally Greek document that gives an account of the teachings of Jesus in the form of a discourse of Jesus and dialogue with two of his disciples, James and Peter. It survives as the second of five tractates of Codex I of the

[1]Wilhelm Schneemelcher, "Gospels: Non-Biblical Material about Jesus," in idem and Edgar Hennecke, eds.; R. McL. Wilson, trans. ed., *New Testament Apocrypha* (2 vols.; Philadelphia: Westminster, 1963) 1. 83.

Coptic Gnostic Library from Nag Hammadi (NHC 1, 2), which was buried in the fourth century and discovered in Egypt in 1945. The *Ap. Jas.* was first published in 1968 in a critical edition in French, with appended translations in German and English.[2] Since then, fresh German[3] and English[4] translations have appeared. A splendid facsimile edition was recently published under the auspices of the Department of Antiquities of the Arab Republic of Egypt, in conjunction with UNESCO;[5] a new critical edition is currently in preparation by the members of the Coptic Gnostic Library Project of the Institute for Antiquity and Christianity at Claremont.[6] The Coptic text is well preserved and the editions of the text are excellent. A fresh assessment of the document would seem to be now in order.

Since the *Ap. Jas.* first became known, most discussions of the text have been attempts to locate its place in the origins of Gnosticism and the rise of Christianity.[7] While these studies have helped clarify certain

[2]Michel Malinine, Henri-Charles Puech, Gilles Quispel, Walter Till, Rodolphe Kasser, R. McL. Wilson, and Jan Zandee, eds., *Epistula Iacobi Apocrypha* (Zurich/Stuttgart: Rascher, 1968). This is cited in the textual apparatus as *ed. pr.*

[3]Hans-Martin Schenke, "Der Jakobusbrief aus dem Codex Jung," *OLZ* 66 (1971) 117–30; and Dankwart Kirchner, "Epistula Jacobi Apocrypha: Die erste Schrift aus Nag-Hammadi-Codex I (Codex Jung)" (Th.D. diss., The Humboldt University of Berlin, 1977).

[4]Francis E. Williams, trans., "The Apocryphon of James (I, *2*)," in James M. Robinson, ed., *NHLE* (New York: Harper & Row, 1977) 29–36; and Ron Cameron, "The Apocryphon of James," in idem, *The Other Gospels: Non-Canonical Gospel Texts* (Philadelphia: Westminster, 1982) 55–64.

[5]*The Facsimile Edition of the Nag Hammadi Codices: Codex I* (Leiden: Brill, 1977).

[6]Harold W. Attridge, ed., *Nag Hammadi Codex I (The Jung Codex)* (NHS; Leiden: Brill, forthcoming).

[7]J. Zandee, "Gnostische trekken in een Apocryphe Brief van Jacobus," *NedThTs* 17 (1962/63) 401–22; Kurt Rudolph, "Gnosis und Gnostizismus, ein Forschungsbericht," *ThR* 34 (1969) 169–75; Scott Kent Brown, "James: A religio-historical study of the relations between Jewish, Gnostic, and Catholic Christianity in the early period through an investigation of the traditions about James the Lord's brother" (Ph.D. diss., Brown University, 1972); Kaikhohen Kipgen, "Gnosticism in Early Christianity: A Study of the Epistula Jacobi Apocrypha with Particular Reference to Salvation" (Ph.D. diss., Oxford University, 1975); Jan Helderman, "Anachorese zum Heil: *Das Bedeutungsfeld der Anachorese bei Philo und in einigen gnostischen Traktaten von Nag Hammadi*," in Martin Krause, ed., *Essays on the Nag Hammadi Texts: In Honour of Pahor Labib* (NHS 6; Leiden: Brill, 1975) 40–55; idem, "*Codex I, Tractate 1: Apocryphon of James*: 'Anapausis in the Epistula Jacobi Apocrypha,'" in R. McL. Wilson, ed., *Nag Hammadi and Gnosis: Papers read at the First International Congress of Coptology (Cairo, December 1976)* (NHS 14; Leiden: Brill, 1978) 34–43; Carsten Colpe, "Heidnische, jüdische und christliche Überlieferung in den Schriften aus Nag Hammadi VII," JAC 21 (1978) 125–46; Karl-Wolfgang Tröger, "Die Passion Jesu Christi in der Gnosis nach den Schriften von Nag Hammadi" (Dr. sc. theol. diss., The Humboldt University of Berlin, 1978) 25–41; and

aspects of the *Ap. Jas.* in terms of the beginnings of Christianity, what has been generally overlooked is the document's clear interest in the sayings-of-Jesus tradition. Scholarly discussions have presupposed that the *Ap. Jas.* is dependent on the NT for its traditions about Jesus. The assessment of Henri-Charles Puech, one of the original editors of the text, that the *Ap. Jas.* "deserves . . . to be ranked among the writings related to the Gnostic gospels or referring to one episode or another of the [canonical] Gospel narrative,"[8] has been generally accepted by subsequent interpreters.[9] This presupposition has precluded any comprehensive analysis of the sayings traditions in the *Ap. Jas.* The *Ap. Jas.* states explicitly that it is providing a written record of those sayings which Jesus revealed to James and Peter. Taking this statement seriously, I propose to analyze the *Ap. Jas.* form-critically in order to clarify the ways in which sayings of Jesus were used and transformed in early Christian communities. This will include a formal isolation of individual sayings, an identification of their traditional and redactional elements, and a reconstruction of the compositional history of the document.

Unlike the four gospels which came to be included in the NT, the body of the *Ap. Jas.* has no narrative structure. Instead, it is composed largely of sayings: similes, prophecies, wisdom sayings, rules of the community, and creedal formulas make up the body of the text. These have been secondarily inserted into an account of a post-resurrection appearance of Jesus and embedded within the frame of a letter, allegedly written by James, for the instruction and edification of an unidentified group of Christians. The *Ap. Jas.* may thus be outlined as follows:

1) 1.1–8: prescript
2) 1.8–2.7: proem
3) 2.7–39: account of the post-resurrection appearance of Jesus
4) 2.39–15.5: the body of Jesus' discourse and dialogue with James and Peter
5) 15.5–16.11: account of the ascension
6) 16.12–30: postscript.

Pheme Perkins, *The Gnostic Dialogue* (New York: Paulist, 1980) 145–56.

[8]Henri-Charles Puech, "Gnostic Gospels and Related Documents," in *NTApo*, I. 335.

[9]S. Brown, "James," 37; Kipgen, "Gnosticism in Early Christianity," 119–20; Perkins, *Gnostic Dialogue*, 145–56; and Rudolph, "Gnosis und Gnostizismus," 175.

In the first half of the *Ap. Jas.*, individual sayings are used to construct a dialogue between Jesus and his disciples. Dialogue is almost completely absent from the discourse of the second half, and, in every case, its use seems to be a secondary literary technique.

Despite having the external appearance of a "letter," the letter frame is a secondary addition by the editor of the *Ap. Jas.*, designed to preface the revelation of Jesus to James and Peter. It is the discourse and dialogue that make up the main body of the document. This is made clear by the fact that this section constitutes three-fourths of the text. The use of the title "Savior" (2.39–40: ⲡⲁϫⲉϥ ⲛ̣̄ϭⲓ ⲡⲥⲱ(ⲧⲏ)ⲣ ϫⲉ ["the Savior said"]) to introduce this section marks the redactional seam of an introduction to a collection of sayings. In composing these sayings in the form of a dialogue, the characteristic title "Lord" is used (4.23 and 31; 5.36 and 6.1; 6.22 and 28; 6.32 and 35; 13.31 and 36).[10] This suggests that the text of the *Ap. Jas.* is intended to be understood principally as a collection of sayings, and that the frame of a letter was constructed to give it the authority of a "secret book" which only the elect were privileged to receive. This interpretation is supported by a comparative analysis of the stages of composition of the sayings traditions in the *Dialogue of the Savior* (NHC 3, 5): the title "Lord" is used exclusively in the dialogue sections (124.22–127.22; 131.16–133.16; 137.3–147.22), whereas "Savior" occurs at the beginning of the dialogue proper (125.1) and at the opening of the entire document (120.2), where it is clearly the work of the final redactor.[11]

The *Ap. Jas.* is, therefore, to be included in the group of texts acknowledged as primary sources of and witnesses to the sayings-of-Jesus tradition. This monograph will endeavor to analyze the *Ap. Jas.* within the context of that tradition. Rather than attempting to deal with the

[10]Except in 2.40, "Savior" occurs only in the editorial frame of the *Ap. Jas.*: in the proem (1.23, 32), account of Jesus' post-resurrection appearance (2.11, 17), and postscript (16.25). The title "Lord" is also found in the proem (1.12) and postscript (16.29), paralleling the title "Savior," but elsewhere is used exclusively in the dialogues in the body of the text. Because "Lord" occurs in every other dialogue in the body of the *Ap. Jas.*, I emend the text of the very first dialogue between Jesus and Peter to ⲟⲩⲱϣⲃ̄ ϫⲉ <ⲡϫⲁ>ⲉⲓⲥ in 3.39, and reconstruct ϩⲁⲡ̣[ϫⲁⲓ̈ⲥ ⲟⲩⲱϣⲃ̄ ⲡⲁ]ϫⲉϥ ϫⲉ in 4.2–3 (for this spelling of ϫⲁⲓ̈ⲥ, cf. 1.12; 6.22).

[11]See Elaine Pagels and Helmut Koester, "Report on the *Dialogue of the Savior* (CG III, 5)," in R. McL. Wilson, ed., *Nag Hammadi and Gnosis: Papers read at the First International Congress of Coptology (Cairo, December 1976)* (NHS 14; Leiden: Brill, 1978) 66–74. The title "Savior" in *Dial. Sav.* 125.18 introduces a fragment (125.17–126.5) which has been secondarily inserted into a dialogue between the "Lord" and his disciples, beginning at 125.4.

entire text in a cursory manner, it seems best to select portions of the text that are indicative of its principal features to examine in some detail. This will lay the foundation for future discussions of the sayings traditions in the *Ap. Jas.* and help prepare the way for further work on the text.

This monograph is composed of three main chapters:

1) Form Criticism of the *Apocryphon of James*;
2) The Use of Sayings to Compose Dialogues; and
3) "Remembering" the Words of Jesus.

Beginning inductively with a formal analysis of originally discrete sayings in the *Ap. Jas.*, the first main chapter will examine three formal traditions that are representative of the discourse portion of the *Ap. Jas.*: three similes (7.24–28; 8.16–23; 12.22–27), a prophecy of judgment (9.24–10.6), and a fragment of a farewell discourse (12.31–13.1). Since all of these passages are found in the discourse of Jesus in the second half of the text, their analysis will provide the opportunity to clarify the ways in which sayings are used to compose discourses of Jesus. The second main chapter will examine the use of sayings to compose three of the dialogues between Jesus and his disciples (2.21–35; 4.22–37; 5.31–6.11). In each case, it seems that originally discrete sayings were used to compose these dialogues. Since all of these passages are found in the dialogues of Jesus in the first half of the *Ap. Jas.*, their analysis will enable us to clarify the mode of composition of dialogues of Jesus. The third main chapter will assess the process of "remembering" the words of Jesus. The opening scene of the *Ap. Jas.* describes a situation in which scribal activity was taking place (2.7–16). Its reference to "remembering" provides the critical clue to the date and character of the tradition, since this term seems to have been used in the early church to describe the process of creating, collecting, and transmitting sayings of Jesus. Chapter three will endeavor to demonstrate how and when "remembering" was employed in the oral and written stages of the transmission of the tradition. This will enable us to assess the conclusions drawn from the formal analysis of the sayings of Jesus in discourse and dialogue and clarify how this tradition was understood and utilized in the composition of the *Ap. Jas.*

1

FORM CRITICISM OF THE *APOCRYPHON OF JAMES*

Individually discrete sayings were used to construct a discourse of Jesus in the *Ap. Jas.* This will be demonstrated by a formal analysis of three sayings traditions representative of the discourse portion of the *Ap. Jas.*: similes, prophecies, and wisdom sayings. Since it is widely held that similes are among the most distinctive forms of the sayings-of-Jesus tradition, the three similes in the *Ap. Jas.* will be considered first. Each is form-critically discrete, secondarily allegorized, and previously unattested. Examination of the prophecy of judgment will provide the opportunity to observe the practice of producing sayings in the name of Jesus. This chapter will conclude with a discussion of wisdom and prophetic sayings traditions which constitute a fragment of a farewell discourse. Since this fragment contains the closest parallel in the *Ap. Jas.* with any saying found in the NT, this analysis will enable us both to consider the relationship of the *Ap. Jas.* to the traditions in the NT and to clarify the use of collections of sayings in the composition of discourses of Jesus.

1.1 SIMILES

In form-critical terms, a "simile" is a general comparison depicting an ordinary situation, illustrating a typical occurrence for the consideration of its hearers. In a simile one point of comparison is intended, and is sometimes made by way of contrast.[1] There are three similes attributed to Jesus in the *Ap. Jas.*, all of which are taken from the agricultural sphere. They are, in the order in which they appear in the text, the simile of the Date-Palm Shoot (7.24–28), the simile of the Grain of Wheat (8.16–23), and the simile of the Ear of Grain (12.22–27). I shall discuss these in reverse order, providing a form-critical analysis, a consideration of the problems of text and translation, and an exegetical discussion of each simile's tradition and redaction.

The Simile of the Ear of Grain

1) Introduction: 12.20–22	
ⲡⲁϫⲉϥ· ϫⲉ	He (Jesus) said:
ⲉⲧⲃⲉ ⲡⲉⲉⲓ ϯϫⲟⲩ ⲙ̅|ⲙⲁⲥ	This is why I say this
ⲛ̅ⲛⲏⲧⲛ̅	to you (pl.),
ϫⲉⲕⲁⲥ ⲉⲣⲉⲧⲛⲁ|ⲥⲟⲩⲱⲛ ⲧⲏⲛⲉ·	that you may know yourselves.
2) Simile: 12.22–27	
ⲧⲙⲛ̅ⲧⲉⲣⲟ ⲅⲁⲣ | ⲛⲙⲡⲏⲩⲉ	For the Kingdom of Heaven
ⲉⲥⲉⲓⲛⲉ ⲛ̅ⲛⲟⲩϩⲙ̅ⲥ	is like an ear of grain
ⲉ|ⲁϥⲣⲱⲧ ϩⲛ̅ⲛ ⲟⲩⲥⲱϣⲉ·	which sprouted in a field.
ⲁⲩⲱ ⲡⲉ|ⲉⲓ ⲛ̅ⲧⲁⲣⲉϥϫⲉⲧⲉ·	And when it ripened,
ⲁϥⲥⲓⲧⲉ ⲙ̅ⲡⲉϥ|ⲕⲁⲣⲡⲟⲥ	it scattered its fruit
ⲁⲩⲱ ⲁⲛ ⲁϥⲙⲟⲩϩ ⲛ̅ⲧⲥⲱ|ϣⲉ	and, in turn, filled the field

[1]See Adolf Jülicher, *Die Gleichnisreden Jesu* (1 vol. in 2 parts; Tübingen: Mohr-Siebeck, 1910; Darmstadt: Wissenschaftliche Buchgesellschaft, 1969) part 1. 69, 80, 98, 101, and passim; followed by Rudolf Bultmann, *The History of the Synoptic Tradition* (2d ed.; New York: Harper & Row, 1963) 170, 174; and Philipp Vielhauer, *Geschichte der urchristlichen Literatur* (Berlin/New York: De Gruyter, 1975) 295. Note that a "simile" (*Gleichnis*, also translated "similitude") is to be distinguished form-critically from a "parable" (*Parabel*), which portrays in a narrative a specific, unique, metaphorical situation that is both imaginative and transparent to the realities of human existence. See, as part of the vast secondary literature, the discussion of Amos N. Wilder, *Jesus' Parables and the War of Myths* (ed. James Breech; Philadelphia: Fortress, 1982) 71–87, and passim.

ⲚϨⲚϨⲘⲤ· ⲀⲔⲈⲢⲀⲘⲠⲈ·	with ears of grain for another year.

3) Application: 12.27–31

ⲚⲦⲰ|ⲦⲚ ϨⲰⲦ· ⲦⲎⲚⲈ	You also:
ϬⲈⲠⲎ· ⲀⲦⲢⲈⲦⲚⲰϨⲤ | ⲚⲎⲦⲚ	be zealous to reap for yourselves
ⲚⲚⲞⲨϨⲘⲤ· ⲚⲰⲚϨ·	an ear of life,
ϪⲈⲔⲀ·|ⲤⲈ ⲈⲢⲈⲦⲚⲀⲘⲞⲨϨ	in order that you may be filled
ⲀⲂⲀⲖ· ϨⲚ ⲦⲘⲚⲦ|ⲢⲢⲞ·	with the Kingdom.

The simile of the Ear of Grain (12.22–27) begins with a transitive verb of comparison (ⲈⲤⲈⲒⲚⲈ), followed by its indefinite direct object and a relative clause. An application (12.27–31)has been appended to the original simile. The imperative (ⲚⲦⲰⲦⲚ ϨⲰⲦ ⲦⲎⲚⲈ ϬⲈⲠⲎ) which introduces the application has transformed the simile (given in the third person singular) into an exhortation to the community (given in the second person plural). This use of the imperative to join an application secondarily to a simile is attested elsewhere in the sayings tradition:[2]

Gos. Thom. (NHC 2, 2) 76b: 46.19–20:
ⲚⲦⲰⲦⲚ ϨⲰⲦ` ⲦⲎⲨⲦⲚ ϢⲒⲚⲈ ⲚⲤⲀ . . .
(appended to the simile of the merchant who found a pearl)

Luke 12:40 (// Matt 24:44):
καὶ ὑμεῖς γίνεσθε ἕτοιμοι . . . [3]
(appended to the simile of the householder and the thief).

This entire passage (12.22–31) has been given a contextually artificial introduction (12.20–22), in which Jesus is presented as speaking in the first person singular. The introduction has nothing to do with the simile, but serves to insert it (by means of ⲄⲀⲢ) into a wider framework, in which the "distress" (Ⲣ ⲖⲨⲠⲈⲒ) of Peter and James (12.17–19) at Jesus' sayings is said to occasion his response.[4]

In this simile (12.22–27), the situation in the reality identified as the Kingdom[5] is compared to the situation of an ear of grain which

[2]Cf. also Mark13:35; Matt 25:13; Luke 10:37b; 16:9; and see Bultmann, *History*, 185.

[3]Matthew prefaces the imperative with διὰ τοῦτο.

[4]For other instances of introductions to which similes and parables have been secondarily attached, cf. Luke 18:1, 9; 19:11; and see Bultmann, *History*, 192–93.

[5]The critical perception that "situations" and "realities" are being compared in similes and parables is seen decisively by Nils Alstrup Dahl, "The Parables of Growth," in

sprouted in a field. The manner in which the ear of grain is depicted, in terms of sprouting, ripening, scattering, and replenishing, suggests that this is the way in which the Kingdom makes its appearance in the world. The situation is an unobtrusive, active one; the ear of grain is portrayed as operative, identifying how the Kingdom is said to happen. The reference to filling the field with ears of grain brings the simile to a climax, providing an image which contrasts with initial appearances and audience expectations. It is in and like such everyday, routine situations, the simile suggests, that the divine dimension is disclosed. No human activity influences the outcome. In this respect, the simile of the Ear of Grain is both formally and materially comparable with other agricultural similes and parables that derive from the earliest stages of the Jesus tradition (cf. esp. Mark 4:26–28, 29; and Mark 4:3–8 par. // *Gos. Thom.* 9: 34.3–13; *1 Clem.* 24.5). Since the simile of the Ear of Grain (12.22–27) displays no source-critical or redaction-critical dependence upon the NT or other early Christian literature, and betrays no influence of the language of the early church, it is to be judged as an independent, primary source of the sayings-of-Jesus tradition.[6]

In the Coptic, the only difficult line is in 12.25–26: ⲁϥⲥⲓⲧⲉ ⲙ̄ⲡⲉϥⲕⲁⲣⲡⲟⲥ, which I have translated: "it scattered its fruit." The verb ⲥⲓⲧⲉ, of course, is synonymous with ϫⲟ (to sow), and generally translates the Greek verb *σπείρειν*. Although ⲥⲓⲧⲉ does not occur in the Sahidic NT—though it does in the Fayyumic and Bohairic translations[7] —it is used twice in the *Gospel of Thomas*, in sayings paralleled in

idem, *Jesus in the Memory of the Early Church* (Minneapolis: Augsburg, 1976) 146; and Earl [James] Breech, "Kingdom of God and the Parables of Jesus," *Semeia* 12 (1978) 21, 26. See also Joachim Jeremias, *The Parables of Jesus* (2d ed.; New York: Scribner's, 1972) 101.

[6]Against Perkins, *Gnostic Dialogue*, 150, who simply assumes that the simile of the Ear of Grain is dependent upon Mark 4:26ff. But even here one must proceed with care, since there can be no doubt that different, pre-Marcan versions of the agricultural simile of the seed growing secretly were in circulation in the early church. It is not yet clear whether Mark's simile of the seed growing secretly originally comprised only Mark 4:26–28, to which the reference to the harvest in vs 29 was appended under the influence of Joel 3:13 (cf. *Gos. Thom.* 21d: 37.17–18; and Rev 14:15), or whether this simile originally did conclude with a reference to the OT (analogous to the Q version of the simile of the mustard seed, Luke 13:18–19), and came to be expanded internally in vss 27–28 (cf. *1 Clem.* 23.4 // *2 Clem.* 11.3). See esp. Heinz-Wolfgang Kuhn, *Ältere Sammlungen im Markusevangelium* (SUNT 8; Göttingen: Vandenhoeck & Ruprecht, 1971) 104–12, who argues for the latter reconstruction.

[7]E.g., Matt 13:18, 27 (F,B), where S has ϫⲟ (= *σπείρειν*). Cf. Crum, *s.v.* ⲥⲓⲧⲉ (360b).

the NT, with this same meaning, "to sow."[8] Yet ever since Herodotus[9] *σπείρειν* has also been used to mean "to scatter, disperse, strew, or spread." This is how I take it here. The image seems to be one of the natural broadcasting of the ripe kernels of grain, "its fruit," throughout the field.[10] Such a scattering would not naturally "fill" a field—at least not in one season. Whether the reference to "another year" is therefore original, or should be understood as an editorial addition of provisions for the future, is not clear. It is possible that this reference has been inserted into the text under the influence of the application (12.27–31), which interprets the simile as an allegory of the salvation which one can attain by "reaping."

It has already been shown on form-critical grounds that the application (12.27–31) has been secondarily added to the original simile. This is also clear in terms of its content. The application introduces the notion of "reaping," which is foreign to the simile, and transposes the agricultural image of "ears of grain" into the redemptive metaphor of "ears of life." This allegorizes the random sameness portrayed in the simile, interpreting the ear of grain as a "cipher for eternal life,"[11] whose life cycle represents a spiritual process of deliverance ("reaping") and salvation ("life"). The reference to filling the field with "ears of grain" has thereby been interpreted as a sort of Gnostic rebirth, in which one is "filled with the Kingdom."[12] The exhortation to "be zealous," moreover, is used editorially here and elsewhere in the *Ap. Jas.* to urge the readers on to saving knowledge (cf. 7.10; 8.10).

[8] *Gos. Thom.* 9: 34.4 // Mark 4:3–8 par.; and *Gos. Thom.* 57: 43.1 // Matt 13:24–30.

[9] Herodotus 7.107. Cf. LSJ, *s.v.* *σπείρω* I.3 (1626a); and BAG, *s.v.* *σπείρω* 2 (761b).

[10] Against Charles W. Hedrick ("Kingdom Sayings and Parables of Jesus in *The Apocryphon of James*: Tradition and Redaction," *NTS* 29 [1983] 9) who takes both ⲁϥⲥⲓⲧⲉ (which he translates: "he sowed") and ⲁϥⲙⲟⲩϩ (which he translates: "[he] filled") to "refer to the action of an unspecified farmer." Although this interpretation may be possible for ⲁϥⲥⲓⲧⲉ, it seems strained for ⲁϥⲙⲟⲩϩ. The attempt to buttress this translation by appealing to an alleged Semitic "non-indication of the change of subject" (analogous to that which Jeremias [*Parables*, 129] has sought to identify in Luke 15:15), moreover, seems tenuous and unnecessary.

[11] The phrase is Hedrick's, "Kingdom Sayings and Parables of Jesus," 13.

[12] "Filling" is a redactional term for the *Ap. Jas.*, as the following lexical references demonstrate: 2.33, 35; 3.8, 36; 4.[1], 2, [4], 7, 9, 10, 11, 12, 13, 15, 16, 19; and 14.31. References to "the Kingdom," moreover, are nearly always juxtaposed in the *Ap. Jas.* with "life": 3.25 and 33–34 (cf. 3.27); 6.6 and 9 (cf. 6.17; 5.32–35); 8.15 and 25; 12.27–29 and 30–31 (cf. 12.15); 13.30, 35 and 34; 14.8 and 10; and 14.15 and 16.

The Simile of the Grain of Wheat

1) Introduction: 8.10–11

ϣⲱⲡⲉ ⲛ̄ⲣⲉϥϭⲉⲡⲏ ϩⲁ ⲡⲣⲁ | ⲙ̄ⲡⲗⲟⲅⲟⲥ	Become zealous about the Word.

2) Catalogue of characteristics of the Word: 8.11–15

ⲡⲗⲟⲅⲟⲥ ⲛ̄ⲅⲁⲣ ϣⲁ|ⲣⲡ̄ ⲙⲉⲛ·	For the Word's first
ⲡⲉϥⲣⲁ ⲡⲉ ⲧⲡⲓⲥⲧⲓⲥ |	characteristic is faith;
ⲡⲙⲁϩⲥⲛⲉⲩ ⲡⲉ ⲧⲁⲅⲁⲡⲏ	the second is love;
ⲡⲙⲁϩ|ϣⲁⲙⲛ̄ⲧ ⲡⲉ ⲛⲉϩⲃⲏⲩⲉ·	the third is works.
ⲉϣⲁϥϣⲱ|ⲡⲉ ⲅⲁⲣ ⲁⲃⲁⲗ ϩⲛ̄ ⲛⲉⲉⲓ ⲛ̄ϭⲓ ⲡⲱⲛϩ̄ |	Now from these comes life.

3) Simile: 8.16–23

ⲡⲗⲟⲅⲟⲥ ⲛ̄ⲅⲁⲣ ⲉϥⲧⲛ̄ⲧⲱⲛ ⲁⲩ|ⲃⲗ̄ⲃⲓⲗⲉ ⲛ̄ⲥⲟⲩⲟ·	For the Word is like a grain of wheat.
ⲡⲉⲉⲓ ⲛ̄ⲧⲁⲣⲉⲟⲩ|ⲉⲉⲓ ϫⲁϥ· ⲁϥⲧⲁⲛϩⲟⲩⲧϥ̄·	When someone sowed it, he believed in it;
ⲁⲩⲱ ⲛ̄|ⲧⲁⲣⲉϥⲣⲱⲧ ⲁϥⲙⲣ̄ⲣⲓⲧϥ̄·	and when it sprouted, he loved it,
ⲉⲁϥⲛⲉⲩ | ⲁϩⲁϩ ⲃ̄ⲃⲗ̄ⲃⲓⲗⲉ·	because he looked (forward to) many grains
ⲁⲡⲙⲁ ⲛ̄ⲟⲩⲉⲓⲉ	in the place of one;
ⲁⲩⲱ | ⲛ̄ⲧⲁⲣⲉϥⲣ̄ ϩⲱⲃ· ⲁϥⲟⲩϫⲉⲉⲓ·	and when he worked (it), he was saved,
ⲉⲁϥ|ⲧⲥⲉⲛⲁϥ ⲛ̄ⲛⲟⲩϩⲣⲉ·	because he prepared it for food.[13]
ⲡⲁⲗⲓⲛ ⲁϥ|ϣⲱϫⲡ̄· ⲁϫⲟ·	Again he left (some grains) to sow.

4) Application: 8.23–27

ⲧⲉⲉⲓ ⲁⲛ ⲧⲉ· ⲑⲉ |	Thus it is also
ⲉⲧⲉ ⲟⲩⲛ̄ ϭⲁⲙ ⲙ̄ⲙⲱⲧⲛ̄ ⲛ̄ϫⲓ ⲁ|ⲣⲱⲧⲛ̄	possible for you (pl.) to receive for yourselves
ⲛ̄ⲧⲙⲛ̄ⲧⲣ̄ⲣⲟ ⲛ̄ⲙ̄ⲡⲏⲩⲉ· |	the Kingdom of Heaven:

[13]Another possible translation of 8.20–22 would be: "and when it produced, he was sustained, because it provided him (with) food."

ⲧⲉⲉⲓ ⲉⲣⲉⲧⲛ̄ⲧⲙ̄ϫⲓⲧⲥ̄·[14]	unless you receive it
ϩⲓ̈ⲧⲛ̄ ⲟⲩⲅⲛⲱ|ⲥⲓⲥ·	through knowledge,
ⲛ̄ⲧⲉⲧⲛⲁϣ ϭⲓⲛ̄ⲧⲥ̄ ⲉⲛ·	you will not be able to find it.

8.11–12 ϣⲁ/ⲣⲡ̄ ⲙⲉⲛ ⲡⲉϥⲣⲁ MS: <ⲡⲉϥⲣⲁ ⲛ̄ϣⲁⲣⲡ̄> Kirchner

The simile of the Grain of Wheat (8.16–23) begins with a transitive verb of comparison (ⲉϥⲧⲛ̄ⲧⲱⲛ), followed by an indefinite direct object (without a relative clause). The subject of the comparison, the ⲗⲟⲅⲟⲥ, does not seem to be original; its absolute use conforms to the vocabulary of the early church (e.g., Mark 4:14–20 par.; *Acts Andr.* 12; Eus. *Hist. eccl.* 1.13.20), and, as an introductory noun of comparison, it is without precedent in the parabolic tradition.

The original form of this simile may be irrecoverable. As the text now stands, the simile's structure consists of (1) three parallel lines, each of which is divided into two equal parts; (2) two circumstantial clauses which modify, respectively, the last two of the parallel lines; and (3) an indefinite concluding statement. The three parallel lines form the core of the simile, and are constructed of two members each: the first depicts, in a temporal clause, an agricultural act ("sowing," "sprouting," and "working"), and the second, the corresponding reaction of an unidentified farmer ("believing," "loving," and "being saved").

It is the third line (8.20–21) that seems to have undergone considerable revision: ⲁⲩⲱ ⲛ̄ⲧⲁⲣⲉϥⲣ̄ ϩⲱⲃ ⲁϥⲟⲩϫⲉⲉⲓ, which I have translated: "and when he worked (it), he was saved." Here, the intransitive verb ⲟⲩϫⲉⲉⲓ (to be saved) is unexpected, breaking the established pattern of relating, in the second half of each parallel line, the farmer's own reaction to the growth of the grain of wheat. If the reference to ⲟⲩϫⲉⲉⲓ is original, this is most likely because the word's ambiguous, double meaning (physically: "to make healthy"—religiously: "to save") reflects an earlier version of this simile that depicted the activity of the grain of wheat without reference to the reaction(s) of the farmer. The text which we now have could be translated, in accordance with that hypothetical earlier version, as follows: "and when it produced (ⲛ̄ⲧⲁⲣⲉϥⲣ̄ ϩⲱⲃ), he was sustained (ⲁϥⲟⲩϫⲉⲉⲓ), because it provided him (ⲉⲁϥⲧⲥⲉⲛⲁϥ) (with) food" (8.20–22). However, the present redaction of the simile is clearly

[14]For the use of the second present conditional clause, negated by -ⲧⲙ-, see Walter C. Till, *Koptische Grammatik (Saïdischer Dialekt)* (2d ed.; Leipzig: VEB Verlag Enzyklopädie, 1961) §§ 448, 402.

designed to emphasize the farmer's reactions to the grain of wheat, being modeled to conform to the catalogue of characteristics of the Word ("faith," "love," and "works" [8.11–15]). Accordingly, the understanding of ⲟⲩϫⲉⲉⲓ as "to save" seems to have transformed the simile into a paradigm of "salvation," highlighting the "working" of the farmer, and transferring the description of the farmer's own activity from the third line of the simile (8.20–21) to the following explanatory circumstantial clause (8.21–22: "because he prepared it for food"). Whether this clause is a gloss or preserves a vestige of a more original reading is difficult to determine.[15] Certainly the previous circumstantial clause (8.19–20: "because he looked [forward to] many grains in the place of one"), which formally parallels this one, seems to be an explanatory insertion with allegorical features.[16]

An application (8.23–27) has been appended to the simile. The comparative words of transition (ⲧⲉⲉⲓ ⲁⲛ ⲧⲉ ⲑⲉ) which introduce this application serve to interpret the simile (given in the third person singular) allegorically (addressed to the community in the second person plural). This comparative formula is the Coptic equivalent of *οὕτως καί*, which was used throughout the NT and other early Christian literature to apply an allegorical meaning to earlier traditions:[17]

Mark 13:29 par.:
οὕτως καὶ ὑμεῖς . . .
(appended to the simile of the fig tree)
Matt 18:35:
οὕτως καὶ ὁ πατὴρ . . . ποιήσει ὑμῖν . . .
(appended to the parable of the unmerciful servant)

[15]Kirchner ("Epistula," 38, 267 n. 337) has recognized the difficulty of this line, but has divided the text differently: he puts a full stop after ⲁϥⲟⲩϫⲉⲉⲓ, translates the circumstantial clause temporally (ⲉⲁϥⲧⲥⲉⲛⲁϥ ⲛ̄ⲛⲟⲩϩⲣⲉ ["after he had prepared food"]), and takes it as dependent upon the following independent clause (ⲡⲁⲗⲓⲛ ⲁϥϣⲱϫⲡ̄ ⲁϫⲟ). Although this is certainly possible, I think that it breaks up the parallelism of the simile.

[16]Cf. *1 Clem.* 24.5: *καὶ ἐκ τοῦ ἑνὸς πλείονα αὔξει καὶ ἐκφέρει καρπόν.*

[17]Cf. within the parabolic tradition: Matt 13:49; 18:14 par.; 20:16; Luke 12:21; *Ap. Jas.* 7.28–29—outside the parabolic tradition: Mark 7:18; Matt 17:12; 23:28; Luke 11:30; 17:26; *2 Clem.* 11.2–4; and see Bultmann, *History*, 184–85.

Luke 14:33:
οὕτως οὖν πᾶς ἐξ ὑμῶν . . .
(appended to the double similes of the tower builder and the king who went to war)
Luke 17:10:
οὕτως καὶ ὑμεῖς . . .
(appended to the simile of the master who had a servant).

This entire composite passage (8.11–27) is framed initially with an imperative (8.10–11), in which the topic of discussion, "the Word," is introduced. The technique of using an imperative to introduce a simile attributed to Jesus belongs to the editorial stage of the tradition, as the following examples attest:[18]

Mark 13:28 (// Matt 24:32):
ἀπὸ δὲ τῆς συκῆς μάθετε τὴν παραβολήν·
(introducing the simile of the fig tree)
Matt 21:33:
ἄλλην παραβολὴν ἀκούσατε.[19]
(introducing the parable of the wicked tenants).

Between the introduction (8.10–11) and the simile (8.16–23) there has been inserted a series of predicates which form a catalogue of characteristics of the Word (8.11–15). The catalogue seems to have been deliberately inserted at this point on the basis of thematic catchword association (**ⲗⲟⲅⲟⲥ**),[20] being joined to the introductory exhortation by means of **ⲛ̄ⲅⲁⲣ**. A traditional triad of nouns ("faith," "love," and "works") is listed as the predicates of the "Word"; their culmination is said to be "life." It is clear from the widespread presence of other such catalogues in Greek, Christian, and Gnostic texts that this particular catalogue is older than its context.[21] Both the catalogue and

[18]Cf. Mark 4:3 par.; and *Ap. Jas.* 7.22–23.

[19]The editorial introductions to the versions of this parable in Mark 12:1 // Luke 20:9 do not use the imperative.

[20]Following the distinctions among "thematic," "associative," and "purely formal" catchword connections made by Martin Dibelius, *James* (Hermeneia; rev. Heinrich Greeven; Philadelphia: Fortress, 1976) 7 with n. 25.

[21]Cf. Clem. Al. *Strom.* 3.10.69.3: *γνῶσις, πίστις, ἀγάπη*, Porphyry *Marc.* 24: *πίστις, ἀλήθεια, ἔρως, ἐλπίς*, *Gos. Phil.* (NHC 2, 3) 79.23–25: **ⲡⲓⲥⲧⲓⲥ, ϩⲉⲗⲡⲓⲥ, ⲁⲅⲁⲡⲏ, ⲅⲛⲱⲥⲓⲥ**; *Ep. Apost.* 43 (54): **ⲡⲓⲥⲧⲓⲥ, ⲁⲅⲁⲡⲏ, ⲭⲁⲣⲓⲥ, ⲉⲓⲣⲏⲛⲏ, ϩⲉⲗⲡⲓⲥ**; 1 Cor 13:13: *πίστις, ἐλπίς, ἀγάπη*, and see Hans Conzelmann, *1 Corinthians* (Hermeneia; Philadelphia: Fortress, 1975) 229 (on 1 Cor 13:13), with the references cited there.

the simile were originally discrete traditions which circulated independently. It is the redactor of the *Ap. Jas.* who placed them together, reworked the simile to conform to the catalogue, and appended his own interpretive application (8.23–27). The reason the original form and meaning of the simile are irrecoverable is that the simile has been revised to correspond to the catalogue. In the present context, the catalogue takes precedence over the simile; it is the latter which is utilized as the interpretive mechanism by which the former is explicated. As a result, at least two modifications have been made in the form of the simile on account of the influence of the catalogue: (1) the subject of the simile has become the Word; and (2) the triad of nouns has come to be interpreted through their verbal counterparts ("believing," "loving," and "working").[22]

Accordingly, the simile of the Grain of Wheat is not understood metaphorically, but functions allegorically as an illustration of the "sowing" of the Word (cf. Mark 4:14–20 par.). Both the catalogue and the simile give way to the application. By giving a Gnostic interpretation to the simile, and by further heightening the soteriological impulse, the application compels the reader to identify the key terms of the catalogue, simile, and application: "life," "salvation," and "the Kingdom." Literarily, therefore, the present edition of the text exhibits the following structure:

1) the catalogue: word → life;
2) the simile: grain of wheat → food (now superseded by "salvation");
3) the application: knowledge → the Kingdom.

The virtual equation of "life" and "the Kingdom" parallels that of the application of the simile of the Ear of Grain (12.27–31), suggesting that both applications were composed by the same circle.[23] There is little reason to think that the simile itself derives from the earliest stages of the Jesus tradition. It seems rather to provide material evidence for the early Christian practice of producing similes, parables, and allegories in Jesus' name.

[22]One should note for comparative purposes that the nouns catalogued in Porphyry *Marc.* 24 (above n. 21), which are said to constitute "four principles" (στοιχεῖα) to be upheld concerning God, are also interpreted through their verbal counterparts in a *sorites* that follows.

[23]Cf. the juxtaposing of "Word," "knowledge," and "life" in *Ap. Jas.* 9.18–20.

The Simile of the Date-Palm Shoot

1) Introduction: 7.22–23

ⲙ̄ⲡⲱⲣ ⲁϩⲱⲕⲙ̄ | ⲛ̄ⲧⲙⲛ̄ⲧⲣ̄ⲣⲟ ⲛ̄ⲙ̄ⲡⲏⲩⲉ· |

Let not the Kingdom of Heaven wither away.

2) Simile: 7.24–28

ⲉⲥⲧⲛ̄ⲧⲁⲛⲧ· ⲛⲅⲁⲣ ⲁⲩ<ϣ>ⲗϩ̄ ⲛⲃⲛ̄|ⲛⲉ·
ⲉⲛⲧⲁϩⲁⲛⲉϥⲕⲁⲣⲡⲟⲥ ϩⲉϯⲉ | ⲙ̄ⲡⲉϥⲕⲱⲧⲉ·
ⲁϥⲧⲉⲩⲟ ⲁⲃⲁⲗ ⲛ̄|ϩⲉⲛϭⲱⲃⲉ·
ⲁⲩⲱ ⲛ̄ⲧⲁⲣⲟⲩϯ ⲟⲩⲱ |
ⲁϩⲟⲩⲧⲣⲉⲧⲁⲧⲉ ϣⲁⲩⲉⲓⲉ·

For it is like a date-palm <shoot>
whose fruits dropped down[24] around it.
It put forth buds
and, when they blossomed,
they (i.e., the fruits) caused the productivity (of the date-palm) to dry up.

3) Application: 7:28–32

ⲧⲉ|ⲉⲓ ⲁⲛ ⲧⲉ ⲑⲉ
ⲙ̄ⲡⲕⲁⲣⲡⲟⲥ ⲛ̄ⲧⲁϩ|ϣⲱⲡⲉ·
ⲁⲃⲁⲗ ϩⲛ̄ ϯⲛⲟⲩⲛⲉ ⲛ̄|ⲟⲩⲱⲧ·
ⲛ̄ⲧⲁⲣⲟⲩⲧⲁⲕ<ⲙ̄>ϥ
ⲁⲩ|ϫⲡⲟ ⲛ̄ϩⲛ̄ⲕⲁⲣⲡⲟⲥ ϩⲓ̈ⲧⲛ̄ ϩⲁϩ· |

Thus it is also
with the fruit which came
from the single root:
when it (i.e., the fruit) was <picked>,
fruits were collected by many.

4) Expansion: 7.33–35

ⲛⲉⲛⲁⲛⲟⲩⲥ ⲙ̄ⲙⲉⲛ ⲡⲉ·
ⲉⲛⲉ | ⲟⲩⲛ̄ ϣϭⲁⲙ ϯⲛⲟⲩ
ⲁⲣ̄ ⲛⲓⲧⲱ|ϭⲉ ⲃ̄ⲃⲣ̄ⲣⲉ· ⲛⲉⲕ
ⲁϭⲛⲧⲥ̄·

It was really good.
Is it (not) possible now
to produce the plants anew for you (sing.),
(and) to find it (i.e., the Kingdom)?

7.24 ⲁⲩⲱⲗϩ̄ MS : Read ⲁⲩ<ϣ>ⲗϩ̄ *ed. pr.* | 24–26 ⲛ<ⲧ>ⲃⲛ̄/ⲛⲉ ⲉⲛⲧⲁϩⲁⲛⲉ<ⲥ> . . . / ⲙ̄ⲡⲉ<ⲥ>ⲕⲱⲧⲉ Schenke : ⲛ<ⲛⲟⲩ>-ⲃⲛ̄/ⲛⲉ Kirchner | 26 ⲁϥⲧⲉⲩⲟ MS : ⲁ<ⲩ>ⲧⲉⲩⲟ Kirchner | 31 ⲧⲁⲕⲛ̄ϥ MS : Read ⲧⲁⲕ<ⲙ̄>ϥ Zandee : ⲧⲁⲕ{ⲛ̄}ϥ Till | 35 ⲛⲉⲕⲁϭⲛⲧⲥ̄ MS : ⲛⲉⲕ <ⲛⲉⲕ>ⲁϭⲛⲧⲥ̄ Williams : ⲛⲉⲕ <ⲛⲉⲕⲛ>ⲁ-ϭⲛⲧⲥ̄ Kirchner

[24]Here and elsewhere I have revised my earlier translation of this passage as printed in "Apocryphon of James," 60.

The simile of the Date-Palm Shoot (7.24–28) begins with a transitive verb of comparison (ⲉⲥⲧⲛ̄ⲧⲁⲛⲧ), followed by its indefinite direct object and a relative clause. An application (7.28–32) follows the simile. The comparative words of transition (ⲧⲉⲉⲓ ⲁⲛ ⲧⲉ ⲑⲉ) which introduce the application are identical with those which preface the application of the simile of the Grain of Wheat (8.23). Unlike the two similes which have already been discussed, however, the concerns of this application are addressed in the third person singular, not directed to the community in the second person plural. An expansion (7.33–35) is attached to the application by means of the affirmative connecting particle ⲙ̄ⲙⲉⲛ.[25] The problems of text, translation, and interpretation in these three lines are particularly acute, and will be treated in some detail below. This entire passage (7.24–35) is introduced with an imperative (7.22–23), as was also the simile of the Grain of Wheat (8.10–11). The image of "withering away"[26] (7.22) is an apt one, since the last line of the simile portrays the "drying up" (7.28) of the date-palm. The introduction, therefore, is a clever summary of the simile that follows. The simile itself is secondarily connected to this introductory exhortation by means of ⲛⲅⲁⲣ. The employment of this connecting conjunction to combine originally discrete sayings is a typical editorial procedure.[27] Accordingly, whether the simile originally made reference to the Kingdom of Heaven must remain an open question.

The expanded account of the Date-Palm Shoot (7.22–35) constitutes an engagingly difficult pericope, both in terms of the history of its text and that of its tradition. Because the Coptic is obscure and, in several places, corrupt, there has been no certainty as to the precise reading of the text—to say nothing of its meaning. ⲱⲗϩ̄ (7.24) and ⲧⲁⲕⲛ̄ϥ (7.31), for example, are unattested as Coptic words; but whereas the former is readily explained,[28] the precise meaning of the latter has been in considerable doubt. The lack of specificity in the use of pronouns throughout the passage, moreover, makes the identification of their

[25]I.e., the Greek *μέν*. This same spelling is found in the *Treat. Res.* (NHC I, 4) 44.8, 27; 45.9.

[26]ϩⲱⲕⲙ̄ (to wither away) is used to translate several Greek words, all of which connote the loss of vitality: love is "extinguished" (Matt 24:12: *ψύχειν*); seed is "burned" (Mark 4:6: *καυματίζειν*); grass "withers" (Sir 43:21: *ἀποσβεννύναι*); and a rich man "fades" (Jas 1:11: *μαραίνειν*).

[27]Cf. within the parabolic tradition: Matt 11:18 par.; 20:1; 25:14; Luke 14:28; *Ap. Jas.* 8.11, 15, 16; 12.22—and outside the parabolic tradition: Matt 6:14; 17:20; Mark 4:22 par.; 9:49.

[28]The transcribing of ⲱⲗϩ̄ instead of ϣⲗϩ̄ in 7.24 is an obvious scribal error.

antecedents problematic, rendering the text ambiguous. In order to be able to interpret the simile, it will be necessary to discuss in some detail certain problems of text and translation. Once a working text has been established, the formal and redactional history of the passage can be more fully traced.

The use of sexual terminology in the simile (7.24–28) has puzzled all interpreters. The text literally speaks of the drying up of "the womb" (7.28: **ⲧ.ⲁⲧⲉ**, which I have translated metaphorically as "the productivity") of the date-palm. The editors of the *editio princeps* understood this to refer to the "pith" of the plant; in this they have been followed by all subsequent translators.[29] It has never been observed, however, that ancient authors customarily used the language of human reproduction to describe the process of the fertilization and cultivation of date-palm trees:[30]

Herodotus 1.193 (5th century BCE):[31]

> There are palm trees there [in Assyria] growing all over the plain, most of them yielding fruit, from which food is made and wine and honey. The Assyrians tend these like figs, and chiefly in this respect, that they tie the fruit of the palm called male by the Greeks to the [female] date-bearing palm, that so the gall-fly may enter the dates and cause them to ripen, and that the fruit of the palm may not fall (*καὶ μὴ ἀπορρέῃ ὁ καρπὸς τοῦ φοίνικος*); for the male palms, like unripened figs, have gall-flies in their fruit.

[29]See Malinine, et al., *Epistula Iacobi Apocrypha*, 57, with their French (p. 15: "la moelle"), German (p. 103: "der Kern [wörtl. Mutterleib]"), and English (p. 121: "the pith") translations. They are followed by Hans-Martin Schenke, "Der Jakobusbrief aus dem Codex Jung," *OLZ* 66 (1971) 123 ("das Mark"); Kirchner, "Epistula," 36 ("die Ursprungszelle"); Francis E. Williams, trans., "The Apocryphon of James (I, *2*)," in James M. Robinson, ed., *NHLE* (New York: Harper & Row, 1977) 32 ("the pith"); Hedrick, "Kingdom Sayings and Parables of Jesus," 13 ("the pith"); and Donald Rouleau, "Les paraboles du royaume des cieux dans l'*Epître apocryphe de Jacques* (NH I,2)," in Bernard Barc, ed., *Colloque international sur les Textes de Nag Hammadi (Québec, 22–25 août 1978)* (Bibliothèque copte de Nag Hammadi, Section "Etudes" 1; Quebec: Laval University Press; Louvain: Peeters, 1981) 185 ("la hampe mère [matrice]").

[30]I owe this observation and the following references to Albert Henrichs.

[31]*Herodotus* (trans. A. D. Godley; 4 vols.; LCL; London: Heinemann; Cambridge: Harvard University Press, 1920) 1. 245.

Theophrastus *Historia plantarum* 2.8.4 (4th-3d century BCE):[32]

> With dates it is helpful to bring the male to the female; for it is the male which causes the fruit to persist and ripen, and this process some call, by analogy, 'the use of the wild fruit.' The process is thus performed: when the male palm is in flower, they at once cut off the spathe on which the flower is, just as it is, and shake the bloom with the flower and the dust over the fruit of the female, and, if this is done to it, it retains the fruit and does not shed it (*διατηρεῖ καὶ οὐκ ἀποβάλλει*). In the case both of the fig and of the date it appears that the 'male' renders aid to the 'female,'—for the fruit-bearing tree is called 'female'—but while in the latter case there is a union (*μῖξις*) of the two sexes, in the former the result is brought about somewhat differently.

Pliny *Naturalis historia* 13.7.34–35 (1st century CE):[33]

> For the rest, it is stated that in a palm-grove of natural growth the female trees do not produce if there are no males (*sine maribus non gignere feminas*), and that each male tree is surrounded by several females with more attractive foliage that bend and bow towards him; while the male bristling with leaves erected impregnates the rest of them by his exhalation and by the mere sight of him, and also by his pollen; and that when the male tree is felled the females afterwards in their widowhood become barren (*sterilescere*). And so fully is their sexual union (*coitus*) understood that mankind has actually devised a method of impregnating them by means of the flower and down collected from the males, and indeed sometimes by merely sprinkling their pollen on the females.

Ammianus Marcellinus *Res gestae* 24.3.12–13 (4th century CE):[34]

> And wherever anyone goes, one constantly sees palm branches with and without fruit, and from their yield an abundance of honey and wine is made. The palms themselves are said to couple, and the sexes may easily be distinguished. It is also said that the female trees conceive when smeared with the seeds of the male, and they assert that the trees take pleasure in mutual love, and that

[32] *Theophrastus: Enquiry into Plants* (trans. Arthur Hort; 2 vols.; LCL; London: Heinemann; New York: Putnam's, 1916) 1. 155.

[33] *Pliny: Natural History* (trans. H. Rackham; 10 vols.; LCL; London: Heinemann; Cambridge: Harvard University Press, 1945) 4. 119.

[34] *Ammianus Marcellinus* (trans. John C. Rolfe; 3 vols.; LCL; London: Heinemann; Cambridge: Harvard University Press, 1937) 2. 429.

> this is evident from the fact that they lean towards each other, and cannot be parted even by gales of wind. And if the female tree is not smeared in the usual way with the seed of the male, it suffers abortion and loses its fruit before it is ripe (*abortus vitio fetus amittit intempestivos*). And if it is not known with what male any female tree is in love, her trunk is smeared with her own perfume, and the other tree by a law of nature is attracted by the sweet odour. It is from these signs that the belief in a kind of copulation is created.

The consistency of these botanical traditions confirms that the author of this simile was familiar with date-palms. Ancient no less than modern observers[35] were aware that the date-palm (*Phoenix dactylifera*) is dioecious—its male and female flowers are borne on separate plants. The inflorescence of the date-palm is organized as a spirally constructed shoot, or flower spathe, produced from a bud in the axil of a foliage leaf which branches out from the stalk of the tree.[36] Only female trees could bear fruit, but unless they were pollinated by a male tree, their stigmae would develop "small, stoneless fruit of little value"[37] that would be lost before ripening, falling unfertilized to the ground. The *Ap. Jas.*'s coupling of the reference to the "dropping down of the fruit" with the "drying up of the womb" (7.24–28) locates its simile within this established tradition of plant-lore.[38]

The text of the application (7.28–32) is also not without its difficulties. It was noted above that the precise meaning of ⲧⲁⲕⲛ̄ϥ (7.31) has been in considerable doubt. A clue to its meaning is provided by the verb's own masculine singular suffix -ϥ (it). Its

[35]See Michael Schnebel, *Die Landwirtschaft im hellenistischen Ägypten*, vol. I: *Der Betrieb der Landwirtschaft* (Münchener Beiträge zur Papyrusforschung und antiken Rechtsgeschichte 7; Munich: Beck, 1925) 294–300; Nicolas Hohlwein, "Palmiers et palmeraies dans l'Egypte romaine," *Etudes de papyrologie* 5 (1939) 3–13; Ingrid Wallert, *Die Palmen im Alten Ägypten* (Münchner ägyptologische Studien 1; Berlin: Hessling, 1962) 11–13; and E. J. H. Corner, *The Natural History of Palms* (Berkeley/Los Angeles: University of California Press, 1966) 322–23, and passim. Note that the custom of using sexual terminology when referring to date-palms has not died out in antiquity: Corner states that when "pollen is blown by wind" the "effect on these dioecious plants is promiscuous" (p. 323)!

[36]See esp. Corner, *Natural History*, 114–38.

[37]So V. H. W. Dowson, *Dates and Date Cultivation of the 'Iraq*, part I: *The Cultivation of the Date Palm on the Shat Al 'Arab* (Cambridge: Heffer, 1921) 27.

[38]The *Ap. Jas.*'s use of stock language to describe the inflorescence of the date-palm confirms that the "shoot" is to be understood as the flower "spathe" produced in a leaf on the stalk of the tree, and not a "sucker," or secondary shoot which arose from the base of the tree trunk and was also used to generate new plants. See Wallert, *Palmen*, 13; and Corner, *Natural History*, 86, 199.

antecedent must surely be the "fruit" (7.29: π.καρποc).[39] This is made clear by the correct emendation of this verb, which, according to all available evidence, is not attested as a Coptic word. Jan Zandee's[40] emendation to **τωκм̄, τακм̄⸗**, which translates such Greek words as *σπᾶν* (to pick, pluck), makes good sense and is confirmed by three Greek documentary papyri which use *κατασπασμός* to refer to the "harvesting" of dates.[41] This reading is corroborated by the reference to the "gathering" of fruit in the very next line of the application—7.31–32: αγϫπο н̄ϩн̄καρποc ϩϊтн̄ ϩαϩ ("fruits were collected by many").[42]

The text of the expansion (7.33–35) is extremely difficult and seems to be garbled. Its uncertain syntax, imprecise use of pronouns, and ambiguous words and phrases combine to make the recovery of its meaning questionable. Since a number of different readings of these lines are possible, it seems best to lay out the various options first, before making a decision on a reading which, given the problems of the text, must necessarily be provisional.

Ambiguous words and phrases:

7.34: р̄-
1) "to make/produce" (= *ποιεῖν*).
2) "to become."[43]

[39]The immediately preceding noun, "root" (**νογνε**), is feminine. The "shoot" (ϣλϩ̄) in 7.24 is masculine, and the "date-palm" (**вн̄νε**) in 7.24–25 is almost always feminine, although Wolfhart Westendorf (*Koptisches Handwörterbuch* [1965; reprint, Heidelberg: Winter, 1977] 25) points to a rare attestation of this word in the masculine gender. See Kirchner, "Epistula," 263 n. 310.

[40]*Epistula Iacobi Apocrypha*, 57.

[41]P. Soterichos Spec. Reg. 3049/11 (no. 4, line 27); P. Ryl. ii. 172 (lines 17, 20–21); and P.S.I. 33 (line 22). See Sayed Omar, ed., *Das Archiv des Soterichos (P. Soterichos)* (Papyrologica Coloniensia 8; Opladen: Westdeutscher Verlag, 1979) 72–83, with Pl. IV (dated 87 CE); J. de M. Johnson, Victor Martin, and Arthur S. Hunt, eds., *Catalogue of the Greek Papyri in the John Rylands Library, Manchester* (2 vols.; Manchester: Manchester University Press, 1915) 2. 206–7, with Pl. 19 (dated 208 CE); and G. Vitelli, ed., *Papiri greci e latini, volume primo (n! 1–112)* (3 vols.; Pubblicazioni della Società italiana; Florence: Ariani, 1912) 1. 76–78 (dated 266/67 CE). See Schnebel, *Landwirtschaft*, 298; and Hohlwein, "Palmiers," 39, 45.

[42]Therefore, the suggested emendation of Till (*Epistula Iacobi Apocrypha*, 57; followed by Kirchner, "Epistula," 263 n. 312) that τακ[н̄]⸗ is an unattested dialectal variant of **τωωϭε** (to plant) is to be rejected. It is not the planting of the date-palm but the harvesting of its fruit that is being discussed here.

[43]See Thomas O. Lambdin, *Introduction to Sahidic Coptic* (Macon: Mercer University Press, 1983) § 26.1.

7.34–35: ⲚⲒⲦⲰϬⲈ ⲂⲂⲢ̄ⲢⲈ
1) "the(se) new (or: young) plants."
2) "neophytes."[44]
3) compounded with Ⲣ̄– (to make): "the(se) plants (a)new."[45]

Pronominal ambiguities (and their possible referents):

7.33: ⲚⲈⲚⲀⲚⲞⲨ⸗ Ⲥ
1) "the root" (7.30: Ϯ.ⲚⲞⲨⲚⲈ).
2) an indefinite reference to what has preceded: "it was good."
3) an indefinite reference to what is to follow:
"it would be good. . . ."[46]

7.35: ϬⲚⲦ⸗ Ⲥ̄
1) "the Kingdom" (7.23: Ⲧ.ⲘⲚ̄ⲦⲢ̄ⲢⲞ).
2) "the root" (7.30: Ϯ.ⲚⲞⲨⲚⲈ).
3) "the productivity" (7.28: Ⲧ.ⲀⲦⲈ).
4) an indefinite reference to what has preceded:
"find it"—that is, the means to produce/become new plants.

Syntactical ambiguities:

7.33: ⲈⲚⲈ
1) the circumstantial of the imperfect (in a condition contrary to fact clause) + the *imperfectum futuri* (7.35: ⲚⲈⲔⲀϬⲚⲦ⸗; or 7.33: ⲚⲈⲚⲀⲚⲞⲨ⸗).
2) the interrogative particle (= εἰ).
3) the generalized circumstantial of the imperfect (with the impersonal verb ⲞⲨⲚ̄ ϢϬⲀⲘ) + some future conjugation of the verb ϬⲒⲚⲈ.

7.35: ⲚⲈ⸗ Ⲕ–Ⲁ–ϬⲚⲦ⸗ Ⲥ̄
1) the *imperfectum futuri.*
2) the dative preposition ⲚⲈ⸗ Ⲕ (for you [masc. sing.]) + the preposition Ⲁ with the infinitive ϬⲚⲦ⸗ (in a construction dependent upon ⲞⲨⲚ̄ ϢϬⲀⲘ, and coordinate with Ⲁ Ⲣ̄–).

[44]See L. Th. Lefort, ed., *S. Pachomii vita bohairice scripta* (CSCO 89/7; Louvain: Durbecq, 1953) 22, line 28: ϨⲀⲚⲦⲰϪⲒ Ⲙ̄ⲂⲈⲢⲒⲚⲈ. Cf. Crum, *s.v.* ⲂⲢⲢⲈ (43a).

[45]Cf. Crum, *s.v.* ⲂⲢⲢⲈ (43b).

[46]For the use of the preterite ⲚⲈ with the suffix verb ⲚⲀⲚⲞⲨ⸗, see Walter C. Till, *Koptische Dialektgrammatik* (2d ed.; Munich: Beck, 1961) § 343.

Given these textual considerations, various translations of these lines will be provided below, following the order in which the syntactical possibilities were listed above, in order to illustrate the variety of interpretations that are possible:

1) *As a condition contrary to fact:*

   a) It was indeed good. If it were (or: had been) possible to produce these new plants now, you (sing.) would find (or: have found) it.
   b) It would indeed be good if it were possible to produce these new plants now; (for then) you (sing.) would find it.[47]

2) *As an interrogative:*

   a) It was really good. Is it (not) possible now to produce the plants anew for you (sing.), (and) to find it?
   b) It was really good. Is it (not) possible now to become the new plants, (and) for you (sing.) to find it?

3) *As a circumstantial:*

   a) It was certainly good. Because it was possible now to become the(se) young plants, you (sing.) were going to find it.[48]
   b) It was certainly good. Although it was possible (for some) to produce the(se) plants anew, (only) you (sing.) are to find it.

With all these possibilities for editing and translating the text of the expansion, one cannot be so confident of recovering its meaning as with the simile and the application. My translation decision (given as no. 2[a] above) will be supported exegetically in the discussion below.

The present text of the simile (7.24–28) does not seem to be in its original form. The first two strophes (lines 24–26) lead directly to the final one (line 28):

[47]This is the translation that I printed in "Apocryphon of James," 60.

[48]For the use of the imperfect of the future to describe an action as imminent in past time, see Thomas O. Lambdin, *Introduction to Sahidic Coptic* (Macon: Mercer University Press, 1983) § 25.1.

ⲉⲥⲧⲛ̄ⲧⲁⲛⲧ· (ⲛⲅⲁⲣ) ⲁⲩ<ϣ>ⲗϩ̄ ⲛⲃⲛ̄|ⲛⲉ·	(For) it is like a date-palm <shoot>
ⲉⲛⲧⲁϩⲁⲛⲉϥⲕⲁⲣⲡⲟⲥ ϩⲉϯⲉ | ⲙ̄ⲡⲉϥⲕⲱⲧⲉ·	whose fruits dropped down around it
. . .	. . .
ⲁϩⲟⲩⲧⲣⲉⲧⲁⲧⲉ ϣⲁⲩⲉⲓⲉ·[49]	so as to cause the productivity (of the date-palm) to dry up.

These three strophes are integral parts of a tradition which used stock language to describe a temporarily infertile date-palm tree. The two middle strophes (7.26–27), however, seem to be extraneous. Not only do the references to the "buds" which "blossom" have no botanical connection with the known facts of the care and (in)fertilization of date-palms, but they also serve no clear metaphorical function, supplying no intrinsic support to the simile. The mentioning of the "putting forth" and "blossoming" of buds, then, can best be explained as an addition from another tradition that has expanded the simile internally.

The plausibility of this suggestion is supported by form-critical analysis of other similes and parables in the sayings-of-Jesus tradition. Heinz-Wolfgang Kuhn has shown that the simile of the seed growing secretly (Mark 4:26–29) reflects the tendency of the tradition to be expanded internally. His reconstruction (from 4:26, 29) of an "earlier form" of a "complete simile," most likely with "a short transition" (vs 27b), is as follows:[50]

. . . ὡς[51] ἄνθρωπος βάλῃ τὸν σπόρον ἐπὶ τῆς γῆς (4:26b)

καὶ βλαστᾷ καὶ μηκύνηται· (vs 27b)

ὅταν δὲ παραδοῖ ὁ καρπός,
εὐθὺς ἀποστέλλει τὸ δρέπανον,
ὅτι παρέστηκεν ὁ θερισμός. (vs 29)

[49]The inflected (causative) infinitive usually denotes purpose or goal. For its less frequent use in a result clause, see Ludwig Stern, *Koptische Grammatik* (Leipzig: Weigel, 1880) § 463. The causative ⲧⲣⲉ– seems to preclude translating this construction as an ersatz passive.

[50]Kuhn, *Ältere Sammlungen*, 108.

[51]Note that the introduction to this simile (Mark 4:26: οὕτως ἐστὶν ἡ βασιλεία τοῦ θεοῦ) may also be secondary. Cf. Mark 13:34; Matt 25:14; and see Bultmann, *History*, 173.

Even if one were to argue that another version of this simile circulated without the concluding reference to the harvest from Joel 3:13 (see n. 6 above), there can be no doubt that the extant text of the seed growing secretly bears witness to the growth of the tradition. Mark's sequential progression, that "the earth" καρποφορεῖ, πρῶτον χόρτον, εἶτεν στάχυν, εἶτεν πλήρη σῖτον ἐν τῇ στάχυϊ (vs 28), documents but one aspect of this development.[52] Additional evidence is provided by Mark's own internal expansion of the second section of the parable of the sower (Mark 4:5–6, 7b par. // *Gos. Thom.* 9: 34.6–9):

Mark 4:5–6, 7b:	*Gos. Thom. 9: 34.6–9:*
5) καὶ ἄλλο ἔπεσεν ἐπὶ τὸ πετρῶδες	ϩⲛ̄ⲕⲟⲟⲩⲉ ⲁⲩϩⲉ ⲉϫⲛ̄ ⲧⲡⲉⲧⲣⲁ
ὅπου οὐκ εἶχεν γῆν πολλήν, καὶ εὐθὺς ἐξανέτειλεν διὰ τὸ μὴ ἔχειν βάθος γῆς·	ⲁⲩⲱ ⲙ̄ⲡⲟⲩϫⲉ ⲛⲟⲩⲛⲉ ⲉⲡⲉⲥⲏⲧ ⲉⲡⲕⲁϩ
6) καὶ ὅτε ἀνέτειλεν ὁ ἥλιος ἐκαυματίσθη καὶ διὰ τὸ μὴ ἔχειν ῥίζαν ἐξηράνθη·	
. . .	
7) καὶ καρπὸν οὐκ ἔδωκεν.	ⲁⲩⲱ ⲙ̄ⲡⲟⲩⲧⲉⲩⲉ ϩⲙ̄ⲥ ⲉϩⲣⲁϊ ⲉⲧⲡⲉ

Mark's second section of the sower, which describes the seed(s) which fell on the rock, exhibits the following secondary features: (1) it is considerably longer than the other three sections of the parable; (2) it disrupts the carefully composed threefold structuring found in every other section; (3) it contains a threefold repetition of the lack of ground; and (4) it presents two conflicting images: that of immediate "scorching" (vs 6a) and that of eventual "withering" on account of the seed's lack of soil/root (vss 5b, 6b).[53] The version in the *Gospel of Thomas*, by

[52]Kuhn (*Ältere Sammlungen*, 107) refers to Mark 4:28 as "the transition of a later narrator to an earlier conclusion of the simile." Cf. *1 Clem* 23.4 // *2 Clem* 11.3: λάβετε ἄμπελον· πρῶτον μὲν φυλλοροεῖ, εἶτα βλαστὸς γίνεται, [in *1 Clement* only: εἶτα φύλλον, εἶτα ἄνθος,] καὶ μετὰ ταῦτα ὄμφαξ, εἶτα σταφυλὴ παρεστηκυῖα.

[53]It may be, as John Dominic Crossan (*In Parables: The Challenge of the Historical Jesus* [New York: Harper & Row, 1973] 39–44) has suggested, that Mark has expanded his source of this section of the parable under the influence of the allegorical interpretation, which uses this section to speak of "tribulation or persecution" which believers are going to face (vss 16–17). Note that Matthew reproduces Mark's version almost verbatim, whereas Luke trims his source (Matt 13:5–6 // Luke 8:6).

contrast, is straightforward and succinct. It is quite possible that this version is closely related to the Gospel of Mark's source, since Mark's insertion of *καὶ καρπὸν οὐκ ἔδωκεν* in vs 7b, which is designed to contrast the threefold failure (vss 3–7) with a threefold harvest (vs 8), presupposes the *Gospel of Thomas*'s ⲁⲩⲱ ⲙ̄ⲡⲟⲩⲧⲉⲩⲉ ϩⲙ̄ⲥ ⲉϩⲣⲁ̈ⲓ̈ ⲉⲧⲡⲉ ("and they did not produce ears of grain" [34.8–9]).

Kuhn[54] rightly notes the importance of supplying a short transitional passage between the introductory and concluding sections of the simile of the seed growing secretly. His inclusion of the text's own reference to the fact that "the seed" *βλαστᾷ καὶ μηκύνηται* (vs 27b) has been modeled on Q's version of the mustard seed (Luke 13:19b: *καὶ ηὔξησεν*), designed to reinforce the observation that this particular pre-Marcan version of the simile emphasized the growth of seed before the harvest. It is striking that the transitional section of the simile of the Date-Palm Shoot also intimates such a potential for productivity—7.26–27: ⲁϥⲧⲉⲩⲟ ⲁⲃⲁⲗ ⲛ̄ϩⲉⲛϭⲱⲃⲉ ⲁⲩⲱ ⲛ̄ⲧⲁⲣⲟⲩϯ ⲟⲩⲱ ("it put forth buds and, when they blossomed . . ."). I would like to suggest that these two middle strophes have been secondarily inserted, prior to the addition of the application, from a separate simile which depicted a situation of growth—not infertility.[55] It is doubtful whether it would be possible to substantiate the conjecture that such a simile may have actually contained the concluding lines of the present application, which refer to the "harvesting" of dates (7.31–32). In any case, many of the problems of text, translation, and interpretation in this passage can be plausibly explained by positing a tradition history which acknowledges that the simile of the Date-Palm Shoot in the *Ap. Jas.* is a fragment of one or more original similes. The continuing growth of the tradition is documented by the addition of the application, expansion, and introductory exhortation.

In this simile (7.24–28), a comparison is made with the situation of a date-palm shoot whose fruits dropped down around it. This situation is conceived as utterly negative; it emphasizes the premature loss of fruit, on account of the temporary infertility of the tree. The application (7.28–32), on the other hand, describes precisely the opposite situation: a rich harvest. It is possible that the author of the application

[54] *Ältere Sammlungen*, 107–8.

[55] Cf. the simile of the fig tree in Mark 13:28–29 par., where the "putting forth of leaves" (*ἐκφύῃ τὰ φύλλα* [= ⲛⲉⲥϭⲱⲃⲉ ϯⲟⲩⲱ]) signifies the onset of the harvest. See Jeremias, *Parables*, 119–20. There is no need, then, to emend with Kirchner ("Epistula," 165–66) the verb ⲁϥⲧⲉⲩⲟ ⲁⲃⲁⲗ (7.26) to ⲁ<ⲩ>ⲧⲉⲩⲟ ⲁⲃⲁⲗ, to make the "fallen fruit" the subject of the entire pericope (including the application).

misunderstood the reference to the "fruits" which "dropped down" around the date-palm, interpreting the image of the downpour to refer to fertility and abundance, rather than, as was actually the case, to the loss of the fruit of the female tree because of infertilization.[56] But this in itself does not fully explain the juxtaposing of botanical, metaphorical, and allegorical language throughout the passage. Whereas the last two lines of the application seem to use botanical language metaphorically when referring to the harvesting of produce (7.31–32), perhaps because they preserve a vestige of an independent simile, the earlier references to the "fruit" and the "single root" (7.29, 30–31) seem to be intended allegorically, to imply that real "offspring" are of Gnostic origin.[57] This suggests that simply separating the simile from the application can help elucidate their discordant images but does not explain the development of the tradition. For that, we must look more carefully at the use of language within the passage and at the choice of the date-palm as a metaphor for comparison.

Ingrid Wallert has shown that the date-palm was one of the oldest motifs in Egyptian art, used to decorate pottery in prehistoric times, cultivated as a fruit tree in predynastic times, and, in the dynastic period, chosen to symbolize the unification of the Kingdom and the vitality of the gods.[58] As a tree which could wither and die, yet be rejuvenated in subsequent years, the date-palm became proverbial of immortality. Its association through puns with the name of the mythological bird (φοῖνιξ) that killed and reanimated itself strengthened this connection.[59] The Greeks made up riddles about the date-palm which traded on the incongruity of its legendary immortality, fertility, and virginity.[60] The Hebrew Bible appropriated the date-palm as a

[56]Similarly, and more recently, Hedrick ("Kingdom Sayings and Parables of Jesus," 16, 18) also interprets the simile with reference to "the abundant and inevitable harvest produced by the Kingdom of God," a "one-of-a-kind yield."

[57]The "root" is a typical Gnostic image used to link the individual with his or her divine origin. Cf. *Gos. Truth* (NHC 1, 3) 17.30; 28.16–18; 41.17, 26; 42.34, 35; *Ap. John* (NHC 2, 1) 30.30; 31.16; and *Hyp. Arch.* (NHC 2, 4) 93.13, 24; 97.15. Bentley Layton ("The Hypostasis of the Archons [Conclusion]," *HTR* 69 [1976] 66 n. 126) calls the root a "consolatory metaphor, expressing the consubstantiality of human *pneuma* with the divine," and compares Plato *Tim.* 90A.

[58]Wallert, *Palmen*, 63–113, 140–45.

[59]E.g., Pliny *Nat. hist.* 13.9.42. Note the interplay between the (fruit of the) tree in Paradise and the "bird which was in Paradise" in *Orig. World* (NHC 2, 5) 118.16–121.13; 121.35–123.1; and *Gen. Rab.* 19.5 (on Gen 3:6). Cf. *b. Sanh.* 108b (on Gen 8:19).

[60]Cf. *Anthologia Graeca* 14.42, 57. See Wolfgang Schultz, *Rätsel aus dem hellenischen Kulturkreise* (2 vols.; Mythologische Bibliothek 3/1, 5/1; Leipzig: Hinrichs, 1909, 1912) 1. 62; 2. 24. Note that Schultz lists these as nos. 90 and 91, respectively.

polyvalent symbol to represent, respectively, the flourishing of the righteous (Ps 92:12–14; cf. Job 29:18 [LXX])[61] and the perishing of the wicked (Joel 1:12). One of the parables attributed to Ahikar makes use of the image of an unproductive date-palm to rebuke his wayward son (*Ahikar* 8.35 [Syriac]).[62] Later Jewish writings used the palm eschatologically of the elect people of God (Sir 24:14; 50:12); according to one apocalyptic vision, the fruit of the tree of life is said to resemble the dates of a palm and be used as food for the elect (*1 Enoch* 24–25).[63]

It is in this context that the simile of the Date-Palm Shoot is to be judged. The image evokes the figure of a proverbial, prolific plant which can thrive yet strangely wither, mysteriously perish yet be immortal. The conflicting images of infertility and abundance in the simile and application, respectively, support the testimony of the Jewish tradition that the date-palm could be used to symbolize judgment and/or blessing.

Form-critically, the simile's (7.24–28) initial verb of comparison (7.24: ⲉⲥⲧⲛ̄ⲧⲁⲛⲧ) seems to be original and indicates that the simile has been formed from a comparison, not a figure.[64] The introduction (7.22–23) is suspiciously appropriate to the application and expansion, and should unquestionably be regarded as inauthentic. As a result, one cannot be certain of the original subject of comparison. The negative image depicted in the simile, however, implies a situation of judgment; it is thus not inconceivable that the subject of the comparison, which has either been lost or simply replaced by the introductory exhortation, was (something like) "this generation" (cf. Matt 11:16 // Luke 7:31; Luke 11:49–51 par.). The text as we have it seems to be a fragment of one or more original similes.

Unlike the simile, the application (7.28–32) envisions a bountiful harvest of dates. Although this may reflect a remnant of another simile which portrayed a situation of harvest, the comparative words of transition which introduce the application make it clear that the tradition is now being used and understood allegorically. The expansion (7.33–35)

[61]See Marvin H. Pope, *Job* (AB 15; Garden City: Doubleday, 1965) 189–90.

[62]A variant of this story appears as the parable of the fig tree in the Gospel of Luke (13:6–9), and elements reappear in an apophthegm about a talking date-palm tree in the *Cologne Mani Codex* (*CMC* 98.8–99.9). See Albert Henrichs, "'Thou Shalt not Kill a Tree': Greek, Manichaean and Indian Tales," *BASP* 16 (1979) 85–108, esp. 104–6.

[63]For the continuation of the tradition, see the examples collected in A. Feldman, *The Parables and Similes of the Rabbis: Agricultural and Pastoral* (Cambridge: Cambridge University Press, 1927) 169–75.

[64]See the distinctions noted in Bultmann, *History*, 168–70, 172.

represents a further stage in the development of the tradition. It recalls that this entire situation really was good, and intimates that there may yet be the possibility of production. This accords with the image of the harvest in the application, and is consistent with the applications of the similes of the Ear of Grain (12.27–31) and the Grain of Wheat (8.23–27). It seems to me most plausible to take the antecedent of the feminine singular pronoun −ⲥ (it), which is suffixed to the verb (ⲛⲉⲕ)ⲁϭⲛⲧ⸗, to be "the Kingdom" (7.23), since this would be consistent with the conclusions of the other two similes in the *Ap. Jas.* and form an inclusio with the introduction.

The fragment of the simile of the Date-Palm Shoot in the *Ap. Jas.* is form-critically isolable and could be very old. The accessibility of the figure of the proverbial palm and the metaphorical use of it in antiquity would seem to support this. The present edition (7.22–35) of the text, however, is clearly the work of a later generation, which seems to have employed the tradition self-critically: the James community is of the Kingdom, but, like the date-palm, is not productive. This is not the fault of the tree, however, nor of its root; they could and at one time did yield bountifully. Both the introduction and the expansion appear to be the work of the redactor of the *Ap. Jas.*, whose exhortation not to let the Kingdom wither away is coupled with the invitation to produce new growth now, in order to "find" it.

1.2 A PROPHECY OF JUDGMENT

Hermann Gunkel was the first to argue in a comprehensive, systematic way that the primary unit of ancient Israelite prophecy was a short, independent saying concerning the future which could be either positive or negative, express weal or woe. As the tradition developed, Gunkel maintained, additional sayings were added to the original unit to state why what was prophesied had to come to pass. Thus, the major elements of prophetic proclamation, the "threat" (*Drohrede*) and the "reproach" (*Scheltrede*), came to be placed together so that the latter could help explain the reason for the negative judgment of God in the former.[1] Following the insights of Gunkel, but modifying his conclusions in a significant way, Claus Westermann has shown that "the

[1] H. Gunkel, "Propheten: II. Seit Amos," *RGG* 4 (1st ed.; 1913) 1866–86, esp. 1878 and 1884. See the fine survey of the history of scholarship in W. Eugene March, "Prophecy," in John H. Hayes, ed., *Old Testament Form Criticism* (Trinity University Monograph Series in Religion 2; San Antonio: Trinity University Press, 1974) 141–57.

'threat' and the 'reproach' are found in the great majority of the prophetic texts, not as two separate genres, but as *one* speech form, i.e., as two constituent parts or members of *one* speech form—the prophetic judgment-speech."[2] The prophetic judgment-speech, which could be directed "to individuals" or, in a further, expanded form, "against Israel,"[3] consists of the following elements:

1) a summons to hear;
2) an accusation (= the "reproach");
3) an introduction to the announcement of judgment ("therefore" + the messenger formula: "thus says the Lord"); and
4) an announcement of judgment (= the "threat").[4]

Some prophecies of judgment also contain (5) a concluding statement, separate from the announcement of judgment, which sums up the pronouncement and brings it to a close (e.g., 1 Kgs 14:11; cf. 12:24; 2 Kgs 1:4, 16; Jer 28:4).[5]

The formal structure of the prophetic judgment-speech can be clearly seen in Amos 7:16–17:[6]

1) Summons to hear: "Now therefore hear the word of the Lord (ועתה שמע דבר־יהוה).
2) Accusation: You say, 'Do not prophesy (לא תנבא) against Israel, and do not preach (ולא תטיף) against the house of Isaac.'
3) Messenger formula: Therefore thus says the Lord (לכן כה־אמר יהוה):

[2]Westermann, *Basic Forms of Prophetic Speech* (Philadelphia: Westminster, 1967) 30.

[3]The "announcement of judgment against Israel" frequently expanded the accusation and/or announcement sections of the "prophetic judgment-speech to individuals." See ibid., 169–89; and Klaus Koch, *The Growth of the Biblical Tradition: The Form-Critical Method* (New York: Scribner's, 1969) 211.

[4]Westermann, *Prophetic Speech*, 131.

[5]Koch, *Biblical Tradition*, 193–94, 212–13. Koch calls this fifth section a "concluding characterization," and refers to the entire prophecy of judgment as a "prophecy of disaster."

[6]Note that this is a prophecy of judgment directed to an individual. For other examples of prophecies to individuals, cf. 1 Kgs 21:18–19; 2 Kgs 1:3–4, 16; Jer 28:13–16; 29:20–23; Isa 22:15–18; and for prophecies against Israel, cf. Amos 4:1–3; and Mic 3:9–12. See Westermann, *Prophetic Speech*, 129–68; and Koch, *Biblical Tradition*, 191–94, 205–7, 210–13.

4) Announcement: 'Your wife shall be a harlot in the city, and your sons and your daughters shall fall by the sword, and your land shall be parceled out by line; you yourself shall die in an unclean land, and Israel shall surely go into exile away from its land.' "

Whereas the accusation (or: reproach) and announcement (or: threat) are the two basic parts of the prophetic judgment-speech, the actual content of the "true word of God"[7] is the announcement of judgment itself, which is indicated and so designated by the messenger formula.

The Christian prophecy of judgment is a continuation of its well-attested Jewish precursor. Donald N. Swanson has analyzed this form in detail, identifying its elements as follows:[8]

1) an introductory attention-getting address (usually pejorative) to the accused;
2) an accusation section which includes or consists of an indignant question and/or a self-incriminating citation from the accused;[9]
3) a self-identification formula of the judge (e.g., "thus says the Lord");
4) a threat or announcement of judgment; and
5) a concluding statement or terse phrase which either (a) reiterates the divine authorization of the prophecy (e.g., "says the Lord") or (b) summarizes or repeats the accusation or threat, terminating the prophecy abruptly on an emphatic note.

The Christian prophecy-of-judgment form has been embedded in several different genres of literature: letters,[10] homilies,[11] apocalypses,[12] literary romances,[13] and written collections of the sayings-of-Jesus tradition.[14] There is one prophecy of judgment attributed to Jesus in the *Ap. Jas.*:

[7]The phrase is Westermann's, *Prophetic Speech*, 132.

[8]Swanson, "Basic Forms of Christian Prophetic Speech" (Th.D. diss., Harvard University, 1981) 15–16.

[9]Swanson notes that "when the form is directed against Israel, it usually contains the equivalent of a historical review of God's fidelity and/or Israel's infidelity" (ibid., 15).

[10]1 Cor 3:16–17; and Rev 2:18–23; 3:14–17.

[11]Melito *Pass. Hom.* 87–93.

[12]*5 Ezra* 1.22–27, 28–32; and *Herm. Sim.* 1.1–2, 3, 4.

[13]Acts 5:9; 13:10–11; and *Acts Pet.* 12.

[14]Q (Luke 3:7–9 par.; Matt 23:29–36 par., 37–39 par.); and *Ap. Jas.* 9.24–10.6.

Ap. Jas. 9.24–10.6:

1) Introductory address to the accused: 9.24–28

<table>
<tr><td>ⲱ̂ ⲛ̄ⲧⲁⲗⲁⲓⲡⲱⲣⲟⲥ</td><td>O you (pl.) wretched!</td></tr>
<tr><td>ⲱ̂ ⲛ̄|ⲕⲁⲕⲟⲇ̣ⲁⲓⲙⲱⲛ</td><td>O you unfortunates!</td></tr>
<tr><td>ⲱ̂ ⲛ̄|ϩϋⲡⲟⲕⲣⲓ̈ⲧⲏⲥ ⲛ̄ⲧⲙⲏⲉ: |</td><td>O you dissemblers of the truth!</td></tr>
<tr><td>ⲱ̂ ⲛ̄ⲣⲙ̄ⲛ̄ⲛⲟⲩϫ ⲛ̄ⲧⲅⲛⲱⲥⲓⲥ· |</td><td>O you falsifiers of knowledge!</td></tr>
<tr><td>ⲱ̂ <ⲙ̄>ⲡⲁⲣⲁⲃⲁⲧⲏⲥ
ⲙ̄ⲡⲛⲉⲩⲙⲁ |</td><td>O you sinners against the spirit!</td></tr>
</table>

2) Accusatory questions: 9.29–36

<table>
<tr><td>ϩⲓ̈ⲉ ϣⲁ ϯⲛⲟⲩ ⲁⲛ</td><td>Do you even now</td></tr>
<tr><td>ⲧⲉⲧⲛ̄ⲣ̄ ϩⲩⲡⲟ|ⲙⲓⲛⲉ ⲁⲥⲱⲧⲙ̄</td><td>dare to listen,</td></tr>
<tr><td>ⲉϣϣⲉ ⲁⲣⲱ|ⲧⲛ̄ ⲁϣⲉϫⲉ</td><td>when it behooved you to speak</td></tr>
<tr><td>ϫⲓⲛ ⲛ̄ϣⲁⲣⲡ̄</td><td>from the beginning?</td></tr>
<tr><td>ϩⲓ̈ⲉ | ϯⲛⲟⲩ ⲁⲛ</td><td>Do you even now</td></tr>
<tr><td>ⲧⲉⲧⲛ̄ⲣ̄ ϩϋⲡⲟⲙⲓⲛⲉ· ⲁⲛ|ⲕⲁⲧⲕⲉ·</td><td>dare to sleep,</td></tr>
<tr><td>ⲉϣϣⲉ ⲁⲣⲱⲧⲛ̄ ⲁⲣⲁⲓ̈ⲥ |</td><td>when it behooved you
to be awake</td></tr>
<tr><td>ϫⲓⲛ ⲛ̄ϣⲁⲣⲡ̄</td><td>from the beginning,</td></tr>
<tr><td>ϫⲉⲕⲁⲥⲉ ⲉⲥⲛⲁ·|ϣⲉⲡ ⲧⲏⲛⲉ·
ⲁⲣⲁⲥ</td><td>in order that the Kingdom
of Heaven</td></tr>
<tr><td>ⲛ̄ϭⲓ ⲧⲙⲛ̄ⲧⲣ̄ⲣⲟ | ⲛⲙⲡⲏⲩⲉ |</td><td>might receive you?</td></tr>
</table>

3) Identification formula: 10.1–2

<table>
<tr><td>ⲥⲉ· ⲙ̄ⲙⲁⲛ ϯϫ̣ⲟⲩ̣ ⲙ̄ⲙⲁⲥ
ⲛⲏⲧⲛ̣̄ | ϫⲉ</td><td>In truth I say to you,</td></tr>
</table>

4) Pronouncement of judgment: 10.2–6

<table>
<tr><td>ⲥⲙⲁⲧⲛ̄ ⲁⲧⲣⲉⲟⲩⲡⲉⲧⲟⲩⲁ|ⲁⲃ·</td><td>it is easier for a holy one</td></tr>
<tr><td>ⲉⲓ ⲁⲡⲓⲧⲛ̄ ⲁⲩϫⲱϩⲙ̄</td><td>to sink into defilement,</td></tr>
<tr><td>ⲁⲩⲱ ⲛ̄|ⲧⲉⲟⲩⲣⲙ̄ⲛ̄ⲟⲩⲁⲉⲓⲛ</td><td>and for a man of light</td></tr>
<tr><td>ⲉⲓ̄ ⲁⲡⲓⲧⲛ̄ | ⲁⲡⲕⲉⲕⲉⲓ</td><td>to sink into darkness,</td></tr>
<tr><td>ⲛ̄ϩⲟⲩⲟ ⲁⲣⲱ̣ⲧⲛ̄ ⲁⲣ̄ ⲣ̄|ⲣⲟ</td><td>than for you to reign—</td></tr>
</table>

5) Conclusion: 10.6

<table>
<tr><td>ⲏ̄ ⲁⲧⲙ̄ⲉⲓⲣⲉ·</td><td>or (even) not to (reign)!</td></tr>
</table>

9.28 <ⲙ̄>ⲡⲁⲣⲁⲃⲁⲧⲏⲥ *ed. pr.* | ⲙ̄<ⲡⲉ>ⲡⲛⲉⲩⲙⲁ *ed. pr.*

Numerous formal parallels to this prophecy of judgment are found in early Christian literature. In order to illustrate the prominence and help clarify the provenance of this form, three examples will be cited below that represent the trajectory of the tradition. The first is a prophecy directed against Israel, embedded in the sayings-of-Jesus tradition, and taken from the Synoptic Sayings Source Q (Luke 3:7–9 par.);[15] the second is a prophecy addressed to an individual and attributed to Paul by the author of the book of Acts (13:10–11);[16] the third is found in an apocalyptic book and, like the saying in *Ap. Jas.* 9.24–10.6, is addressed to the church (*Herm. Sim.* 1.3).[17]

Luke 3:7–9:

1) Introductory address to the accused: 3:7b
   γεννήματα ἐχιδνῶν,

2) Accusatory question (with a self-incriminating citation): 3:7c–8b
   τίς ὑπέδειξεν ὑμῖν φυγεῖν ἀπὸ τῆς μελλούσης ὀργῆς;
   ποιήσατε οὖν καρποὺς ἀξίους τῆς μετανοίας·
   καὶ μὴ ἄρξησθε λέγειν ἐν ἑαυτοῖς·
   πατέρα ἔχομεν τὸν Ἀβραάμ·

3) Identification formula: 3:8c
   λέγω γὰρ ὑμῖν ὅτι

4) Pronouncement of judgment: 3:8d–9a
   δύναται ὁ θεὸς ἐκ τῶν λίθων τούτων ἐγεῖραι τέκνα τῷ Ἀβραάμ.
   ἤδη δὲ καὶ ἡ ἀξίνη πρὸς τὴν ῥίζαν τῶν δένδρων κεῖται·

5) Conclusion: 3:9b
   πᾶν οὖν δένδρον μὴ ποιοῦν καρπὸν καλὸν
   ἐκκόπτεται καὶ εἰς πῦρ βάλλεται.

As was noted above,[18] the accusation section of prophecies directed against Israel is frequently expanded to contain the equivalent of a historical review of God's fidelity and/or Israel's infidelity. In this particular saying, the accusatory question (vs 7c) is coupled with a historical reference which takes the form of a self-incriminating citation (vs 8b: πατέρα ἔχομεν τὸν Ἀβραάμ).[19] The accompanying exhortation

[15]The other examples of Christian prophecies of judgment directed against Israel are: Matt 23:29–36 par., 37–39 par.; Melito *Pass. Hom.* 87–93; and *5 Ezra* 1.22–27, 28–32.

[16]The other examples of Christian prophecies of judgment addressed to an individual are: Acts 5:9; and *Acts Pet.* 12.

[17]The other examples of Christian prophecies of judgment addressed to the church are: 1 Cor 3:16–17; Rev 2:18–23; 3:14–17; and *Herm. Sim.* 1.1–2, 4.

[18]See nn. 3, 9.

[19]Examples from the OT of an accusatory question with a self-incriminating citation are: Isa 37:23–29; and Jer 5:7–14. For examples of a self-incriminating citation alone,

(vs 8a: ποιήσατε . . . καρποὺς ἀξίους τῆς μετανοίας) is reflected in the pronouncement of judgment (vs 9a) and resumed in the concluding statement (vs 9b). The precise paralleling of this conclusion with a saying attributed to Jesus in Matt 7:19 raises the question whether Q's attribution of this prophecy of judgment to John the Baptist is accurate. This suspicion is heightened by the fact that the introductory address to the accused (vs 7b) and the accusatory question (vs 7c) are also paralleled in a prophecy of judgment attributed to Jesus in Matt 23:33. At the very least, the form and content of this prophecy permit the observation that its attribution to John—and not Jesus—was accidental,[20] owing perhaps to Q's tendency to present John the Baptist in a positive light. Moreover, the fact that there is no reference to a messiah in this prophecy indicates that it is a very early tradition, which is to be understood against the pre-exilic prophetic tradition of Israel.[21]

Acts 13:10–11:

1) Introductory address to the accused: 13:10a
ὦ πλήρης παντὸς δόλου καὶ πάσης ῥᾳδιουργίας,
υἱὲ διαβόλου,
ἐχθρὲ πάσης δικαιοσύνης,

2) Accusatory question: 13:10b
οὐ παύσῃ διαστρέφων τὰς ὁδοὺς τοῦ κυρίου τὰς εὐθείας;

3) Identification formula: 13:11a
καὶ νῦν ἰδοὺ

4) Pronouncement of judgment: 13:11bc
χεὶρ κυρίου ἐπὶ σέ,
καὶ ἔσῃ τυφλὸς μὴ βλέπων τὸν ἥλιον ἄχρι καιροῦ.

One of the distinctive features of this prophecy of judgment is that it is permeated with biblical language.[22] The accusatory question, in fact, is based on a combination of Prov 10:9 and Hos 14:10, both of which

---

cf. Amos 4:1–3; 7:16–17; Hos 2:5–7; Mic 3:9–12; and Jer 29:15–17.

[20]See Bultmann, *History*, 117; followed by Dieter Lührmann, *Die Redaktion der Logienquelle* (WMANT 33; Neukirchen: Neukirchener Verlag, 1969) 31.

[21]See Joseph A. Fitzmyer, *The Gospel According to Luke (I–IX)* (AB 28; Garden City: Doubleday, 1981) 464.

[22]See Ernst Haenchen, *The Acts of the Apostles: A Commentary* (Philadelphia: Westminster, 1971) 400.

already intimate an indictment of the accused. The identification formula (with ἰδού) is a "characteristic substitute"[23] for the prophetic messenger formula ("thus says the Lord"). The introductory address to the accused (vs 10a: ὦ πλήρης παντὸς δόλου . . .) consciously contrasts the ψευδοπροφήτης Bar-Jesus (vs 6), against whom this prophecy is directed, with Paul, who is πλησθεὶς πνεύματος ἁγίου (vs 9; cf. vss 1–3, 4) and thus sanctioned to pronounce such a judgment. This means that the "Holy Spirit" is understood here as the spirit of prophecy, in accordance with the widespread tradition in early Christianity that the possession of the spirit empowered one to prophesy.[24] The pronouncement of judgment itself (vs 11bc) is paradigmatic of the function of prophecy in general, that is, the exercise of "jurisdiction over the conditions of divine forgiveness and soteriological security."[25]

Herm. Sim. 1.3:

1) Introductory address to the accused:
ἄφρον καὶ δίψυχε καὶ ταλαίπωρε ἄνθρωπε,

2) Accusatory question:
οὐ νοεῖς,
ὅτι ταῦτα πάντα ἀλλότριά εἰσι
καὶ ὑπ᾽ ἐξουσίαν ἑτέρου εἰσίν;

3) Identification formula:
ἐρεῖ γὰρ ὁ κύριος τῆς πόλεως ταύτης·

4) Pronouncement of judgment:
οὐ θέλω σε κατοικεῖν εἰς τὴν πόλιν μου,
ἀλλ᾽ ἔξελθε ἐκ τῆς πόλεως ταύτης,

5) Conclusion:
ὅτι τοῖς νόμοις μου οὐ χρᾶσαι.

[23]So Swanson, "Christian Prophetic Speech," 15. Note that the pronouncement of judgment begins with χεὶρ κυρίου. Cf. ἰδού in the identification formulas of prophecies of judgment in Matt 23:34; Acts 5:9; Rev 2:22; and also in the citations of Christian prophetic interpretations of Scripture in Clem. Al. *Paed.* 1.2.5.3; and *Barn.* 9.5.

[24]E.g., Iren. *Adv. haer.* 3.11.9; Tertullian *Res. carn.* 63.7, 9; Orig. *Comm. in Matt.* 10.18, 22; *Princ.* 2.7.2; Eus. *Hist. eccl.* 5.16.8; Theophilus *Ad Autol.* 2.9; and in the NT: Luke 1:67; 1 Cor 12:3; 14:37–39; and Mark 3:28–29 par. // *Gos. Thom.* 44: 40.26–31 // *Did.* 11.7. Helmut Koester (*Synoptische Überlieferung bei den apostolischen Vätern* [TU 65; Berlin: Akademie-Verlag, 1957] 215–17) observes that the "unforgivable sin" in Mark 3:28–29 par. is "blasphemy" against the "spirit of prophecy."

[25]Swanson, "Christian Prophetic Speech," 12.

This prophecy of judgment is part of a series of admonitions and warnings that constitute the first "similitude" of *Hermas.* Whether this prophecy originally circulated independently of its context or is a purely literary imitation of its Jewish counterparts is not completely clear. Only its inclusion within the framework of *Hermas* identifies it as addressed to the church; nothing distinctively Christian characterizes this passage at all. The fact that it is placed alongside two other prophecies of judgment (*Sim.* 1.1–2, 4) which treat the common theme of life in this world as a sojourn in a strange land,[26] without reference to a particular situation, suggests that it is a secondary composition.[27] In this respect, this prophecy is comparable to the prophecies of judgment addressed in letters to the churches of Thyatira and Laodicea (Rev 2:18–23; 3:14–17, respectively), which seem to be composed by the author of the entire Apocalypse of John.[28] However, whereas those prophecies address real, concrete situations, this one in *Hermas* is nonspecific, directed to the church at large.

The prophecy of judgment in *Ap. Jas.* 9.24–10.6 is part of that well-established Jewish and Christian tradition which regarded pronouncements of the prophets as divinely commissioned announcements of God's threats and reproaches. This particular saying rests uncomfortably in a context which moves abruptly from a preceding set of exhortations which promise solace (9.18–23), to the outright condemnation in this prophecy of certain unnamed persons who are said to feign the truth, falsify knowledge, and sin against the spirit (9.24–10.6), to a subsequent series of loosely connected first person statements and second person commands pertaining to the speaker's relationship with his hearers (10.6–21). Form-critically, the introductory address to the accused (9.24–28) comprises a fivefold pejorative summons. The accusatory questions (9.29–36) are also carefully structured, coupling a pair of allegations (their daring "to listen" and "to sleep") and indictments (it behooved them "to speak" and "to be awake") in a reproach for not being receptive to the Kingdom. The reference to the Kingdom (9.35: ⲧⲙⲛ̄ⲧⲣ̄ⲣⲟ) is resumed in the pronouncement of judgment itself (10.2–6), which announces that the fall of the elect (a "holy one") and enlightened (a "man of light") is more fathomable than the kingship (10.5–6: ⲣ̄ ⲣ̄ⲣⲟ) of the accused.[29] The

[26]Cf. Philo *Rer. div. her.* 82; *Agric.* 64–65; *Abr.* 62, 66–67; *Vit. cont.* 18–20; *Conf. ling.* 76; and *Cher.* 120. See also Martin Dibelius, *Der Hirt des Hermas* (HNT; Tübingen: Mohr-Siebeck, 1923) 550–51.

[27]See Dibelius, *Hermas*, 550.

[28]See Elisabeth Schüssler Fiorenza, "Revelation, book of," *IDBSup* 744–45.

[29]For the construction "it is easier for . . . than for . . . " (= εὐκοπώτερόν ἐστιν . . .

concluding phrase (10.6) tersely exaggerates the crux of the pronouncement, bringing the prophecy to an abrupt halt.

The *Ap. Jas.* preserves this prophecy among the sayings of Jesus. The context presents the risen Lord as speaking in the first person singular, identifying himself with the "amen" formula (10.1–2: ϲⲉ ⲙ̄ⲙⲁⲛ ϯϫ̣ⲟⲩ ⲙ̄ⲙⲁⲥ ⲛⲏⲧⲛ̣̄ ϫⲉ).[30] According to Joachim Jeremias,

> The only substantial analogy to ἀμὴν λέγω ὑμῖν that can be produced is the messenger-formula 'Thus says the Lord,' which is used by the prophets to show that their words are not their own wisdom, but a divine message. In a similar way, the ἀμὴν λέγω ὑμῖν that introduces the sayings of Jesus expresses his authority. The novelty of the usage, the way in which it is strictly confined to the sayings of Jesus, and the unanimous testimony by all the strata of tradition in the gospels show that here we have the creation of a new expression by Jesus.[31]

Given the tendency and testimony of the prophetic tradition, however, one must ask whether such a "divine alter ego"[32] actually reflects the authentic cry of Jesus' prophetic self-understanding or the voice of Christian prophecy in the name of the risen Lord. Evidence for the acknowledgment of the risen Lord as the source of Christian prophecy abounds in early Christianity. According to the Gospel of Matthew, the church will be graced with the abiding presence of the Lord in its corporate life (18:20) as well as its teaching ministry (28:18–20). Those sayings formulated by the community which refer to the "Lord" and "prophecy" demonstrate that it is the risen Lord who is the inspiration

---

ἤ + the accusative and infinitive), see Mark 10:25 par.; Luke 16:17; and cf. 1 Macc 3:18. For the expression "man of light," cf. *Gos. Thom.* 24: 38.8–10; *Pist. Soph.* 3.132; and see the discussions of Bertil Gärtner, *The Theology of the Gospel According to Thomas* (New York: Harper & Brothers, 1961) 206–9; and Stevan L. Davies, *The Gospel of Thomas and Christian Wisdom* (New York: Seabury, 1983) 50–56. For the image of "sinking" into "defilement" and "darkness," see Hans Jonas, *The Gnostic Religion* (2d ed.; Boston: Beacon, 1963) 57–58, 62–65.

[30]The *Ap. Jas.* transmits the "amen" formula two ways: ϩⲁⲙⲏⲛ (truly: 2.29; 6.2; 12.9) and ϲⲉ ⲙ̄ⲙⲁⲛ (in truth: 6.14; 10.1, 15; 13.8; 14.14).

[31]Joachim Jeremias, *New Testament Theology* (New York: Scribner's, 1971) 36; following T. W. Manson, *The Teaching of Jesus* (Cambridge: Cambridge University Press, 1931) 207, 105–7. For a critique of the insistence of Jeremias (*Theology*, 35 n. 8, 36 n. 2) and others that ἀμήν is used only as a responsory affirmative in Hebrew literature, see John Strugnell, "'Amen, I say unto you' in the Sayings of Jesus and in Early Christian Literature," *HTR* 67 (1974) 177–82, and the literature cited there.

[32]The phrase is Swanson's, "Christian Prophetic Speech," 49.

for Christian prophetic activity in Matthew's community (7:21, 22–23; 24:5, 11; cf. 10:19–20).[33]

The Gospel of John announces that Jesus will return in the figure of the Paraclete, the "*spirit* of *truth*" (16:12–13; 14:16–17, 25–26), who will "guarantee the lasting presence of revelation in the community."[34] The "spirit" is said to be given to the disciples when the risen Lord "breathes" on them (20:22; cf. 7:39), empowering them with the legal right to forgive or retain sins (vs 23). Their commission to exercise this jurisdiction is announced by the Lord in the form of parallel prophetic sentences of holy law:

> ἄν τινων ἀφῆτε τὰς ἁμαρτίας, ἀφέωνται αὐτοῖς·
> ἄν τινων κρατῆτε, κεκράτηνται. (20:23)[35]

Whereas John takes this saying from the cultic-liturgical setting of Christian public worship and attributes it to the risen Lord, Matthew applies it indiscriminately to the earthly Jesus (16:19; 18:18).[36] When

[33]See Ferdinand Hahn, *Christologische Hoheitstitel: Ihre Geschichte im frühen Christentum* (FRLANT 83; 3d ed.; Göttingen: Vandenhoeck & Ruprecht, 1966) 97–98; and Swanson, "Christian Prophetic Speech," 57, 233.

[34]Helmut Koester, *Introduction to the New Testament* (2 vols.; Foundations and Facets; Philadelphia: Fortress, 1982; Berlin/New York: De Gruyter, 1983) 2. 191.

[35]Against Ernst Käsemann, "Sentences of Holy Law in the New Testament," in idem, *New Testament Questions of Today* (London: SCM, 1969) 66–81; and Klaus Berger, "Zu den sogenannten Sätzen heiligen Rechts," *NTS* 17 (1970/71) 10–40, Swanson ("Christian Prophetic Speech") has shown that a definitive feature of the sentence of holy law derives from the prophecy-of-judgment form, namely, "its negative focus on the conditions under which believers forfeit their soteriological security" (p. 175). Its positive counterpart (e.g., Matt 6:14; John 20:23a) is restricted to sentence-of-holy-law "couplets, one member of which reflects the form's characteristic negative function" (ibid.). And like the accusation section of many prophecies of judgment, the sentence of holy law is "characteristically undergirded by a Scriptural allusion" (p. 184). For the sentences of holy law in John 20:23, cf. the scriptural allusions in Isa 22:22 and Sir 28:1. Note that John 20:22 and 23 seem to have been added to an appearance story (vss 19–21) which properly ends with vs 21. See C. H. Dodd, *Historical Tradition in the Fourth Gospel* (Cambridge: Cambridge University Press, 1963) 143–44, 347–49.

[36]Günther Bornkamm ("The Authority to 'Bind' and 'Loose' in the Church in Matthew's Gospel: The Problem of Sources in Matthew's Gospel," in David G. Buttrick, ed., *Jesus and Man's Hope* [2 vols.; Perspective; Pittsburgh: Pittsburgh Theological Seminary, 1970] 1. 48) observes that Matt 16:17–19 presupposes (1) the resurrection of Jesus, (2) the delay of the parousia, and (3) the "continuation of the church as an empirical entity characterized by an authoritative apostolic teaching tradition." For other instances in which the authority to forgive or retain sins is at issue in the church, cf. within the sayings tradition: Matt 6:14–15; Luke 6:37; 7:47 (cf. vs 39!); *1 Clem.* 13.2; Mark 2:5b–10a par.—and outside the sayings tradition: Luke 24:47; Rev 3:7; 1 John 5:16;

Jesus is said to entrust this authority to the entire community, the saying is introduced with the prophetic "amen" formula:

ἀμὴν λέγω ὑμῖν,
ὅσα ἐὰν δήσητε ἐπὶ τῆς γῆς ἔσται δεδεμένα ἐν οὐρανῷ,
καὶ ὅσα ἐὰν λύσητε ἐπὶ τῆς γῆς ἔσται λελυμένα
ἐν οὐρανῷ. (18:18)

This means that the formal function of this sentence of holy law "can be defined in terms of a dominically authorized adaptation of Scripture for the purpose of disclosing the circumstances under which divine acceptance can be jeopardized or secured."[37] It indicates further that the use of ἀμὴν λέγω ὑμῖν as a prophetic identification formula is not restricted to the authentic sayings-of-Jesus tradition.

The virtual equation of the earthly Jesus with the risen Lord helped give rise to the creative power of the Jesus tradition, leading to the spirited production of sayings in the name, and under the authority, of Jesus. The prophetic sayings of the exalted Jesus in Rev 3:3b and 16:15a have thus been reformulated as (inauthentic) sayings of the earthly Jesus in Matt 24:43–44 // Luke 12:39–40:[38]

Rev 3:3b:

ἐὰν (οὖν) μὴ γρηγορήσῃς,
ἥξω ὡς κλέπτης,
καὶ οὐ μὴ γνῷς ποίαν ὥραν ἥξω ἐπὶ σέ.

Rev 16:15a:

ἰδοὺ
ἔρχομαι ὡς κλέπτης·

This saying clearly presupposes a belief in the second coming of Christ, and yet can either be cited as a word of a Christian prophet in *Did.* 16.1[39] or attributed to Jesus in Q (Matt 24:43–44 // Luke 12:39–40) and *Gos. Thom.* 21b: 37.6–10.[40] The tendency to transfer Christian prophetic words from the Lord to the sayings-of-Jesus tradition signals an

Heb 6:4–6; 10:26; and *Herm. Vis.* 2.2.4–8.

[37] Swanson, "Christian Prophetic Speech," 198.

[38] See Bultmann, *History*, 127, 163.

[39] See Koester, *Überlieferung*, 174–79.

[40] This tradition is also found in the eschatological sections of 1 Thess 5:2 and 2 Pet 3:10, with reference to the "coming" of the ἡμέρα κυρίου, which Epiphanius and Didymus the Blind preserve as a dominical saying: Epiph. *Ancor.* 21.2: λέγει [ὁ υἱός] γάρ· ὡς κλέπτης ἐν νυκτὶ ἔρχεται ἡ ἡμέρα ἐκείνη—and Didym. *Trin.* 3.22: καὶ εἰπών [ὁ υἱός]· ὡς κλέπτης ἐν νυκτὶ ἔρχεται ἡ τελευταία ἡμέρα. See Alfred Resch, *Agrapha: Aussercanonische Schriftfragmente* (TU 30/3–4; 2d ed.; Leipzig: Hinrichs, 1906) 146 (numbered "Agraphon 101").

important stage in the development of the tradition. In a prophecy of judgment embedded in a late layer[41] of Q (Matt 23:29–36 // Luke 11:47–51), the announcement of judgment is introduced as follows:

Matt 23:34:	*Luke 11:49:*
1) Identification formula:	
διὰ τοῦτο ἰδοὺ	διὰ τοῦτο καὶ ἡ σοφία τοῦ θεοῦ εἶπεν·
2) Pronouncement of judgment:	
ἐγὼ ἀποστέλλω . . .	ἀποστελῶ . . .

Whereas the Q version (as recorded by Luke) introduces what seems to be a citation from a now lost "wisdom-apocalypse,"[42] where it was given as a pronouncement of personified Wisdom, Matthew has clearly transformed the introductory formula to identify Jesus with Wisdom herself.[43] This identification is made even more explicit by Matthew's insertion of the ἀμὴν λέγω ὑμῖν formula in the concluding statement of the prophecy (23:36), reiterating the divine authorization of the message and associating that message with Jesus himself. But it is obvious that Jesus could not really have been the speaker, because the speaker is the one who sent the Hebrew prophets (23:34a, 35 par.). Accordingly, just as the Hebrew prophets' כה־אמר יהוה came to be understood to express not their own words but the actual message of God, so the Jesus tradition's ἀμὴν λέγω ὑμῖν reflects the transference of Christian prophetic authority from announcements made in the name of the Lord to their attribution to Jesus himself—concurrent with his coming to be identified not just as Wisdom's messenger, but as Wisdom herself.

The prophecy of judgment in *Ap. Jas.* 9.24–10.6 is a previously unattested saying which is included in the sayings-of-Jesus tradition. The

[41]So Lührmann, *Logienquelle*, 97; followed by Arland D. Jacobson, "The Literary Unity of Q," *JBL* 101 (1982) 383.

[42]So M. Jack Suggs, *Wisdom, Christology, and Law in Matthew's Gospel* (Cambridge: Harvard University Press, 1970) 19; Bultmann, *History*, 114; and Adolf Harnack, *The Sayings of Jesus* (New York: Putnam's; London: Williams & Norgate, 1908) 103. Against Lührmann, *Logienquelle*, 46 n. 3. Cf. the quotation formula (introducing a citation of the text of Prov 1:23–33) in *1 Clem.* 57.3: οὕτως γὰρ λέγει ἡ πανάρετος σοφία.

[43]See James M. Robinson, "Jesus as Sophos and Sophia: Wisdom Tradition and the Gospels," in Robert L. Wilken, ed., *Aspects of Wisdom in Judaism amd Early Christianity* (University of Notre Dame Center for the Study of Judaism and Christianity in Antiquity 1; Notre Dame/London: University of Notre Dame Press, 1975) 1–16.

fact that it had a prior history of independent circulation as an utterance by a Christian prophet is suggested by the following observations:[44]

1) form-critical analysis of parallel Jewish and Christian prophetic speeches has demonstrated that, except for occasional literary imitations, such sayings were announced orally prior to their being written down;
2) this saying is inserted in a literary context which is clearly composite;
3) it is included in a document which is concerned with preserving and transmitting traditional (though, in many instances, hitherto unattested) dominical sayings; and
4) precedent for the circulation of originally independent prophetic utterances can be found as early as Q and the letters of Paul[45] and as late as the Montanist movement.[46]

The reference to "sinning against the spirit" (9.28) in the introductory address to the accused locates this saying within the tradition that identified the spirit as the spirit of prophecy. Accordingly, the first indictment in the accusatory questions, that they failed "to speak" (9.31: ϣⲉϫⲉ), must be understood as a reproach for failing to prophesy. The use of the verb λαλεῖν in technical discussions of prophesying (1 Cor 12:3; 14:29; *Did.* 11.7, 8) would seem to verify this observation. This indicates that the saying has a legal provenance.

The second indictment, that they failed "to be awake" (9.33: ⲣⲁ̈ⲓⲥ), reinforces the first allegation, using the language of prophetic sayings (cf. Rev 3:3; Matt 24:42, 43 par.) to emphasize readiness for exercising the gift of prophecy. The coupling of the imagery of "sleeping" and "being awake," moreover, seems to locate the symbolism of this accusation within a Gnostic milieu, which employed the correlative themes of sleep and awakening in a programmatic way to represent, respectively, the plight of the ignorant and the "call from without."[47]

[44]See Swanson, "Christian Prophetic Speech," 60–61.

[45]Prophecies of salvation: 1 Thess 4:15–17 // 1 Cor 15:51–52; Rom 11:25–26a; sentences of holy law: 1 Cor 14:38 // *Gos. Thom.* 3b: 32.26–33.1; and a sentence of holy law embedded in a prophecy of judgment: 1 Cor 3:16–17.

[46]Tertullian *De anima* 9.3–4; *Res. carn.* 11.2; and Eus. *Hist. eccl.* 5.16.4, 6–10, 12–15, 17, 18–19, 20–21.

[47]E.g., the *Hymn of the Pearl* (*apud Acts Thom.* 109.35; 110.43; 111.53). See Hans Jonas, *The Gnostic Religion* (2d ed.; Boston: Beacon, 1963) 68–91; and George W. MacRae, "Sleep and Awakening in Gnostic Texts," in Ugo Bianchi, ed., *Le origini dello gnosticismo: Colloquio di Messina, 13–18 Aprile 1966* (Leiden: Brill, 1970) 496–507 (with special attention to *Ap. John* [NHC 2, 1] 31.5–25). This imagery is, of course, used elsewhere in a non-Gnostic sense (e.g., 1 Thess 5:6–10).

Parallels with the language of Eph 5:14, widely regarded as a fragment of a baptismal hymn (or homily) taken from a Gnostic source,[48] may suggest a cultic context for this saying. The book of Acts attests to the tradition that Christian initiates were expected to prophesy on the occasion of their baptism (8:12–17; 19:2–6; cf. 2:38; 10:44–48),[49] and several early Christian circles recognized—as John the Baptist did—the prophetic prerogative to baptize.[50] Accordingly, the seeming removal of the "head of prophecy" with the decapitation of John the Baptist (*Ap. Jas.* 6.19–7.1) signifies not the termination of prophetic activity but its proper localization in the community.[51] This would indicate that the prophecy of judgment in *Ap. Jas.* 9.24–10.6 has a liturgical provenance as well. Its *Sitz im Leben* is oral prophecy during public worship, perhaps in conjunction with baptism. The implication of the accusatory statement that the purpose of "speaking" and "being awake" is to be "received" by the Kingdom (9.34–36), and hence "to reign"

[48]See Rudolf Bultmann, *Theology of the New Testament* (2 vols.; London: SCM, 1952) 1. 174–75; Hans Conzelmann, "*φῶς*," *TDNT* 9 (1974) 348; and MacRae, "Sleep and Awakening," 503–7.

[49]In Acts, it is the baptized who receive the "spirit," enabling them "to speak in tongues," which is identical with "prophesying" (19:5–6; cf. 8:16–17). Those instances in which the reception of the spirit is separated from baptism (2:38; 8:16; 10:44; cf. 11:15; and 19:2–6) are Lucan theological constructions that actually presuppose the correlation of baptism and spirit, designed (1) to parallel the descent of the Spirit at Pentecost (2:4) with the dispensation of the Spirit to the Gentiles (10:44–48); (2) to present the apostles of the Jerusalem church as being in control of the church in outlying areas such as Samaria (8:12–17); (3) to portray a united front by harmonizing the ministries of Peter (10:44–48) and Paul (19:2–6); and (4) to contrast John's baptism of repentance with Christian baptism in the name of the Lord Jesus (19:2–6). See Haenchen, *Acts*, 184, 304, 554 (on 2:38; 8:16; and 19:6, respectively); and Hans Conzelmann, *Die Apostelgeschichte* (HNT 7; Tübingen: Mohr-Siebeck, 1963) 55, 111 (on 8:16; and 19:5–6).

[50]E.g., the followers of Elchasai (Hipp. *Ref.* 9.13.3–4; 9.15.1–16.4); Marcus (Iren. *Adv. haer.* 1.13.2–6; 1.21.2–3); and Heracleon (Orig. *Comm. in Joh.* 6.23.123–26). On Marcus and Heracleon, see Elaine H. Pagels, *The Johannine Gospel in Gnostic Exegesis: Heracleon's Commentary on John* (SBLMS 17; Nashville/New York: Abingdon, 1973) 57–65; and François-M.-M. Sagnard, *La Gnose valentinienne et le témoignage de saint Irénée* (Etudes de philosophie médiévale 36; Paris: Vrin, 1947) 416–25, 513–14.

[51]Against Klaus Koschorke, "Eine neugefundene gnostische Gemeindeordnung: Zum Thema Geist und Amt im frühen Christentum," *ZThK* 76 (1979) 36 n. 28, 53–54 (with special attention to *Interpretation of Knowledge* [NHC 11, 1]). Origen (*Comm. in Matt.* 10.18, 22, on Matt 13:53–58; 14:1–11) uses exactly the same metaphor to describe the transferal of the gift of prophecy from the Jews to the Gentiles. Since *προφήτης ἐν τῇ ἰδίᾳ πατρίδι τιμὴν οὐκ ἔχει*, he says, the *προφητικὸν λόγον* was surrendered to the Gentiles (10.18.24). The beheading of John, moreover, meant the elimination of the *προφητικὴ κεφαλή* among the Jewish people, the relinquishing of the *προφητικὴ χάρις* to the Christians: *τὴν δὲ κεφαλὴν τῆς προφητείας Ἰουδαῖοι οὐκ ἔχουσι, τὸ κεφάλαιον πάσης προφητείας Χριστὸν Ἰησοῦν ἀρνούμενοι* (10.22.30).

(10.5–6), is that participation in the Kingdom requires prophetic certification. Parallels with those Christian prophetic sayings of the Jesus tradition that have been embedded in the letters of Paul and the Synoptic Sayings Source Q would suggest an early date for the production and circulation of this utterance in the name of the Lord.

1.3 WISDOM AND PROPHETIC SAYINGS TRADITIONS

Ap. Jas. 12.31–13.1:

ⲁⲩⲱ ⲉⲫⲟⲥⲟⲛ ⲙⲉⲛ ⲉⲉⲓϣⲟⲟⲡ | ϩⲁⲧⲉ ⲧⲏⲛⲉ·	As long as I am with you (pl.),
ⲡⲣⲟⲥⲉⲭⲉ ⲁⲣⲁⲉⲓ | ⲁⲩⲱ ⲛ̄ⲧⲉⲧⲛ̄ⲡⲉⲓⲑⲉ ⲛⲏⲉⲓ·	give heed to me and obey me.
ⲡⲥⲁ|ⲡ̄ ⲛ̄ⲇⲉ· ⲉϯⲛⲁⲟⲩⲁⲉⲓⲉ ⲁⲣⲱⲧⲛ̄ |	But when I am to depart from you,
ⲉⲣⲓ ⲡⲁⲙⲉⲉⲩⲉ·	remember me.
ⲉⲣⲓ ⲡⲁⲙⲉⲉⲩⲉ ⲇⲉ |	And remember me
ⲁⲃⲁⲗ ϫⲉ ⲛⲉⲉⲓϣⲟⲟⲡ ϩⲁⲧⲛ̄ ⲧⲏⲛⲉ |	because I was with you
ⲙ̄ⲡⲉⲧⲛ̄ⲥⲟⲩⲱⲛⲧ·	without your knowing me.
ⲥⲉⲛⲁϣⲱ|ⲡⲉ ⲙ̄ⲙⲁⲕⲁⲣⲓⲟⲥ[1]	Blessed are those
ⲛ̄ϭⲓ ⲛⲉⲛⲧⲁϩ|ⲥⲟⲩⲱⲛⲧ̄·	who have known me.

[1]Here and five other times in the *Ap. Jas.* the gnomic future ⲥⲉⲛⲁϣⲱⲡⲉ ⲙ̄ⲙⲁⲕⲁⲣⲓⲟⲥ is used (cf. 1.25–26; 3.18–19; 11.14–15; 12.40–41; 13.11–12). The use of a gnomic future to express a general truth is well known (e.g., Rom 5:7a). See BDF § 349(1); and Herbert Weir Smyth, *Greek Grammar* (rev. Gordon M. Messing; Cambridge: Harvard University Press, 1956) § 1914. Translating a general truth expressed in the present tense in Greek with a gnomic future in Coptic is also a common technique (e.g., Ps 83:13 [LXX]; 1 John 2:8; John 6:27; 15:5; and Luke 14:26 // *Gos. Thom.* 55: 42.25–27; note that Luke 14:14 and Jas 1:25 are not gnomic futures). The use of the verb ϣⲱⲡⲉ (to become) in the future tense with ⲙⲁⲕⲁⲣⲓⲟⲥ seems to be a translational idiosyncrasy, occurring inconsistently within the *Ap. Jas.* itself with no perceptible distinction in meaning from other verbal constructions of "blessing" (cf. the juxtaposing of ⲥⲉⲛⲁϣⲱⲡⲉ ⲙ̄ⲙⲁⲕⲁⲣⲓⲟⲥ with the normal suffix verb ⲛⲉⲉⲓⲉⲧ⸗ in 3.18–19 and 30–31). The only other instance of this usage that I have found is the macarism in *Great Pow.* (NHC 6, 4) 42.23–24. The fact that it never occurs elsewhere in those tractates (1, 3, and 5) in the Jung Codex which were copied by the same scribe is, unfortunately, not conclusive, since there is only one other macarism in this entire folio (*Gos. Truth* [NHC 1, 3] 30.14–15: ⲟⲩⲙⲁⲕⲁⲣⲓⲟⲥ ⲡⲉ).

ⲟⲩⲁⲉⲓ ⲛ̄ⲛⲉⲉⲓ ⲛ̄ⲧⲁϩ|ⲥⲱⲧⲙ̄	Woe to those who have heard
ⲁⲩⲱ ⲙ̄ⲡⲟⲩⲣ̄ ⲡⲓⲥⲧⲉⲩⲉ·	and have not believed!
ⲥⲉ|ⲛⲁϣⲱⲡⲉ· ⲙ̄ⲙⲁⲕⲁⲣⲓⲟⲥ	Blessed are those
ⲛ̄ϭⲓ ⲛⲉ|ⲧⲉ ⲙ̄ⲡⲟⲩⲛⲉⲩ	who have not seen
ⲁ[ⲗⲗ] ⲁ̣ ⲁⲩ̣[ⲛⲁϩⲧⲉ] |	[but] have [had faith].

12.36 <ⲉ>ⲛⲉⲉⲓϣⲟⲟⲡ Schenke | 37 <ⲁⲩⲱ> ⲙ̄ⲡⲉⲧⲛ̄ⲥⲟⲩⲱⲛⲧ Quispel | 13.1 ⲁ[ⲗⲗ] ⲁ̣ ⲁⲩ̣[ⲛⲁϩⲧⲉ] Attridge : ⲁ[ⲗ] ⲗ̣ⲁ [ⲁⲩⲛⲁϩ-ⲧⲉ] *ed. pr.* : ⲁ[ⲩ] ⲧ̣ⲁⲛ̣[ϩⲟⲩⲧ] Kirchner

Ap. Jas. 12.31–13.1 seems to be a composite piece. The first section (12.31–39) comprises three separate but interrelated statements (12.31–35, 35–37, 37–39), each with a first person singular pronoun, arranged thematically by the repetition of certain key words or phrases:

12.31–32: ⲉⲉⲓϣⲟⲟⲡ ϩⲁⲧⲉ ⲧⲏⲛⲉ	. . . 12.36: ⲛⲉⲉⲓϣⲟⲟⲡ ϩⲁⲧⲛ̄ ⲧⲏⲛⲉ
12.35: ⲉⲣⲓ ⲡⲁⲙⲉⲉⲩⲉ	. . . 12.35: ⲉⲣⲓ ⲡⲁⲙⲉⲉⲩⲉ
12.37: ⲙ̄ⲡⲉⲧⲛ̄ⲥⲟⲩⲱⲛⲧ	. . . 12.38–39: ⲛⲉⲛⲧⲁϩⲥⲟⲩⲱⲛⲧ̄

The thematic arrangement indicates that the construction of this piece of discourse is distinguished by antitheses: "to be with" and "to depart" (12.31, 36 and 34); "to not know" and "to know" (12.37 and 38–39). Pronominal references identify the revealer him/herself as speaking in the first person singular. The blessing (or: macarism) in 12.37–39 may be a secondary addition. The second section (12.39–13.1), consisting of a paired woe (12.39–40) and blessing (12.40–13.1), is also marked by antitheses:

12.39: ⲟⲩⲁⲉⲓ	. . . 12.40–41 (cf. 12.37–38): ⲥⲉⲛⲁϣⲱⲡⲉ ⲙ̄ⲙⲁⲕⲁⲣⲓⲟⲥ
12.40: ⲙ̄ⲡⲟⲩⲣ̄ ⲡⲓⲥⲧⲉⲩⲉ	. . . 13.1: ⲁⲩ̣[ⲛⲁϩⲧⲉ]

Whether these two sayings were already joined in the tradition is not completely clear. However, the fact that they make no reference to the speaker may suggest that they have had a compositional history separate from that of the first section.

Heinz Becker[2] has argued that antitheses such as these characterize the style of the "revelation discourse source" of the Gospel of John (e.g., 3:18a, 31, 36; 4:13–14; 5:43; 8:23; 9:39; 11:9–10; 15:2). Although the existence of such a source has been almost unanimously rejected by subsequent scholarship,[3] Becker's analysis can be used, in conjunction with the formal observation that independent sayings were collected and expanded into larger units of discourse and dialogue in the Gospel of John, to help clarify the compositional history of such writings as John's Gospel. *Ap. Jas.* 12.31–13.1 is particularly well suited for such an investigation since it contains, embedded in a discourse, the closest parallel in the *Ap. Jas.* with any saying found in the NT: the macarism in *Ap. Jas.* 12.40–13.1 // John 20:29.

The presence of first person references in the initial section of this discourse (12.31–39) provides a clue to the origin and history of the tradition. The speaker makes reference first to a sojourn (12.31) among an unidentified "you" (pl.) and then to an imminent departure (12.34). The injunctions to "give heed" and "obey" when the speaker is present, heightened by the exhortation to "remember" once the speaker has departed, highlight the contingency of the message. The tension between presence and absence, not knowing and knowing, creates a spiraling[4] effect which culminates with a blessing on those who do know who the speaker is. This is a description of the fate of Wisdom, uttered with her own voice. The blessing on those (few) who have known her (12.37–39) may represent a response to an earlier tradition, reflected in the preceding statement (12.36–37: "I was with you [pl.] without your knowing me"), that Wisdom in fact had been totally rejected, had found no habitation on earth (cf. *1 Enoch* 42.1–2, 3; Matt 23:37 par.).[5] If so, this blessing, though secondary, would

[2] *Die Reden des Johannesevangeliums und der Stil der gnostischen Offenbarungsrede* (FRLANT, NS, 50; Göttingen: Vandenhoeck & Ruprecht, 1956) 24, 65. See Rudolf Bultmann, *The Gospel of John: A Commentary* (Philadelphia: Westminster, 1971) 140 n. 2, and passim.

[3] See Raymond E. Brown, *The Gospel according to John (i–xii)* (AB 29; Garden City: Doubleday, 1966) xxviii–xxxii; and Rudolf Schnackenburg, *The Gospel according to St John* (3 vols.; HTCNT; New York: Herder and Herder, 1968) 1. 48–52.

[4] See Becker, *Reden*, 56.

[5] See Rudolf Bultmann, "Der religionsgeschichtliche Hintergrund des Prologs zum Johannes-Evangelium," in idem, *Exegetica* (Tübingen, Mohr-Siebeck, 1967) 13–19. Gerhard von Rad (*Wisdom in Israel* [Nashville: Abingdon, 1972] 160 n. 17) disagrees, but does make reference to the return to Olympus of two disappointed goddesses in Hesiod's *Works and Days* 197–201. Cf. *Odes Sol.* 42.3, 4; and *Ap. Jas.* 10.15–20.

accord with the subsequent tradition that a righteous remnant did respond to her call (e.g., Sir 1:10, 15; 24:8–32; Bar 3:36–4:1; Wis 7:14, 21; and John 1:12). The injunction to "remember" her (cf. Sir 24:20) is a summons to come to know her (cf. Sir 24:19; 6:26–27).

The first section (12.31–39) of this discourse, therefore, is a fragment of a farewell speech of Wisdom. The injunction to "remember" identifies this fragment as part of an invitation or call of Wisdom. How much of the speech has been lost is impossible to know. Extant examples of wisdom speeches range from those with extensive summonses and elaborate autodoxologies (e.g. Prov 8:4–21, 32–36; Sir 24:3–34)[6] to ones with a terse direct address and summons (e.g., Prov 9:4–6). It is also not clear whether the imperatives are meant to indicate reproach. In the wisdom speech in Prov 1:22–33, for example, the invitation has been completely reworked, via the prophetic tradition, to emphasize a twofold threat (vss 24–26, 29–31) and a reproach (vss 22b–23a).[7] But the temporal references in that speech (vs 22: ὅσον χρόνον) are part of the prophetic reproach (*Scheltrede*),[8] whereas those in the *Ap. Jas.* are integral to the contrast between Wisdom's own presence and absence, and seem to present the possibility of her call's being received. At least this much can be said: the way from "ignorance" to "knowledge" of Wisdom is identified in this fragment with her departure (12.33–35, 35–37). Individually isolable wisdom sayings are not recoverable;[9] the fragment, as a unity, comprises the wisdom speech. But it is possible that the first two statements, which make reference to Wisdom's sojourn and departure (12.31–35, 35–37), were originally separate

[6]The independent wisdom hymn in Prov 8:22–31 comprises a separate autodoxology which was probably added at a later date. See Martin Hengel, *Judaism and Hellenism* (2 vols.; Philadelphia: Fortress, 1974) 1. 153; and Becker, *Reden*, 41–42. For a discussion of the parallels between Sir 24:3–7 and the Isis aretalogies, see Hengel, *Judaism and Hellenism*, 1. 157–62; and Hans Conzelmann, "The Mother of Wisdom," in James M. Robinson, ed., *The Future of our Religious Past: Essays in Honour of Rudolf Bultmann* (New York: Harper & Row, 1971) 230–43.

[7]See Becker, *Reden*, 44–48.

[8]Cf. Jer 4:14, 21; 12:4; 31:22; Hab 2:6; and Matt 23:37 par.

[9]Therefore, the examples of Christian adaptations of older wisdom sayings that are found in the Gospel of John (e.g., 7:33–34; cf. 13:13; 14:19; 16:16), whose temporal references are editorial additions designed to give structure to the Gospel narrative by dramatizing the references to Jesus' impending departure, are not true parallels to *Ap. Jas.* 12.31–39. Cf. *Gos. Thom.* 38: 40.2–7; Cyprian *Testim. ad Quir.* 3.29; and Helmut Koester, "Gnostic Writings as Witnesses for the Development of the Sayings Tradition," in Bentley Layton, ed., *The Rediscovery of Gnosticism: Proceedings of the International Conference on Gnosticism at Yale, New Haven, Connecticut, March 28–31, 1978* (2 vols.; NumenSup 41; Leiden: Brill, 1980) 1. 238–44.

from the macarism (12.37–39), since the testimony of the tradition would lead us to expect the latter to be included in a final crisis saying (*Krisenspruch* [e.g., Prov 8:32, 34]), where references to Wisdom's own activity are not usually found.

Ap. Jas. 12.31–13.1 concludes with a paired woe (12.39–40) and blessing (12.40–13.1). The blessing (or: macarism) is obviously the same saying as that which climaxes[10] the Gospel of John:

> λέγει αὐτῷ (Θωμᾷ) ὁ Ἰησοῦς·
> ὅτι ἑώρακάς με πεπίστευκας;
> μακάριοι οἱ μὴ ἰδόντες καὶ πιστεύσαντες. (20:29)

The formulation of this verse is clearly the work of the Evangelist, who characteristically prepared questions to correct a false or misguided "opinion or attitude of the one addressed,"[11] followed by sayings or comments which provided his own theological interpretation for the readers of the Gospel. This can be seen in an exemplary way in John's invitation to the reader to "come and see" at the beginning of the Gospel (1:50 [cf. vs 51]—with which John 20:29 provides an inclusio in form as well as in content):[12]

> ἀπεκρίθη Ἰησοῦς καὶ εἶπεν αὐτῷ (Ναθαναήλ)·
> ὅτι εἶπόν σοι ὅτι εἶδόν σε ὑποκάτω τῆς συκῆς, πιστεύεις;
> μείζω τούτων ὄψῃ. . . . (1:50)

Scholarly consensus holds that the story of Jesus' appearance to Thomas (John 20:24–29) did not circulate as an independent pericope.[13] Certainly the story in its present form presupposes the resurrection account in John 20:19–21, 22–23, a self-contained unit which is told in such a way that no one would ever imagine that Thomas was missing. The parallel structure and (sometimes verbatim) language of these two stories demonstrate that the former (vss 24–29) has been

[10]According to C. H. Dodd, John 20:29 "is the true climax of the gospel; the rest, however true and however moving, is mere postscript" (*The Interpretation of the Fourth Gospel* [Cambridge: Cambridge University Press, 1968] 443).

[11]Bultmann, *John*, 695 n. 6.

[12]Cf. John 4:35; 6:61–62; 16:19–20, 31–32.

[13]See C. H. Dodd, "The Appearances of the Risen Christ: An Essay in Form-Criticism of the Gospels," in D. E. Nineham, ed., *Studies in the Gospels: Essays in Memory of R. H. Lightfoot* (Oxford: Blackwell, 1967) 20; and Raymond E. Brown, *The Gospel according to John (xiii–xxi)* (AB 29A; Garden City: Doubleday, 1970) 1031. Bultmann (*John*, 693–94) is hesitant.

modeled on the latter. It may be that the Thomas episode is designed, in part, to personify the doubt of (some of) the disciples.[14] But there are still some seemingly unresolved problems:

1) the characterization of Thomas as *εἷς ἐκ τῶν δώδεκα* (vs 24) is curious, since "the *δώδεκα* are otherwise scarcely mentioned in this Gospel"[15] (cf. 6:13, 67, 70, 71), and Thomas has already been introduced in the narrative in John 11:16; 14:5 (cf. 21:2);
2) even if Thomas is portrayed as the personification of doubt, the motif of doubting the resurrection is firmly fixed elsewhere in the gospel tradition (cf. Matt 28:17; Luke 24:11, 25, 37–38, 41; *Gos. Pet.* 13.56; *Ep. Apost.* 10–12 [21–23]; Mark 16:14; and *Gos. Heb.* frg. 7 [*apud* Jerome *De vir. inl.* 2], where it is presupposed), and is not dependent on John 20:19–21; and
3) the reference to the fact that Jesus *ἔδειξεν καὶ τὰς χεῖρας καὶ τὴν πλευρὰν αὐτοῖς* (vs 20)[16] is unmotivated, making sense only in light of the Thomas story in vss 25, 27.

Raymond E. Brown's suggestion that the showing of Jesus' hands and side (vs 20) was originally preceded by an expression of doubt (as in Luke 24:37–39), which the Evangelist has transferred to a separate episode and personified in Thomas, gives a plausible solution to most of these problems.[17] It does not, however, answer the history-of-religions question of the purpose of narrating such a story.

The story of Jesus' appearance to Thomas "originally was designed to demonstrate the physical reality of the resurrection through the touching of Jesus' body."[18] The reference to the fact that Jesus "showed" (*ἔδειξεν*) the (eleven) disciples his hands and side (vs 20) is designed to dispel doubt by "demonstrating" the physicality of the resurrection. The legend preserved in Ignatius (*Smyrn.* 3.2–3) and the Gospel of Luke (24:36–43) confirms this:[19]

[14]So Dodd, "Appearances," 20; and Brown, *John (xiii–xxi)*, 1028, 1032.

[15]Bultmann, *John*, 694.

[16]The secondary reference to the *πλευράν*, rather than the *πόδας* (cf. Luke 24:39), is probably dependent on John 19:34.

[17]Brown, *John (xiii–xxi)*, 1032. However, his suggestion (p. 1024) that the phrase "one of the twelve" could be an imitation of "one of the disciples" (cf. John 6:8; 12:4; 13:23) overlooks the fact that *μαθηταί* is an important term in John.

[18]Helmut Koester, "Apocryphal and Canonical Gospels," *HTR* 73 (1980) 125.

[19]See Koester, *Überlieferung*, 45–56. Note that Jerome's reference (*De vir. inl.* 16) to this passage was not taken from a Jewish-Christian gospel but from Eusebius's quotation of Ignatius (*Hist. eccl.* 3.36.11). See Philipp Vielhauer, "Jewish-Christian Gospels," in *NTApo*, 1. 128–29.

Ign. Smyrn. 3.2–3:	*Luke 24:36–43:*
καὶ ὅτε πρὸς τοὺς περὶ Πέτρον ἦλθεν,	36) ταῦτα δὲ αὐτῶν λαλούντων αὐτὸς ἔστη ἐν μέσῳ αὐτῶν καὶ λέγει αὐτοῖς· εἰρήνη ὑμῖν.[20]
	37) πτοηθέντες δὲ καὶ ἔμφοβοι γενόμενοι ἐδόκουν πνεῦμα θεωρεῖν.
ἔφη αὐτοῖς·	38) καὶ εἶπεν αὐτοῖς· τί τεταραγμένοι ἐστὲ καὶ διὰ τί διαλογισμοὶ ἀναβαίνουσιν ἐν τῇ καρδίᾳ ὑμῶν;
λάβετε,	39) ἴδετε τὰς χεῖράς μου καὶ τοὺς πόδας μου ὅτι ἐγώ εἰμι αὐτός·
ψηλαφήσατέ με καὶ ἴδετε, ὅτι οὐκ εἰμὶ δαιμόνιον ἀσώματον.	ψηλαφήσατέ με καὶ ἴδετε, ὅτι πνεῦμα σάρκα καὶ ὀστέα οὐκ ἔχει καθὼς ἐμὲ θεωρεῖτε ἔχοντα.
καὶ εὐθὺς αὐτοῦ ἥψαντο καὶ ἐπίστευσαν,	40) καὶ τοῦτο εἰπὼν ἔδειξεν αὐτοῖς τὰς χεῖρας καὶ τοὺς πόδας.[21]
κραθέντες τῇ σαρκὶ αὐτοῦ καὶ τῷ πνεύματι. . .[22]	
	41) ἔτι δὲ ἀπιστούντων αὐτῶν ἀπὸ τῆς χαρᾶς καὶ θαυμαζόντων εἶπεν αὐτοῖς· ἔχετέ τι βρώσιμον ἐνθάδε;
μετὰ δὲ τὴν ἀνάστασιν συνέφαγεν αὐτοῖς καὶ συνέπιεν ὡς σαρκικός, καίπερ πνευματικῶς	42) οἱ δὲ ἐπέδωκαν αὐτῷ ἰχθύος ὀπτοῦ μέρος· 43) καὶ λαβὼν ἐνώπιον αὐτῶν ἔφαγεν.
ἡνωμένος τῷ πατρί.	

[20]This line (Luke 24:36c), missing in D and Itala, may well have been inserted by a later scribe on the basis of John 20:19, 26.

[21]This verse (Luke 24:40) is missing in D Itala syr$^{s.c}$ Marcion, and may well have been inserted by a later scribe on the basis of John 20:20.

[22]Here Ignatius (*Smyrn.* 3.2) inserts his own interpretive comment: διὰ τοῦτο καὶ θανάτου κατεφρόνησαν, ηὑρέθησαν δὲ ὑπὲρ θάνατον.

The similarities of language and narrative structure prove that Ignatius and Luke have transmitted the same story:[23]

Language (verbatim): *ψηλαφήσατέ με καὶ ἴδετε*

Narrative structure:
1) resurrection appearance
2) mistaking Jesus for a "ghost"
3) demonstration by touching[24]
4) concluding report of Jesus' eating.[25]

The variants (especially in the saying attributed to Jesus) indicate that these are independent accounts of this shared tradition.[26] Together they bear witness to the objective of the story which John has presupposed,[27] that is, doubts about the physical reality of the resurrection could be silenced by touching (*ψηλαφᾶν, ἅπτεσθαι*) the risen Jesus' body.[28] Since the story of Jesus' appearance to Thomas is explicable only in this history-of-religions context, the Thomas episode (John 20:24–29) can best be understood not simply as a secondary adaptation of the story of Jesus' appearance to the eleven (John 20:19–21,

[23]So Koester, *Überlieferung*, 46–49.

[24]This is presupposed, though not actually stated, in Luke 24:39, 40. Cf. *Ep. Apost.* 11–12 (22–23).

[25]Cf. *Gos. Heb.* frg. 7 (*apud* Jerome *De vir. inl.* 2).

[26]See Koester, *Überlieferung*, 47–48: Ignatius would not have changed Luke's *πνεῦμα* and *σάρξ* (Luke 24:39) to *δαιμόνιον ἀσώματον*, for: (1) the terms "flesh and spirit" are almost formulaic in Ignatius (e.g., *Magn.* 1.2; 13.1; *Trall.* 12.1); (2) the phrase *σαρκικός τε καὶ πνευματικός* is used elsewhere in Ignatius of Jesus (*Eph.* 7.2; *Smyrn.* 12.2), but *σῶμα* and *σωματικός* are not; and (3) Ignatius's only other use of *ἀσώματος* and (the adjective) *δαιμονικός* occurs in the characterization of his opponents in *Smyrn.* 2.1, where he introduced it from and on account of the resurrection tradition in *Smyrn.* 3.2. Against Philipp Vielhauer, "Jewish-Christian Gospels," in *NTApo*, 1. 130.

[27]Against Brown, (*John [xiii–xxi]*, 1046), who maintains that in "a later generation" there "developed a tradition that Thomas or the disciples actually touched Jesus," and makes reference to Ign. *Smyrn.* 3.2 and *Ep. Apost.* 11–12 (22–23), but does not mention Luke 24:36–43.

[28]Cf. the corroborating history-of-religions tradition in Philostr. *Vit. Ap.* 8.12: when Apollonius "appeared" (8.10: *ἐφάνη*) to Demetrius and Damis, after having "vanished" (8.5: *ἠφανίσθη*) from the court, he said (*ἔφη*): "*λαβοῦ μου . . . κἂν μὲν διαφύγω σε, εἴδωλόν εἰμί σοι ἐκ Φερσεφάττης ἥκον . . . εἰ δὲ ὑπομείναιμι ἁπτόμενον, πεῖθε καὶ Δάμιν ζῆν τέ με καὶ μὴ ἀποβεβληκέναι τὸ σῶμα.*" Philostratus then continues: they were no longer able "to disbelieve" (*ἀπιστεῖν*), but got up, "clung to him" (*ἐξεκρέμαντο*), and kissed him.

22–23). Rather, both of these episodes are to be regarded as variants of an earlier appearance story which spoke of touching Jesus' body.

The demand of Thomas for a tangible demonstration of the resurrected Lord (vs 25) is not simply doubt, but a refusal to believe,[29] tantamount to faith based merely on "signs." Thomas thus personifies the theological position that the Evangelist consistently attempts to correct throughout the Gospel, as seen, for example, in the redactional interpolation into the source of the story of the healing of the court official's son (4:48: ἐὰν μὴ σημεῖα καὶ τέρατα ἴδητε, οὐ μὴ πιστεύσητε; cf. 2:23–25).[30] Even though John does not state that Thomas actually did touch Jesus (the inference being that he did not), and does report that Thomas made a (Johannine) confession of faith (vs 28), Thomas is still one who must see in order to believe (vs 29a). He therefore does not receive a blessing. The blessing on those who have not seen but have come to faith is directed to future generations. Instead of telling the traditional resurrection-appearance story with its original ending, the Evangelist has replaced the ending with a saying (vs 29b) which rejects the physical realism of the story, a realism, in fact, which is anticipated in the narrative itself (vss 25, 27).[31] John's use of the macarism is unquestionably redactional, an early Christian appropriation of a traditional saying designed to provide continuity with the now distant past, in order to assure persons who were not eyewitnesses that they are the ones to be blest with faith.

> For the Evangelist, it is those Christians of a later generation, who have seen neither the earthly nor the risen Jesus, but only received the message through the tradition and became believers by that means, who are in fact the true Christians. Therefore they, and not Thomas, are blest. The faith of Thomas attempts to gain custody of God as a present thing of the world. Inasmuch as the Evangelist does not yet bless this faith, he corrects the presentation of faith as it has been transmitted in the tradition. Naturally, even that tradition, which like Luke 24:36–43 seeks to overcome doubt by a tangible proof of the perceptible, is thereby rejected as incomplete.[32]

[29]See George W. MacRae, *Invitation to John* (Garden City: Doubleday, 1978) 225.

[30]See James M. Robinson, "The Johannine Trajectory," in idem and Helmut Koester, *Trajectories through Early Christianity* (Philadelphia: Fortress, 1971) 246, 252–55.

[31]Note that the Evangelist's hand can also be detected in the preceding empty tomb and appearance stories (20:11–18, 19–23), in that references to touching (vs 17) are replaced by seeing (vss 18, 20). This indicates that the stories in this entire chapter have been reworked, not just the story of Jesus' appearance to Thomas (vss 24–29).

[32]Ernst Haenchen, *Das Johannesevangelium: Ein Kommentar* (Tübingen: Mohr-Siebeck,

The *Ap. Jas.* preserves this macarism (12.40–13.1) as part of the concluding section (12.39–13.1) of a fragmentary discourse of a departing revealer. Only the context implies that Jesus is the revealer; not even a pronominal reference is made in this section to the "I" of the speaker, in either the blessing or its accompanying woe. Accordingly, these two sayings have nothing to do with hearing or seeing *Jesus*, but with a prophetic response to faith in the revealed word. There are no indicators here of Johannine redactional influence on the *Ap. Jas.* John has taken this macarism from the tradition and used it in a programmatic way to climax the entire Gospel, providing at once a critique of the aretalogical tradition and a blessing on future generations, by inserting it as the conclusion of a revised resurrection-appearance story and introducing it with his own distinctive corrective question (vs 29a: *ὅτι ἑώρακάς <u>με</u> πεπίστευκας*).[33] John's redaction of this saying and story supports his understanding that "seeing" Jesus is not observing the miraculous but perceiving Jesus' "glorious" manifestation of the Father (cf. 1:18; 2:11; 6:46; 11:40; 14:7–9; 20:8, 18, 20). All elements which John adds to the Thomas story convey distinctively Johannine theological themes.[34]

The woe in *Ap. Jas.* 12.39–40 probably should also be regarded as a traditional prophetic saying (cf. *Herm. Vis.* 4.2.6). Whether the editor of this entire passage (12.31–13.1) received the woe and blessing as a pair, and attached them to the wisdom speech on the basis of catchword association (12.37–38, 40–41: ⲥⲉⲛⲁϣⲱⲡⲉ ⲙ̄ⲙⲁⲕⲁⲣⲓⲟⲥ), is not certain. It may be that they were included here after the pattern of the wisdom speeches in Prov 1:22–33; 8:4–21, 32–36, which typically were concluded with a threat and a promise (the crisis sayings in Prov 1:32–33; 8:32–36). However, the fact that those threats and promises contain first person singular references to the speaker, whereas *Ap. Jas.* 12.39–13.1 does not, implies that its woe and blessing are to be form-critically distinguished from such speeches.[35] *Ap. Jas.* 12.31–13.1,

---

1980) 574.

[33]John 20:29 is not the only place the Evangelist has inserted a traditional saying into his narrative by means of the corrective question. Cf. John 1:51 (secondarily appended to the corrective question and comment in vs 50); and John 4:35, which is similar to the saying about the harvest found independently in Q (Matt 9:37–38 // Luke 10:2) and *Gos. Thom.* 73: 46.6–9. See Wayne A. Meeks, "The Man from Heaven in Johannine Sectarianism," *JBL* 91 (1972) 50–52 (on John 1:51); and Dodd, *Historical Tradition*, 391–405 (on John 4:35).

[34]Jesus' exhortation (20:27), Thomas's confession (20:28), and Jesus' macarism (20:29).

[35]Dodd (*Historical Tradition*, 354–55) tried to relate the macarism in John 20:29 to the Q saying in Matt 13:16 // Luke 10:23 (cf. *Ps. Sol.* 17.44). That saying, however, belongs

therefore, is a mixed form, a combination of a fragmentary wisdom speech (12.31–39) and a collection of prophetic sayings (12.39–13.1) molded into a discourse which is now attributed to Jesus. Rather than being a "strange echo"[36] of John 20:29, *Ap. Jas.* 12.40–13.1 preserves this macarism independently of John, in a less-redacted form, as part of a discourse of a departing revealer.

---

rather to the complex of revelation sayings in Q, the *Gospel of Thomas*, and the (now lost) wisdom book(s) which the Corinthian church "knew and used in the context of their wisdom theology" (Helmut Koester, "Gnostic Writings as Witnesses for the Development of the Sayings Tradition," in Bentley Layton, ed., *The Rediscovery of Gnosticism: Proceedings of the International Conference on Gnosticism at Yale, New Haven, Connecticut, March 28–31, 1978* [2 vols.; NumenSup 41; Leiden: Brill, 1980] 1. 249). Note also that the farewell speech at the beginning of the discourse and dialogue in *Ap. Jas.* 2.39–3.38 represents a development of the sayings tradition in *Ap. Jas.* 12.39–13.1 // John 20:29, since explicit reference is made there to the one ("the [Son of] Man") who was seen (3.13–24). So also *5 Ezra* 1.35–37; *Ep. Apost.* 29 (40); and the counterfeit "Letter of Jesus to Abgar" (*apud* Eus. *Hist. eccl.* 1.13.10; on which see Walter Bauer, *Orthodoxy and Heresy in Earliest Christianity* [Philadelphia: Fortress, 1971] 1–43).

[36]As asserted by Brown, *John (xiii–xxi)*, 1051.

2

THE USE OF SAYINGS TO COMPOSE DIALOGUES

Originally discrete sayings were used to compose some of the dialogues between Jesus and his disciples in the *Ap. Jas.* This will be demonstrated by an analysis of three dialogues. The saying or sayings which underlie each dialogue will be isolated and discussed (1) by clarifying the elements of redaction and the use of tradition; (2) by identifying the formal parallels of the saying(s), or, in those instances in which a particular saying may not have been preserved elsewhere, by citing parallel sayings which preserve the same form; and (3) by examining the *Sitz im Leben* and formal history of the saying(s), concluding with a consideration of the use of the saying(s) in the composition of each dialogue.

2.1 THE DIALOGUE IN *AP. JAS.* 2.21–35

Ap. Jas. 2.21–35:

1) *Question of the Disciples:*

a) Introduction: 2.21–22

. . . ⲡⲁϫⲉⲛ | ⲛⲉϥ ϫⲉ	. . . We said to him:

b) Question: 2.22

ⲁⲕⲃⲱⲕ ⲁⲕⲟⲩⲁⲉⲓⲉ ⲁⲣⲁⲛ |	"Have you gone and departed from us?"

2) *Response of Jesus:*

a) Introduction: 2.23

ⲓⲏ(ⲥⲟⲩ)ⲥ ⲇⲉ ⲡⲁϫⲉϥ ϫⲉ	And Jesus said:

b) Response: 2.23–26

ⲙⲡⲉ· ⲁⲗⲗⲁ |	"No, but
ϯⲛⲁⲃⲱⲕ ⲁⲡⲧⲟⲡⲟⲥ	I shall go to the place
ⲛ̄ⲧⲁϩⲓ̈ⲉⲓ ⲙ̄|ⲙⲉⲩ	from which I have come.
ϣⲡⲉ ⲧⲉⲧⲛ̄ⲟⲩⲱϣⲉ· ⲉⲉ̂ⲓ |	If you (pl.) desire to come
ⲛ̄ⲙ̄ⲙⲏⲉ̂ⲓ ⲁⲙⲏⲧⲛ̄	with me, come."

3) *Response of the Disciples:*

a) Introduction: 2.26–27

ⲁϩⲟⲩ<ⲟⲩ>ⲱϣⲃ̄ | ⲧⲏⲣⲟⲩ ⲡⲁϫⲉⲩ ϫⲉ	They all answered and said:

b) Response: 2.27–28

ϣⲡⲉ ⲕⲣ̣̄ ⲕ̣ⲉ̣|ⲗⲉⲩⲉ ⲛⲉⲛ	"If you bid us,
ⲧⲛ̄ⲛ̄ⲏⲟⲩ	we'll come."

4) *Response of Jesus:*

a) Introduction: 2.28

ⲡⲁϫⲉϥ ϫ̣[ⲉ] |	He said:

b) Response: 2.29–35

ϩⲁⲙⲏⲛ ϯϫⲟⲩ ⲙ̄ⲙⲁⲥ ⲛⲏⲧⲛ̄ ϫ̣[ⲉ] |	"Truly I say to you (pl.),
ⲙⲛ ⲗⲁⲁⲩⲉ ⲁⲛⲏϩⲉ ⲛⲁⲃⲱⲕ ⲁϩⲟⲩ̣[ⲛ] |	no one ever will enter

ⲁⲧⲙⲛⲧⲣ̄ⲣⲟ ⲛ̄ⲙ̄ⲡⲏⲩⲉ·	the Kingdom of Heaven
ⲉⲉⲓϣⲁⲛ̣[ⲣ] | ⲕⲉⲗⲉⲩⲉⲓ ⲛⲉϥ·	if I bid him,
ⲁⲗⲗⲁ ⲁⲃⲁⲗ ϫⲉ̣ | ⲧ̣ⲉⲧⲛ̄ⲙⲏϩ ⲛ̄ⲧⲱⲧⲛ̄·	but rather because you yourselves are full.
ⲁⲣⲓ ⲥⲩⲅⲭⲱⲣⲓ | ⲛⲏï	Let me have
ⲛ̄ïⲁⲕⲱⲃⲟⲥ ⲙⲛ̄ ⲡⲉⲧⲣⲟⲥ |	James and Peter,
ϫⲉⲕⲁⲥⲉ ⲉⲉⲓⲛⲁⲙⲁϩⲟⲩ	in order that I may fill them."

2.26 ⲁϩⲟⲩ<ⲟⲩ>ⲱϣⲃ̄ *ed. pr.* | 32 ⲕⲉⲗⲉⲩⲉⲓ, ⲓ inserted secondarily

This passage exhibits the formal features of a composite piece. The main indicators of compositional redaction are the following:

1) the introductory references to the disciples alternate between "we" (2.21) and "they" (2.26–27);
2) the use of the formula "answered and said" (2.26–27) is reminiscent not only of the redactional introductions to sayings in the Synoptics and John but also of those preserved independently of the NT;[1] and

[1]In Jesus traditions independent of the NT: *P. Egerton 2* frg. 1 (verso, lines 17–18); *Gos. Pet.* 11.46 (contrast Matt 27:24); *2 Clem.* 5.3; *Dial. Sav.* 132.19–20; *P. Oxy. 840* (recto, lines 30–31); *Gos. Eg.* frg. 4 (*apud* Clem. Al. *Strom.* 3.9.66.2).

In Jesus traditions which are, at least in part, dependent on the NT: *Gos. Naz.* frg. 15a (*apud* Jerome *Adv. Pelag.* 3.2—contrast Matt 18:22); *Prot. Jas.* 23.1; *Acts Pil.* 2.3; *Ep. Apost.* 4 (15), 17 (28) and passim.

In early Christian literature not composed of sayings of Jesus: *Herm. Sim.* 9.7.5 and passim; *Acts Pet. 12 Apost.* (NHC 6, 1) 4.11, 29–30 and passim; *Gos. Mary* 10.7, 13–14 and passim; *Thom. Cont.* (NHC 2, 7) 138.29, 36 and passim; *Ep. Pet. Phil.* (NHC 8, 2) 134.19–20; 138.17; *Acts Thom.* 39; *Asc. Isa.* 7.26, 27; *Apoc. Paul* (NHC 5, 2) 22.30–23.1 and passim; *Ap. John* (NHC 2, 1) 25.18–19; *Ap. John* (NHC 4, 1) 40.24–25; *Hyp. Arch.* 91.23; *Orig. World* 112.31; 115.20–21; 120.1; *1 Jeu* 1 and passim; *2 Jeu* 44; *Pist. Soph.* 1.17 and passim.

In non-Christian texts: 2 Esdr 4:1–2 and passim; *T. Levi* 19.2; *Ahikar* 8.35 (Syriac) and passim; *Man. Ps.* 16.1; *1 Enoch* 25 and passim.

Therefore, this formula does not necessarily suggest that the *Ap. Jas.* is "echoing" or "imitating" the style of the NT, and it certainly does not presuppose dependence on the NT. Against Puech, *Epistula Iacobi Apocrypha*, xxix; idem, "Gnostic Gospels and Related Documents," 335; Perkins, *Gnostic Dialogue*, 145–56; Kipgen, "Gnosticism in Early Christianity," 119–20; and S. Brown, "James," 37.

3) the three main verbs in the dialogue (ⲃⲱⲕ [to go], ⲉⲓ [to come], and ⲣ̄ ⲕⲉⲗⲉⲩⲉ[ⲓ] [to bid]) are found in the questions and responses of both the disciples and Jesus, indicating that the dialogue has been constructed by means of repeating these verbs in a progressive series of questions and answers:

ⲃⲱⲕ:	2.22 (Disciples)	. . . 2.24 (Jesus)
ⲉⲓ:	2.24, 25, 26 (Jesus)	. . . 2.28 (Disciples)
ⲣ̄ ⲕⲉⲗⲉⲩⲉ(ⲓ):	2.27–28 (Disciples)	. . . 2.31–32 (Jesus).

The presence of these verbs in the individual responses of Jesus as well as the editorial questions and comments of the disciples leads us to suspect that the latter may have been constructed out of the former. This would suggest that the basis of this dialogue is one or more traditions which have been quoted and reformulated to construct a dialogue.

The main indicator of the use of traditions is the fact that the two responses of Jesus use the language, style, and formal structure of sayings attested elsewhere in early Christian literature:

A) 2.24–25: "I shall go to the place from which I have come"; and
B) 2.29–33: "Truly I say to you (pl.), no one ever will enter the Kingdom of Heaven if I bid him, but rather because you yourselves are full."

Isolating these sayings and identifying their formal features will enable us to trace the compositional history of this entire passage from originally discrete sayings to an expanded dialogue.

A) *Ap. Jas.* *2.24–25:*

ϯⲛⲁⲃⲱⲕ ⲁⲡⲧⲟⲡⲟⲥ	I shall go to the place
ⲛ̄ⲧⲁϩⲓ̈ⲉⲓ ⲙ̄|ⲙⲉⲩ	from which I have come.

This first person singular saying is a discrete unit, capable of standing independently. As the first statement made by Jesus in the *Ap. Jas.*, it sets the stage for the entire discussion which follows. The occurrence of this same saying in a discourse of Jesus near the end of the *Ap. Jas.* (14.20–22) forms an inclusio which frames the body of Jesus' private revelation to James and Peter:

Ap. Jas. 14.20–22:

ⲉⲉⲓⲛⲁⲃⲱⲕ ⲁϩⲣⲏ̈ⲓ̈ ⲁⲡⲧⲟⲡⲟⲥ[2] ⲛ̄ⲧⲁϩⲓ̈ⲉⲓ ⲙ̄ⲙⲁϥ·	I shall ascend to the place from which I have come.

Redactional elements:

The use of ⲙⲡⲉ ⲁⲗⲗⲁ (2.23) at the beginning of Jesus' response (2.23–26) is redactionally secondary, serving to connect the saying (2.24–25) to the initial question of the disciples (2.22). This connection is made even more neatly through the use of the word ⲃⲱⲕ (to go) in both the question and the response (2.22, 24). The catchword ⲃⲱⲕ is derived from the traditional saying that provides the answer to the disciples' question. The form of this piece of dialogue (2.21–26), therefore, is the chria: a traditional saying is introduced by a question or remark that secondarily frames the saying.[3] The *Ap. Jas.* preserves this traditional saying as a response of Jesus to a question of the disciples. The concluding remark of Jesus (2.25–26: "if you [pl.] desire to come with me, come") is a secondary addition which repeats the verb ⲉⲓ as a catchword on which to build the subsequent response of the disciples (2.26–28).

Formal parallels:

A most instructive comparison can be made with the chria in the *Apoc. Paul* 22.30–23.10:

1) *Question:*

a) Introduction: 22.30–23.2

ⲁ̣ϥⲟⲩⲱ|ϣⲃ̄ ⲛ̄ϭⲓ ⲡⲓϩⲗ̄ⲗⲟ ⲉϥϫⲱ ⲙ̄ⲙⲟⲥ ⲛⲁ[ⲓ̈] | ϫⲉ	The old man answered, saying to [me]:

[2]The temporal reference ϯⲛⲟⲩ ⲇⲉ (but now) in 14.20 is redactionally secondary. The use of the directional adverb ⲁϩⲣⲏ̈ⲓ̈ does not alter the form or content of the saying. Except in 2.30 where ⲃⲱⲕ ⲁϩⲟⲩ̣[ⲛ] means "to enter" and 10.19–20 where ⲃⲱⲕ ⲁϩⲣⲏⲉⲓ ϩⲓ̈ϫⲙ means "to descend upon," ⲃⲱⲕ always means "to go (up)" or "ascend" in the *Ap. Jas.*, with or without ⲁϩⲣⲏ̈ⲓ̈. For ⲃⲱⲕ: 2.22, 24; 7.38; 10.23; 14.23; 15.6, 33. For ⲃⲱⲕ ⲁϩⲣⲏ̈ⲓ̈: 14.21, 40–41; 15.35; 16.8.

[3]See Martin Dibelius (*From Tradition to Gospel* [New York: Scribner's, 1934] 152–53), who refers to Xenoph. *Mem.* 3.13; Luc. *Demon.* 12–62; Diog. L. 4.7.47–51; and Philostr. *Vit. Soph.* 1.19 (§ 511); 1.25 (§§ 537–39); 2.4 (§ 568).

b) Question: 23.2

ⲉⲕⲛⲁⲃⲱⲕ ⲉⲧⲱⲛ ⲡⲁⲩⲗⲟⲥ |. . .	"Where are you (sing.) to go, Paul?". . .

2) *Answer:*

a) Introduction: 23.8–9

ⲁⲩⲱ ⲁϊⲟⲩⲱϣⲃ̄ ⲉϊϫⲱ ⲙ̄ⲙⲟⲥ | ⲙ̄ⲡⲓϩⲗ̄ⲗⲟ ϫⲉ	And I answered, saying to the old man:

b) Answer: 23.9–10

ⲉϊⲛⲁⲃⲱⲕ ⲉⲡⲧⲟⲡⲟⲥ | ⲛ̄ⲧⲁϊⲉ͡ⲓ ⲉⲃⲟⲗ ⲛ̄ϩⲏⲧϥ̄	"I shall go to the place from which I have come."

Both the *Apocalypse of Paul* and the *Ap. Jas.* preserve the traditional saying in its first person singular form in a secondary setting of questions and answers. Whereas the *Apocalypse of Paul* attributes this saying to Paul, as he ascends through the seventh heaven (22.23–23.30), the *Ap. Jas.* attributes it to Jesus, five hundred and fifty days after he arose from the dead (2.19–21).[4]

Other texts transmit further developments of this saying:

Gos. Pet. 13.56:

. . . ἀνέστη γὰρ καὶ ἀπῆλθεν ἐκεῖ ὅθεν ἀπεστάλη.

Ap. John (BG 8502, 2) 19.15–16:

ⲡⲙⲁ ⲛⲧ̣ⲁϥⲉ̣ⲓ̣ ⲙ̣ⲙ̣ⲟ̣ϥ ⲁ̣ϥⲃⲱⲕ ⲟ̣ⲛ̣ ⲉ̣[ⲣ] ⲟ̣ϥ	The place from which he has come, to it he has gone again.

In both these instances, the change of pronoun from the first to the third person singular is not original, but is dictated by the context, in which a third party speaks to one or more disciples, in the past tense, about the resurrection or ascent of Jesus. The traditional saying is used here to help formulate secondary narrative scenes. Nevertheless, in all these cases the saying "I shall go to the place from which I have come" is used to refer to an individual's heavenly ascent. In related contexts,

[4]Irenaeus states that, according to the Valentinians (*Adv. haer.* 1.3.2.) and the Ophites (1.30.14), the risen Lord lingered on earth for eighteen months after he arose from the dead and before he ascended into heaven, in order to teach the elect among his disciples. Cf. *Asc. Isa.* 9.16 ("545 days"); and see the discussion in Adolf Harnack, "Chronologische Berechnung des 'Tags von Damaskus,'" SPAW 37 (1912) 673–82.

the saying can be used with reference to the ascent of the soul.

The *First Apocalypse of James* (NHC 5, 3) preserves this saying (34.17–18) in a series of five questions and answers presented as part of a "revelation" of Jesus to James (32.28–34.20). The questions and answers function as a catechism, providing an anticipatory reenactment of a future triumph over the powers of death, thus enabling the soul to return to the Pre-existent Father:

1 Apoc. Jas. 33.11–34.20:[5]

"When you come into their power [i.e., that of the celestial "toll collectors" who "take away souls by theft"],
[1] one of them who is their guard will say to you (sing.):
'Who are you or where are you from?'
You are to say to him:
'I am a son, and I am from the Father.'
[2] He will say to you:
'What sort of son are you, and to what father do you belong?'
You are to say to him:
'I am from the Pre-[existent] Father, and a son in the Pre-existent One.'
[3] [When he says] to you:
[. . .]
you are to [say to him:]
[. . .]
[4] [. . .]
[. . .]
You are to say to him:
'They are not entirely alien,
but they are from Achamoth, who is female.
And these she produced as she brought this race
down from the Pre-existent One. . . .[6]

[5]William R. Schoedel, trans., "The (First) Apocalypse of James: V,*3*: 24,10–44,10," in Douglas M. Parrott, ed., *Nag Hammadi Codices V, 2–5 and VI with Papyrus Berolinensis 8502, 1 and 4* (NHS 11; Leiden: Brill, 1979) 84–89, adapted.

[6]The didactic passage in *1 Apoc. Jas.* 34.7–15 is a fragment of a theological treatise dealing with the myth of the fall of Wisdom, which has been inserted (apparently by the editor of the *First Apocalypse of James*) into the catechism on the basis of its similarity in content. Not only does this passage break up the question and answer form, it also expands the answer with a clarification of what is and is not "alien." This passage has no parallel in Irenaeus and Epiphanius.

[5] When he also says to you:
'Where are you to go (ⲉⲕⲛⲁⲃⲱⲕ ⲉⲧⲱⲛ)?',
you are to say to him:
'To the place from which I have come (ⲉⲡⲙⲁ ⲉⲧⲁⲓ̈ⲉⲓ̂ ⲉⲃⲟⲗ ⲙ̄ⲙⲁⲩ),
there again I shall go (ⲉⲓ̈ⲛⲁⲃⲱⲕ ⲟⲛ ⲉⲙⲁⲩ).'
And if you say these things, you will escape from their attackers."

This same tradition is preserved in Irenaeus's discussion of the Marcosians (*Adv. haer.* 1.21.5) and Epiphanius's discussion of the Heracleonites (*Pan.* 36.3.2). According to Irenaeus, this is a liturgical formula of "redemption" taught to a dying Gnostic in connection with a rite of unction. Its recitation will enable the "inner *anthrōpos*" to elude and escape from the powers after death:

Iren. Adv. haer. 1.21.5:	*Epiph. Pan. 36.3.2:*
Ego filius a Patre,	ἐγὼ υἱὸς ἀπὸ Πατρός,
Patre qui ante fuit,	Πατρὸς προόντος,
filius autem in eo qui ante fuit.	υἱὸς δὲ ἐν τῷ π<ρο>όντι·[7]
Veni autem videre omnia	ἦλθον <δὲ> πάντα ἰδεῖν
quae sunt mea et aliena;	τὰ ἴδια καὶ τὰ ἀλλότρια,
non autem aliena in totum,	καὶ οὐκ ἀλλότρια δὲ παντελῶς,
sed sunt Achamoth,	ἀλλὰ τῆς Ἀχαμώθ,
quae est faemina,	ἥτις ἐστὶν θήλεια
et haec sibi fecit:	καὶ ταῦτα ἑαυτῇ ἐποίησεν.
deducit enim genus ex eo qui ante fuit,	κατάγ<ει>[8] δὲ τὸ γένος ἐκ τοῦ προόντος
et eo rursus in mea	καὶ πορεύομαι πάλιν εἰς τὰ ἴδια,
unde veni.	ὅθεν ἐλήλυθα.

It is clear that the tradition preserved in the *First Apocalypse of James* is identical with that in Irenaeus and Epiphanius. The questions and answers in the *First Apocalypse of James* correspond both in sequence and content with the liturgical formula in Irenaeus and Epiphanius. On source-critical grounds, all three texts are probably independent of one another, deriving from a common tradition.[9] Their main difference is

[7]Epiphanius reads: παρόντι.

[8]Epiphanius reads: κατάγω.

[9]Alexander Böhlig and Pahor Labib, eds., *Koptisch-gnostische Apokalypsen aus Codex V von Nag Hammadi* (Wissenschaftliche Zeitschrift der Martin-Luther-Universität; Halle-Wittenberg, 1963) 32: "The source of Irenaeus is not our text [*First Apocalypse of James*];

one of form: the *First Apocalypse of James* presents the tradition in a series of questions and answers, whereas Irenaeus and Epiphanius preserve only answers, not questions. But as Irenaeus himself makes clear, the answers presuppose questions ascribed to the evil "principalities and powers." In all three texts, older materials are used for the formation of secondary units. What each gives as the last response to the evil powers is an answer derived from the traditional saying "I shall go to the place from which I have come." It is the *First Apocalypse of James* which has preserved this saying in a more original form than the others, retaining the reference to "the place" (ⲉⲡⲙⲁ) rather than to one's "own" (*in mea*; εἰς τὰ ἴδια).

Sitz im Leben and Formal history:

The traditional saying, with its first person singular reference to going to the place from which one has come, presupposes a version of a myth of the descent and ascent of Wisdom. The revelatory character of the "I" style and implicit dualism inherent in the notion of an otherworldly origin suggest that the *Sitz im Leben* of this saying was esoteric teaching within a wisdom-school tradition.[10] This is certainly the way the *Ap. Jas.* and the *Apocalypse of Paul* understood the saying, and it seems to be the way the *Gospel of Peter* and the *Apocryphon of John* made use of it. The inclusion of the saying in a catechetical series of questions and answers in the *First Apocalypse of James* and parallel liturgical formulas (connected with a rite of unction) in Irenaeus and Epiphanius shows how the saying was taken over for use in Christian Gnostic liturgical traditions. In every case, a traditional saying has been quoted and reformulated as an answer to a (real or implied) question. A "dialogue" has thus been constructed out of an originally independent tradition.

---

rather, both have probably used cultic traditional pieces of Gnostic origin." Kurt Rudolph ("Der gnostische 'Dialog' als literarisches Genus," in *Probleme der koptischen Literatur* [Wissenschaftliche Beiträge, Martin-Luther-Universität; Halle-Wittenberg, 1968/1 (K2)] 99) conjectures that this piece of tradition stems from a written Valentinian text.

[10]See the discussion of wisdom and revelatory sayings, in conjunction with school traditions, in Helmut Koester, "The Structure and Criteria of Early Christian Beliefs," in *Trajectories*, 219–23.

B) *Ap. Jas. 2.29–33:*

ϩⲁⲙⲏⲛ ϯϫⲟⲩ ⲙ̄ⲙⲁⲥ ⲛⲏⲧⲛ̄ ϫ̣[ⲉ] |	Truly I say to you (pl.),
ⲙⲛ ⲗⲁⲁⲩⲉ ⲁⲛⲏϩⲉ ⲛⲁⲃⲱⲕ ⲁϩⲟⲩ̣[ⲛ] |	no one ever will enter
ⲁⲧⲙⲛⲧⲣ̄ⲣⲟ ⲛⲙ̄ⲡⲏⲩⲉ·	the Kingdom of Heaven
ⲉⲉⲓϣⲁⲛ̣[ⲣ] | ⲕⲉⲗⲉⲩⲉⲓ ⲛⲉϥ·	if I bid him,
ⲁⲗⲗⲁ ⲁⲃⲁⲗ ϫⲉ̣ | ⲧⲉⲧⲛ̄ⲙⲏϩ ⲛ̄ⲧⲱⲧⲛ̄·	but rather because you yourselves are full.

The Amen-saying which concludes this initial dialogue in the *Ap. Jas.* is a prophetic pronouncement. It can be formally analyzed as follows:

a) identification formula: *Truly I say to you (pl.),*
b) negative future apodosis: *no one ever will enter the Kingdom of Heaven*
c) positive conditional protasis: *if I bid him,*
d) positive causal qualification of the protasis: *but rather because you yourselves are full.*

Section (d) thus functions as an alternative protasis and a de facto qualification of the apodosis.

Redactional elements:

As the text now stands, I know of no exact parallel with this saying in the Jesus tradition, not only in terms of its content but also in terms of its form. But its beginning, sections (a) and (b), certainly has all the earmarks of a real saying: "Truly I say to you (pl.), no one ever will enter the Kingdom of Heaven. . . ." Sections (c) and (d) provide several clues which indicate that the saying has undergone considerable editorial revision. Identifying these will permit us to reconstruct, with a reasonable degree of confidence, a likely original, and to trace the history of the saying to its present form:

1) The causal qualification of (c) by means of (d) is rare and, to my knowledge, unattested elsewhere in parallel prophetic pronouncements.
2) This qualification creates a tension within the saying, pitting one's inability to enter the Kingdom at the Lord's "bidding" (c) against the feasibility of entering if one is "full" (d).

3) This qualification further introduces an irregular change from the third person singular ("no one . . . him") to the second person plural ("you yourselves").
4) The juxtaposition of a positive protasis (c) and a negative apodosis (b) is also unexpected. One would anticipate a conditional sentence with a protasis and apodosis which are either both positive ("if . . . then") or both negative ("unless . . . then not").[11]

If one assumes that (d) has been added onto an original Amen-saying which regularly had its three sections (a)-(c), then all of these problems can be solved. The removal of (d) would eliminate the futile search for other sayings with qualifications of the protasis;[12] it would clarify the editor's clear intention to debate, in the name of the Lord, whether one can enter the Kingdom at the Lord's "bidding" or only because one is "full"; it would do away with the asymmetric change of person and number; and it would solve the problem of the extraordinary juxtaposing of positive and negative in protasis and apodosis. Accepting the thesis that (a) and (b) are original, and that the addition of (d) has created the inconcinnities between (a)-(b) and (c), one can reconstruct the original saying to have most likely read:

a) identification formula: *Truly I say to you (pl.),*
b) negative future apodosis: *no one ever will enter the Kingdom of Heaven*
c) negative conditional protasis: *<unless> I bid him.*

Its reconstruction in Greek is given *exempli gratia*:

a) *ἀμὴν λέγω ὑμῖν,*
b) *οὐδεὶς εἰσελεύσεται εἰς τὴν βασιλείαν τῶν οὐρανῶν πώποτε*
c) *ἐὰν <μὴ> κελεύσω αὐτόν.*

[11]Examples in the Jesus tradition of conditional sentences with positive protases and negative apodoses (e.g., John 8:51, 52; cf. 11:25, 26) belong to those sayings in which the fulfillment of the condition in the protasis results in the promised protection of the apodosis. This is quite the opposite of the saying in *Ap. Jas.* 2.29–33, where the resultant apodosis is not protection but virtual destruction.

[12]The prophetic saying about entering the Kingdom in Matt 7:21 par. is worthy of comparison, with its qualification of *οὐ πᾶς ὁ λέγων . . . ἀλλ' ὁ ποιῶν. . . .* But this saying has neither identification formula nor conditional protasis and apodosis. It should rather be compared with its parallels in Luke 6:46; 13:26–27; *Gos. Naz.* frg. 6 (in the "Zion Gospel" Edition); *Ps.-Clem. Hom.* 8.7.4.; *Recog.* 4.5.4; and *2 Clem.* 4.5.

The reconstruction suggested here requires only minimal emending of the text: the addition of the expected negative in the protasis. Its omission is easily explained: the addition of (d) demanded it. The reversal of the order of protasis and apodosis is to be expected in sayings which begin with *οὐδείς* (= ⲘⲚ ⲖⲀⲀⲨⲈ [e.g., John 3:13; 14:6; cf. 1 Cor 12:3]). The reference to "bidding" in (c) is not an important term in the *Ap. Jas.*, appearing only in the narrative frame (2.27–28, 31–32; 15.39). The reference to being "full" in (d), on the other hand, is an important theological term for the editor of the *Ap. Jas.*, being found almost exclusively in the body of the text:[13] twice in the farewell speech at the beginning of the discourse and dialogue (3.8, 36); twelve times in the subsequent disquisition on "fullness" and "diminution" (4. [1], 2, [4], 7, 9, 10, 11, 12, 13, 15, 16, 19); and once each in the simile of the Ear of Grain and its allegorical application (12.26, 30). The traditional (reconstructed) saying about entering the Kingdom at the Lord's "bidding" thus seems to have been transformed by the secondary addition of the notion of being "full." The plausibility of this reconstruction will be supported in the analysis below, in which I shall seek to trace the formal history of this saying and demonstrate its use in the composition of the dialogue.

Formal parallels:

The closest formal parallel to this Amen-saying is another prophetic pronouncement found in several different versions in early Christian literature (Matt 18:3 // John 3:3a, 5b // Just. *1 Apol.* 61.4 // Mark 10:15 // Luke 18:17). For the purposes of comparison the first two texts will be cited here:

Matt 18:3:	*John 3:3a, 5b:*
a) identification formula: ἀμὴν λέγω ὑμῖν,	ἀμὴν ἀμὴν λέγω σοι,
b) negative conditional protasis: ἐὰν μὴ στραφῆτε καὶ γένησθε ὡς τὰ παιδία,	ἐὰν μή τις γεννηθῇ ἄνωθεν, . . .

[13]In 14.30–31 ⲀⲦⲢⲀⲘⲞⲨϨ is different.

c) negative future apodosis:

οὐ μὴ εἰσέλθητε	*οὐ δύναται εἰσελθεῖν*
εἰς τὴν βασιλείαν τῶν οὐρανῶν.	*εἰς τὴν βασιλείαν τοῦ θεοῦ.*

A synoptic comparison clearly reveals that these two texts independently give variants of a single saying, which apparently was originally composed in Aramaic.[14] Matthew's version of this saying seems to have been transmitted independently of that in Mark 10:15 // Luke 18:17.[15] The fact that John is dependent on tradition for his saying is suggested by the phrase *βασιλεία τοῦ θεοῦ*, which occurs nowhere else in John, and is confirmed by the variant of this saying, in a less-developed form, in Just. *1 Apol. 61.4*:[16]

> *καὶ γὰρ ὁ Χριστὸς εἶπεν·*
> *ἂν μὴ ἀναγεννηθῆτε,*
> *οὐ μὴ εἰσέλθητε εἰς τὴν βασιλείαν τῶν οὐρανῶν.*

Justin's identification formula (*ὁ Χριστὸς εἶπεν*), use of the verb *ἀναγεννηθῆτε* in the protasis, and reading of *τῶν οὐρανῶν* in the apodosis all differ from John's text; there can thus be no doubt that Justin knows of this saying independently of John.[17] The context in which Justin quotes this saying and his use of *ἀναγεννᾶν* (cf. 1 Pet 1:3, 23) indicate that its *Sitz im Leben* is baptism.[18]

John has taken this traditional dominical saying and quoted it twice, with different readings, in a dialogue with Nicodemus:

[14]See most recently Barnabas Lindars, "John and the Synoptic Gospels: A Test Case," *NTS* 27 (1981) 287–94. The critical argument for postulating an original Aramaic composition of this saying is the observation that Matthew's use of *στραφῆτε καὶ γένησθε* seems to be a Semitism for "become again." See also Jeremias, *Theology*, 155; and Matthew Black, *An Aramaic Approach to the Gospels and Acts* (2d ed.; Oxford: Clarendon, 1954) 253, who cites Paul Joüon, "Notes philologiques sur les évangiles," *RechSR* 18 (1928) 347–48.

[15]See Lindars, "John and the Synoptic Gospels," 287.

[16]See Bultmann, *John*, 135 n. 4.

[17]Ibid.; Helmut Koester, "History and Cult in the Gospel of John and in Ignatius of Antioch," *JTC* 1 (1965) 118–20; A. J. Bellinzoni, *The Sayings of Jesus in the Writings of Justin Martyr* (NovTSup 17; Leiden: Brill, 1967) 134–38; and Leslie Lee Kline, *The Sayings of Jesus in the Pseudo-Clementine Homilies* (SBLDS 14; Missoula: Scholars, 1975) 134–40.

[18]See Bultmann, *John*, 135 n. 4; and Koester, "History and Cult," 118–20.

1) γεννηθῇ ἄνωθεν in vs 3a has been changed to γεννηθῇ ἐξ ὕδατος καὶ πνεύματος in vs 5a; and
2) εἰσελθεῖν εἰς in vs 5b has replaced ἰδεῖν in vs 3b.[19]

The secondary ἰδεῖν (vs 3b) seems to be a reference to a heavenly journey (*Himmelsreise*) tradition, which only the Son of Man, who has descended from heaven (vs 13; cf. 1:51), could have experienced.[20] Whether the tradition which John received contained the expression γεννηθῇ ἄνωθεν (vs 3a) is not certain. The precise understanding of the meaning of γεννηθῇ ἄνωθεν (or its equivalent) in John's tradition is also not clear. Rudolf Bultmann argued that John's "source dealt with the question of the origin of faith in the Spirit" (cf. vs 6), and that it was John who "*transformed the idea of 'being begotten from above' . . . into the idea of 'rebirth,'*"[21] in accordance with the practice of the developing Christian tradition. It seems more likely, however, that the saying's original meaning of "rebirth" (as preserved in Justin) came to be formulated in John's tradition to mean "begotten from above" (cf. 1:13), and that John retained this understanding and heightened its ambiguity through a pun on ἄνωθεν (cf. vs 31). The replacement of ἄνωθεν (vs 3a) with ἐξ ὕδατος καὶ πνεύματος (vs 5a) may simply be another way of referring to "being begotten by the Spirit," for when John uses the terms "water" and "spirit" elsewhere in the Gospel he seems to use them as synonyms for the Spirit (7:37–39).[22]

The original baptismal *Sitz im Leben* of the traditional saying has receded into the background in John's formulation. The very first time the saying is quoted (John 3:3) it is given in an altered form. The use of the saying to compose a dialogue between Jesus and Nicodemus has transformed this prophetic pronouncement into a riddle (vs 3) which Nicodemus cannot solve (vs 4).[23] The pun on γεννηθῇ ἄνωθεν gives rise to misunderstanding, heightened by the contrast between "flesh" and "spirit" in vs 6. Nicodemus's literal-minded incredulity cannot fathom the symbolic meaning of the spirit (vss 4, 6–9). A traditional saying has thus been transformed in the construction of a quintessentially Johannine enigmatic discourse.[24]

[19]John's double ἀμήν and singular σοι (vss 3, 5) are redactionally secondary.

[20]See Meeks, "Man from Heaven," 52–53.

[21]Bultmann, *John*, 135 n. 4 (emphasis his).

[22]See MacRae, *Invitation to John*, 56.

[23]See Herbert Leroy, *Rätsel und Missverständnis: Ein Beitrag zur Formgeschichte des Johannesevangeliums* (BBB 30; Bonn: Hanstein, 1968) 124–36.

[24]See Meeks, "Man from Heaven," 55–57.

Sitz im Leben and Formal history:

The original (reconstructed) saying in *Ap. Jas.* 2.29–33 is an Amen-saying which speaks about entering the Kingdom at the Lord's bidding. The presence of "Amen" in the identification formula, use of the first person singular pronoun in the protasis, and reference to "entering" the Kingdom in the apodosis are clues to the formal function of this saying. In the previous discussion of the prophecy of judgment in *Ap. Jas.* 9.24–10.6, it was argued that ἀμὴν λέγω ὑμῖν was frequently employed as an identification formula by Christian prophets who spoke in the name, and under the authority, of the Lord. It was also observed that a widespread tradition in early Christianity understood the Holy Spirit to be the spirit of prophecy, and that possession of the spirit was thought to empower one to prophesy. References to "entering" the Kingdom are found in prophetic sayings in the Synoptic tradition (e.g., Matt 7:21; 23:13),[25] and in connection with baptism in the saying in John 3:3a, 5b. The tradition of sayings of Jesus which spoke of "entering"[26] the Kingdom through baptism, by treading on the "garment of shame" (e.g. *Gos. Eg.* frg. 5 [*apud* Clem. Al. *Strom.* 3.13.92.2]; *Gos. Thom.* 37: 39.27–40.2; 21a: 36.33–37.6)[27] and/or making the "two (male and female) one" (e.g., *Gos. Thom.* 22: 37.20–35; *2 Clem.* 12.2, 6),[28] confirms that sayings such as these were used liturgically, most likely by Christian prophets, as part of their exercise of "jurisdiction over the conditions of divine forgiveness and soteriological security."[29] This suggests that *Ap. Jas.* 2.29–33 is an early Christian

[25]See Hans Windisch, "Die Sprüche vom Eingehen in das Reich Gottes," *ZNW* 27 (1928) 163; and Bultmann, *History*, 116, 113. Note that Bultmann considers Mark 10:15 par. to be a wisdom saying secondarily inserted into Mark 10:13–16 (pp. 75, 32), and John 3:3, 5 to be a "rule of piety" (p. 146). For the relation of Mark 10:15 to the baptismal context of John 3:3, 5, see Morton Smith, *Clement of Alexandria and a Secret Gospel of Mark* (Cambridge: Harvard University Press, 1973) 169.

[26]*Gos. Thom.* 22: 37.35; 114: 51.25–26; and *Acts Phil.* 140 (34). Variants of this saying speak of one's "recognizing" (*Acts Pet.* 38 // *Mart. Pet.* 9) or the "coming" (*2 Clem.* 12.6) of the Kingdom.

[27]Cf. other instances of this aspect of the tradition in *Gos. Thom.* 114: 51.18–26; and *Dial. Sav.* 138.11–20; 143.11–24.

[28]Cf. other instances of this aspect of the tradition in *Acts Phil.* 140 (34); *Acts Thom.* 147; *Acts Pet.* 38 // *Mart. Pet.* 9; *Gos. Phil.* 67.30–34; and Gal 3:26–28 // 1 Cor 12:13. See the analysis of the tradition in Dennis Ronald MacDonald, "There is No Male and Female: Galatians 3:26–28 and Gnostic Baptismal Tradition" (Ph.D. diss., Harvard University, 1978). For Paul's use of the tradition see also Hans Dieter Betz, *Galatians* (Hermeneia; Philadelphia: Fortress, 1979) 181–201.

[29]Swanson, "Christian Prophetic Speech," 12. Such jurisdiction includes the prophetic prerogative to supervise public worship, engage in church discipline, conduct baptismal

prophetic saying pronounced in the name of the Lord. The reference to "bidding" (ⲣ ⲕⲉⲗⲉⲩⲉⲓ) implies a legal provenance;[30] but a more specific liturgical context (such as baptism) cannot be determined.

The original (reconstructed) saying implies that one can enter the Kingdom only if the Lord "bids." The addition of the positive causal qualification of the protasis (d) has transformed the original meaning to state, instead, that one can enter the Kingdom only if one is "full." This addition is the work of the editor of the *Ap. Jas.*, who has used a traditional saying to formulate a secondary response of Jesus (2.29–33) in order to correct a previous comment of the disciples (2.27–28). The secondary reference to being "full" is picked up in the editor's appended remark which concludes the initial dialogue between Jesus and the disciples in the *Ap. Jas.*: "Let me have James and Peter, in order that I may fill them"(2.33–35). This draws the post-resurrection scene to a close and leads to the disclosure of Jesus' private revelation to James and Peter, which constitutes the body of the *Ap. Jas.*: "And when he called (ⲛ̄ⲧⲁⲣⲉϥⲙⲟⲩⲧⲉ) these two, he took them aside, and commanded (ⲁϥⲟⲩⲉϩⲥⲁϩⲛⲉ) the rest to busy themselves with that with which they had been busy" (2.35–39).

Form-critically, this scene constitutes an invitation to esoteric instruction.[31] As the text now stands, a traditional prophetic saying about entering the Kingdom has been secondarily transformed and, through the use of the catchword ⲣ̄ ⲕⲉⲗⲉⲩⲉ(ⲓ), reformulated to create a dialogue in which the disciples do not come with Jesus if he bids, but only if they are made full. The initial comment of the disciples (2.27–28) is thus corrected by a redacted saying of Jesus (2.29–33). This Amen-saying, with its reference to "going into" (ⲃⲱⲕ ⲁϩⲟⲩ̣[ⲛ]) the Kingdom, also points back to the dialogue's initial saying of Jesus (2.24–25), which referred to his "going" to the place from which he had "come."[32] One dominical saying thus

---

services, and modify or even invent baptismal praxis (pp. 112–23, 205–14, and passim).

[30]Against Malinine et al., *Epistula Iacobi Apocrypha*, 41; followed by Klaus Berger, *Die Amen-Worte Jesu: Eine Untersuchung zum Problem der Legitimation in apokalyptischer Rede* (BZNW 39; Berlin: De Gruyter, 1970) 134. They simply assume that the reference to ⲣ ⲕⲉⲗⲉⲩⲉⲓ is to be associated with the biographic legend about Peter in Matt 14:28.

[31]Such scenes, in which Jesus gives instructions privately to one or more of his disciples, are not uncommon in the sayings-of-Jesus tradition (e.g., Mark 4:10–11, 34; 7:17–18a; 10:10–11a; 13:3–5a; Matt 5:1–2; *Gos. Thom.* 13: 35.7–8). Cf. also, in the narrative tradition: Mark 9:28–29a; *Secret Mark* (folio 2 recto, lines 5–10). See Bultmann, *History*, 330; and Smith, *Clement*, 199. Call stories, such as those narrated at the beginning of the Gospels of the NT (Mark 1:16–20 // Matt 4:18–22; Luke 5:1–11; and John 1:35–50), belong to a different tradition.

[32]The play on words is possible in Greek or Coptic. The Coptic plays on ⲃⲱⲕ (2.24)

functions to interpret another. The editor has combined terms used in the initial invitation to "come" to Jesus (2.25–26) and the final saying about his "bidding" (2.31–32) to create the disciples' intermediate, misguided response (2.27–28). Once James and Peter have been chosen (2.33–35) and "called" (2.35–39) as the disciples privileged to become "full," the frame of the post-resurrection appearance of Jesus (2.7–39) is brought to a conclusion. The stage is set for Jesus' private revelation to James and Peter, in discourse and dialogue.

---

and ⲂⲰⲔ ⲀϨⲞⲨ[Ⲛ] (2.30); if the original Greek of ⲂⲰⲔ read *πορεύεσθαι*, then the word play would instead be with *ἔρχεσθαι* (= ⲈⲒ: 2.24) and *εἰσέρχεσθαι* (= ⲂⲰⲔ ⲀϨⲞⲨ̣[Ⲛ] : 2.30).

2.2 THE DIALOGUE IN *AP. JAS.* 4.22–37

Ap. Jas. 4.22–37:

1) *Comment of a Disciple:*

a) Introduction: 4.22–23

ⲁϩⲓ̈ⲟⲩⲱ|ϣⲃ̄ ⲇⲉ ⲡⲁϫⲏⲓ̈ ⲛⲉϥ ϫⲉ	And I (James) answered and said to him:

b) Comment: 4.23–31

ⲡϫⲁⲉⲓⲥ | ⲟⲩⲛ̄ ϭⲁⲙ ⲙ̄ⲙⲁⲛ ⲁⲡⲓⲑⲉ ⲛⲉⲕ |	"Lord, we can obey you
ϣⲡⲉ ϩⲛⲉⲕ	if you wish.
ⲁϩⲛ̄ⲕⲱⲉ ⲅⲁⲣ ⲛ̄|ⲥⲱⲛ	For we have forsaken
ⲛⲛⲉⲛⲉⲓⲁϯ ⲛ̄ϩⲁⲟⲩⲧ· |[1]	our fathers
ⲙⲛ̄ ⲛⲉⲛⲙⲉⲉⲩ	and our mothers
ⲙⲛ̄ ⲛⲉⲛϯⲙⲉ |	and our villages
ⲁϩⲛ̄ⲟⲩⲁϩⲛ̄ ⲛ̄ⲥⲱⲕ	and have followed you.
ϯ ⲑϩⲉ ϭ̣[ⲉ] | ⲛⲉⲛ	Grant us, [therefore],
ⲁⲧⲙ̄ⲧⲣⲟⲩⲡⲓⲣⲁⲍⲉ ⲙ̄ⲙⲁⲛ |	not to be tempted
ⲁⲃⲁⲗ ϩⲓ̈ⲧⲟⲟⲧϥ̄ ⲙ̄ⲡⲇⲓⲁⲃⲟⲗⲟⲥ· ⲉ|ⲑⲁⲩ·[2]	by the wicked devil."

[1]Literally: "our male fathers." The plural noun ⲉⲓⲁϯ can, of course, mean "parents," and so the adjective ϩⲁⲟⲩⲧ (male) has been added to restrict the reference to the "male parents," i.e., the "fathers." The only other instance of ⲉⲓⲁϯ ⲛ̄ϩⲁⲟⲩⲧ that I know of occurs in an unpublished MS from the J. Pierpont Morgan Library (M. 595, folio 129 recto, col. 1, line 3, which appears on p. 259 of the photographic facsimile), in which ⲛⲉⲩⲉⲓⲟⲧⲉ ⲛϩⲟⲟⲩⲧ (their fathers) is paralleled with ⲛⲉⲩⲉⲓⲟⲧⲉ ⲛⲥϩⲓⲙⲉ (their mothers) in lines 4–5. Crum, *s.v.* ⲉⲓⲱⲧ (86b) cites this MS as Mor 43 259. Cf., on the preceding page, M. 595, folio 128 verso, col. 2, lines 28–31 (p. 258): ϩⲉⲛϩⲙϩⲁⲗ ⲛϩⲟⲟⲩⲧ ⲙⲛ ϩⲉⲛϩⲙϩⲁⲗ ⲛⲥϩⲓⲙⲉ (male servants and female servants); and Rev 12:5: *υἱὸν ἄρσεν* = ⲟⲩ.ϣⲣ̄ϩⲟⲟⲩⲧ (S) = ⲡⲓ.ϣⲏⲣⲓ ⲛ̄ϩⲱⲟⲩⲧ (B) (male child, son). The translation ("fathers") given here corrects my previous translation, "forefathers" ("Apocryphon of James," 58), which is in error.

[2]The Coptic expression ⲁⲃⲁⲗ ϩⲓ̈ⲧⲟⲟⲧϥ̄ ⲙ̄ⲡⲇⲓⲁⲃⲟⲗⲟⲥ ⲉⲑⲁⲩ shows that the *Ap. Jas.* was originally written in Greek. According to Francis E. Williams, "the Greek original probably read *ὑπὸ τοῦ διαβόλου τοῦ πονηροῦ*, with the last phrase intended appositionally. The Coptic translator took it as an attributive adjective" ("The Apocryphon of James: I, *2*: 1,1–16,30," in Harold W. Attridge, ed., *Nag Hammadi Codex I [The Jung Codex]* [NHS; Leiden: Brill, forthcoming] on 4.30–31).

2) *Response of Jesus:*

a) Introduction: 4.31–32

ⲁϥⲟⲩⲱϣⲃ̄ ⲛ̄ϭⲓ ⲡϫⲁⲉⲓⲥ | ⲡⲁϫⲉϥ ϫⲉ	The Lord answered and said:

b) Response: 4.32–37

ⲉϣ ⲡⲉ ⲡⲉⲧⲛ̄ϩⲙⲁⲧ |	"What is your (pl.) merit
ⲉⲣⲉⲧⲛ̄ⲉⲓⲣⲉ ⲙ̄ⲡⲟⲩⲱϣⲉ ⲙ̄ⲡⲓⲱⲧ· |	when you do the will of the Father
ⲉⲩⲧⲙ̄ϯ ⲛⲏⲧⲛ̄	as if it had not been given to you[1]
ⲁⲃⲁⲗ ϩⲓ̈ⲧⲟⲟⲧϥ̄ ϩⲛ̄ | ⲟⲩⲙⲉⲣⲟⲥ ⲛ̄ⲇⲱⲣⲉⲁ·	by him as a gift,
ϩⲙ̄ ⲡⲧⲣⲟⲩ|ⲡⲓⲣⲁⲍⲉ ⲙ̄ⲙⲱⲧⲛ̄	while you are tempted
ⲁⲃⲁⲗ ϩⲓ̈ⲧⲟⲟⲧϥ̄ | ⲙ̄ⲡⲥⲁⲧⲁⲛⲁⲥ . . .	by Satan? . . ."

4.28 ⲑϩⲉ ϭ̣[ⲉ] *ed. pr.* : ⲑϩⲉⲥ̣ Mueller | 35 ⲛ̄<ⲧ>ⲇⲱⲣⲉⲁ Schenke

This passage is also a composite piece. The comments attributed to James include fragments of two traditional sayings:

A) 4.25–28: "For we have forsaken our fathers and our mothers and our villages and have followed you"; and
B) 4.28–31: "Grant us, [therefore], not to be tempted by the wicked devil."

It is important to observe that, in this dialogue, the tradition is preserved solely in the form of a comment and a request of a disciple. The response of Jesus (4.32–37) contains no originally discrete traditional elements.

A) Ap. Jas. 4.25–28:

ⲁϩⲛ̄ⲕⲱⲉ ⲅⲁⲣ ⲛ̄|ⲥⲱⲛ	For we have forsaken
ⲛⲛ̄ⲉⲛⲉⲓⲁϯ ⲛ̄ϩⲁⲟⲩⲧ· |	our fathers
ⲙⲛ̄ ⲛⲉⲛⲙⲉⲉⲩ	and our mothers
ⲙⲛ̄ ⲛⲉⲛϯⲙⲉ |	and our villages
ⲁϩⲛ̄ⲟⲩⲁϩⲛ̄ ⲛ̄ⲥⲱⲕ	and have followed you.

[1]This also corrects my previous translation ("if it is not given to you") in "Apocryphon of James," above n. 1.

This is a fragment of a saying which is also found in the Synoptic tradition (Mark 10:28–30 // Matt 19:27–28a, 29 // Luke 18:28–30).

Redactional elements:

This fragment is secondarily connected to the initial comment of James (4.23–25) by means of ⲅⲁⲣ. The use of the connective ⲅⲁⲣ to attach originally discrete sayings to a larger context occurs throughout the sayings tradition, as the following examples attest:

Matt 6:14: an independent sentence of holy law appended in Matthew to the Lord's prayer (Matt 6:9–13 // Luke 11:2–4)

Matt 17:20b: a Q saying (// Luke 17:6; cf. Mark 11:22 par.) appended in Matthew to the story of the healing of an epileptic child (Mark 9:14–29 // Matt 17:14–19 // Luke 9:37–43a)

Mark 4:22 // Luke 8:17 // *Gos. Thom.* 5b: 33.13–14 and 6b: 33.21–22: an eschatological saying appended in Mark and Luke to a traditional proverb (Mark 4:21 // Luke 8:16), and in the *Gospel of Thomas*, to a doublet of another eschatological saying.

Formal parallels:

This saying is found in the Synoptic tradition (Mark 10:28–30 par.) in a collection of sayings on the riches and rewards of discipleship.[4] The collection itself has been appended to the apophthegm of the rich young man and Jesus (Mark 10:17–22 par.). The Synoptic tradition formulates this saying as a chria:

Mark 10:28–30:

1) *Comment of a Disciple:*

a) Introduction: 10:28a
ἤρξατο λέγειν ὁ Πέτρος αὐτῷ·

b) Comment: 10:28b
ἰδοὺ ἡμεῖς ἀφήκαμεν πάντα
καὶ ἠκολουθήκαμέν σοι.

[4]Mark 10:23–25, 26–27, 28–30, 31. See Bultmann, *History*, 21–22, 110–11.

2) *Response of Jesus:*

a) Introduction: 10:29a

ἔφη ὁ Ἰησοῦς·

b) Response: 10:29b–30

ἀμὴν λέγω ὑμῖν,
οὐδείς ἐστιν ὃς ἀφῆκεν
οἰκίαν ἢ ἀδελφοὺς ἢ ἀδελφὰς
ἢ μητέρα ἢ πατέρα ἢ τέκνα ἢ ἀγροὺς
ἕνεκεν ἐμοῦ καὶ ἕνεκεν τοῦ εὐαγγελίου,
ἐὰν μὴ λάβῃ ἑκατονταπλασίονα
νῦν ἐν τῷ καιρῷ τούτῳ
οἰκίας καὶ ἀδελφοὺς καὶ ἀδελφὰς
καὶ μητέρας καὶ τέκνα καὶ ἀγροὺς
μετὰ διωγμῶν,
καὶ ἐν τῷ αἰῶνι τῷ ἐρχομένῳ
ζωὴν αἰώνιον.

This dialogue between Jesus and Peter has been secondarily constructed out of a saying.[5] Whether Peter's question in vss 28 is a "connecting link, deriving its form from the traditional saying" in vss 29–30, or is "the original introduction to an ancient apophthegm, in which the original saying of Jesus has been substituted" by vss 29–30, is not certain.[6] The response of Jesus in vss 29–30 nowhere makes mention of "following."[7] As the text now stands, vs 28 is secondary to vss 29–30, constructed to introduce the saying attributed to Jesus. The saying in vss 29–30 seems to have originally ended with ἑκατονταπλασίονα (vs 30a), since what follows introduces a contrast between the rewards in

[5]Note that, unlike the apophthegm of the rich young man and Jesus in Mark 10:17–22 par., the dialogue between Jesus and Peter in Mark 10:28–30 is not a genuine apophthegm. It contains no narrative account which serves as the vehicle for the saying, no context which sets the stage for an epigram or aphorism. In contradistinction to controversy, scholastic, or biographical dialogues, which are typically introduced by editorializing questions composed by the tradent(s) of the tradition, this dialogue is created entirely from an original saying. Therefore, I am using Dibelius's formal category of "chriae" (*Tradition*, 151–64), rather than Bultmann's "apophthegmata" (*History*, 11–69).

[6]Bultmann, *History*, 22.

[7]The only saying attributed to Jesus that I know of which speaks both of "forsaking" and "following," terms which together are not attested as part of a dominical saying in the Synoptic tradition, is found in *Dial. Sav.* 141.8–12. Here, the saying has been used to construct a dialogue between Jesus and Matthew in 141.2–12. Cf. *Bruce Codex* 15.

this age and those in the age to come that is at odds with the futuristic implication of the "hundredfold" reward.[8]

Matthew and Luke preserve the dialogue as given in Mark with a few alterations. Matthew characteristically inserts an isolated Q saying (Matt 19:28 // Luke 22:28–30; cf. Rev 3:21) into his narrative to complete his understanding of the scene.[9] Mark's statement that all is to be forsaken ἕνεκεν ἐμοῦ καὶ ἕνεκεν τοῦ εὐαγγελίου (vs 29; cf. 8:35) is clearly an expansion of the older saying. The reference to the "gospel," moreover, is not read by Matthew or Luke,[10] and was probably introduced at a later stage of the development of Mark's Gospel text.[11] Matthew and Luke also omit Mark 10:30b (including the reference to "persecutions"), most likely because this verse simply repeats the list of people and places which, once forsaken, the disciple will receive anew.

Sitz im Leben and Formal history:

Sayings such as that in *Ap. Jas.* 4.25–28 // Mark 10:28–30 par. seem to have been formulated as general rules of the community in the early stages of the Jesus movement, perhaps among itinerant Christian prophets.[12] Matthew and Luke indicate that different versions of this saying were transmitted in early Christianity.[13] Numerous other sayings

[8]See Bultmann, *History*, 110; and Ernst Lohmeyer, *Das Evangelium des Markus* (MeyerK; Göttingen: Vandenhoeck & Ruprecht, 1957) 216–17.

[9]Cf. Matt 8:11–12 (// Luke 13:28–29), inserted into the Q narrative of the healing of the centurion's παῖς (Matt 8:5–10, 13 // Luke 7:2a, 6b–10); and Matt 12:11–12a (// Luke 14:5; cf. 13:15), inserted into the narrative of the healing of the man with the withered hand (Mark 3:1–5 // Matt 12:9–10, 12b–13 // Luke 6:6–10).

[10]Matt 19:29 (cf. 7:22; 10:22; 18:20): ἕνεκεν τοῦ ὀνόματός μου—and Luke 18:29 (cf. 4:43; 8:1; 9:2, 11, 60, 62): ἕνεκεν τῆς βασιλείας τοῦ θεοῦ. The Gospel of Luke does not use the noun εὐαγγέλιον.

[11]See Helmut Koester, "History and Development of Mark's Gospel (From Mark to *Secret Mark* and 'Canonical' Mark)," in Bruce Corley, ed., *Colloquy on New Testament Studies: A Time for Reappraisal and Fresh Approaches* (Macon: Mercer University Press, 1983) 35–57; and the discussion of the term "gospel" in Willi Marxsen, *Mark the Evangelist* (Nashville: Abingdon, 1969) 117–50.

[12]Argued most forcefully by Gerd Theissen, *Sociology of Early Palestinian Christianity* (Philadelphia: Fortress, 1978); and Howard Clark Kee, *Community of the New Age: Studies in Mark's Gospel* (Philadelphia: Westminster, 1977). This saying is a general charismatic announcement, not a specific prophetic pronouncement.

[13]Cf. the quotation of Mark 10:28–30 in Clem. Al. *Quis div. salv.* 4.10 (cf. 21.5–25.8), which shows contaminations from the readings of Matthew and Luke. These contaminations may be seen graphically in Appendix F in Smith, *Clement*, 368–69. See the discussion, with special attention to Clement's own redactional emphases (e.g., χρήματα), in

about discipleship are also attributed elsewhere to Jesus himself.[14]

Ap. Jas. 4.25–28 preserves the tradition as a comment of James. It is the response of Jesus (4.32–37) which is an editorial product. Although the tendency of the tradition is to introduce sayings into a larger (narrative) context by means of a question or comment of one or more disciples (e.g., Mark 4:10; 7:17; 9:11, 28; 10:10; 13:3), there are instances in which traditional material is not merely used to formulate secondary questions, but is actually preserved in such questions. A good example is found in the following Q tradition:

Matt 18:21–22:	*Luke 17:3–4:*
τότε προσελθὼν ὁ Πέτρος εἶπεν αὐτῷ·	
κύριε, ποσάκις ἁμαρτήσει εἰς ἐμὲ ὁ ἀδελφός μου καὶ ἀφήσω αὐτῷ; ἕως ἑπτάκις;	ἐὰν ἁμάρτῃ ὁ ἀδελφός σου ἐπιτίμησον αὐτῷ, καὶ ἐὰν μετανοήσῃ ἄφες αὐτῷ.
λέγει αὐτῷ ὁ Ἰησοῦς· οὐ λέγω σοι ἕως ἑπτάκις	καὶ ἐὰν ἑπτάκις τῆς ἡμέρας ἁμαρτήσῃ εἰς σὲ
ἀλλὰ ἕως ἑβδομηκοντάκις ἑπτά.	καὶ ἑπτάκις ἐπιστρέψῃ πρὸς σὲ λέγων· μετανοῶ, ἀφήσεις αὐτῷ.

Matthew has clearly transformed the saying in Q (as preserved by Luke) to create a dialogue between Jesus and Peter. This saying has been inserted into one of Matthew's five "great discourses" of Jesus (Matt 18:1–35) as a transitional passage between Matthew's special sayings material (18:15–17, 18, 19, 20) dealing with church discipline and his parable of the unmerciful servant (18:23–35). Whereas the Q version in Luke formulated this saying as two parallel conditional sentences[15] which addressed the general duty of forgiveness, Matthew has radicalized the saying to emphasize the necessity of continuous

---

M. Mees, *Die Zitate aus dem Neuen Testament bei Clemens von Alexandrien* (Quaderni di "Vetera Christianorum" 2; Bari: Instituto di Letteratura Cristiana Antica-Universita di Bari, 1970) 1. 59–62.

[14]E.g., Matt 10:37 // Luke 14:26 // *Gos. Thom.* 55a: 42.25–27 and 101a: 49.32–33; Matt 10:38 // Luke 14:27; and Mark 8:34 // Matt 16:24 // Luke 9:23 // *Gos. Thom.* 55b: 42.27–29.

[15]Bultmann (*History,* 86) suggests that it is possible that Luke 17:4 is a "later expansion" of vs 3.

forgiveness, turning the saying into a dialogue between Jesus and Peter.[16] A synoptic comparison with Luke 17:3–4 reveals that the question of Peter (Matt 18:21) preserves the tradition, not Jesus' answer (18:22).[17] This means that Matthew has taken a traditional saying and made it into a question of a disciple. Like Matt 18:21, *Ap. Jas.* 4.25–28 also preserves the tradition as a remark of a disciple. Unlike Matt 18:22, however, the response of Jesus (*Ap. Jas.* 4.32–37) does not continue the tradition of this saying, but follows up on the subsequent request of James (4.28–31).

B) *Ap. Jas. 4.28–31:*

ⲧ ⲑⲉⲉ ϭ̣[ⲉ] | ⲛⲉⲛ ⲁⲧⲙ̄ⲧⲣⲟⲩⲡⲓⲣⲁⲍⲉ ⲙ̄ⲙⲁⲛ | ⲁⲃⲁⲗ ϩⲓ̈ⲧⲟⲟⲧϥ̄ ⲙ̄ⲡⲇⲓⲁⲃⲟⲗⲟⲥ· ⲉ|ⲑⲁⲩ·	Grant us, [therefore], not to be tempted by the wicked devil.

This is a fragment of the final petitions of the "Lord's prayer" (Matt 6:13 // Luke 11:4 // *Did.* 8.2).

Redactional elements:

This fragment is secondarily connected to James's previous comment by means of the postpositive ϭⲉ (= οὖν). The use of οὖν to attach originally discrete traditions to a larger context is attested elsewhere in the sayings tradition. In Matt 6:9, for example, it connects the Lord's prayer to Matthew's introductory exhortations, but it is absent from the parallel in Luke 11:2. And in Matt 7:12, it connects the "golden rule"

[16]See Dibelius, *Tradition*, 160.

[17]Note that, despite the parallels between Luke 17:3 and Matt 18:15a (ἐὰν δὲ ἁμαρτήσῃ εἰς σέ), one should not regard Matt 18:15a as taken from Q, but from Matthew's special material. The sayings in 18:15–17 have been transmitted as a unity, and are tradition-historically secondary to Luke 17:3–4. Against Adolf Harnack, *The Sayings of Jesus* (New York: Putnam's; London: Williams & Norgate, 1908) 94–95. Despite Matthew's frame (18:12–14, 21–22, 23–35), Matt 18:15–17 does not discuss forgiveness, but excommunication. Apparently Matthew understood these verses as detailing a step-by-step procedure for repentance. See the discussion in Lührmann, *Logienquelle*, 111–14, 116; Gerhard Barth, "Matthew's Understanding of the Law," in idem, Günther Bornkamm, and Heinz Joachim Held, *Tradition and Interpretation in Matthew* (Philadelphia: Westminster, 1963) 84; W. D. Davies, *The Setting of the Sermon on the Mount* (Cambridge: Cambridge University Press, 1964) 391–92; and Bultmann, *History*, 141.

to the preceding instructions about prayer, but it again is missing in the Lucan parallel (6:31).

The use of the passive voice in *Ap. Jas.* 4.29–30 (ⲁⲧⲙ̄ⲧⲣⲟⲩⲡⲓⲣⲁⲍⲉ ⲙ̄ⲙⲁⲛ ⲁⲃⲁⲗ ϩⲓ̈ⲧⲟⲟⲧ≠) reflects those traditions in which any responsibility for temptation is removed from God.[18] Marcion's text of Luke also used the passive (*apud* Tertullian *Marc.* 4.26: *μὴ ἄφες ἡμᾶς εἰσενεχθῆναι εἰς πειρασμόν*),[19] and this evidently became customary in early Christian citations of this saying.[20]

Formal parallels:

The Lord's prayer is found in the Synoptic Sayings Source Q (Matt 6:9–13 // Luke 11:2–4) and, independently, in *Did.* 8.2.[21] The *Ap. Jas.* preserves a variant of the final two petitions of the longer version of this prayer:

Matt 6:13:	*Luke 11:4:*	*Did. 8.2:*
καὶ μὴ εἰσενέγκῃς ἡμᾶς εἰς πειρασμόν, ἀλλὰ ῥῦσαι ἡμᾶς ἀπὸ τοῦ πονηροῦ.	καὶ μὴ εἰσενέγκῃς ἡμᾶς εἰς πειρασμόν.	καὶ μὴ εἰσενέγκῃς ἡμᾶς εἰς πειρασμόν, ἀλλὰ ῥῦσαι ἡμᾶς ἀπὸ τοῦ πονηροῦ·

It is well known that Luke's version of this prayer (Luke 11:2–4) contains only five petitions, whereas Matthew's has seven (Matt 6:9–13). Whether it was Matthew's community which expanded its Q version with two additional requests (vss 10bc, 13b) to create a sevenfold arrangement is not certain, Matthew does favor sevenfold structures,[22]

[18]Cf. 1 Cor 10:13; Jas 1:12–14; *b. Ber.* 60b; and Jeremias, *Theology*, 202.

[19]Reconstructed by Adolf von Harnack from Tertullian *Marc.* 4.26: *non sinet nos deduci in temptationem* (*Marcion: Das Evangelium vom fremdem Gott* [TU 45; 2d ed.; Leipzig: Hinrichs, 1924] 207*).

[20]Texts and references are given in Alfred Resch, *Aussercanonische Paralleltexte zu den Evangelien* (TU 10/3; Leipzig: Hinrichs, 1895) 2. 239–43. See the discussions in Ernst Lohmeyer, *Das Vater-unser* (3d ed.; Göttingen: Vandenhoeck & Ruprecht, 1952) 134–46; and Erich Klostermann, *Das Matthäusevangelium* (HNT 4; 2d ed.; Tübingen: Mohr-Siebeck, 1927) 55–59.

[21]See Koester, *Überlieferung*, 203–9.

[22]The beatitudes are expanded from three to seven (Matt 5:3–9; vs 10 is to be taken with vss 11–12 and regarded with them as a creation of the post-Easter church) by supplementing the Q version (Luke 6:20b–21) with additional macarisms from Matthew's special material. The collection of parables in Matthew 13 is expanded to seven by supplementing the one in Mark 4 with additions and replacements from Q and M. The woes in Matt 23:13–31 are also expanded to seven (cf. Luke 11:39–44, 46, 52).

and his third petition (vs 10bc: *γενηθήτω τὸ θέλημά σου, ὡς ἐν οὐρανῷ καὶ ἐπὶ γῆς*) seems to reflect a secondary development, paralleled in the Matthean version of the address (vs 9b), to transform a prayer of Jesus into a catechetical prayer of the community. The fact that each of the three additions in Matthew comes at the same place in the text may indicate a consistent tendency to expand the tradition at similar junctures:[23]

1) at the end of the address (Matt 6:9b);
2) at the end of the petitions in the second person (Matt 6:10bc); and
3) at the end of the petitions in the first person plural (Matt 6:13b).

Nevertheless, the final petition in Mattthew (vs 13b), which stands in antithetical parallelism to that in Q (vs 13a), is paralleled in pre-Christian Jewish prayers, and does not necessarily reflect the eschatological orientation of a Christian community:[24]

Add Esth 14:19:
καὶ ῥῦσαι ἡμᾶς ἐκ χειρὸς τῶν πονηρευομένων

11QPs^{a} Plea xix 15–16:[25]

Let not Satan rule over me (אל תשלטבי שכן),
nor an unclean spirit (ורוח טמאה).

Even if the final petition in Matthew (6:13b) is not an original part of the prayer of Jesus, it is a very early tradition[26] which is also attested in *Did.* 8.2. The *Ap. Jas.*'s reference to "the wicked devil" shows that it, too, contains a portion of the tradition that is not found in Luke.

Sitz im Leben and Formal history:

The "Lord's prayer" is almost certainly an authentic prayer of Jesus, most likely originally spoken in Aramaic.[27] Its *Sitz im Leben* in the early

[23]See Jeremias, *Theology*, 195.
[24]Against Rudolf Bultmann, *Jesus and the Word* (1934; reprint, New York: Scribner's, 1958) 181.
[25]J. A. Sanders, *The Psalms Scroll of Qumrân Cave 11* (DJD 4; Oxford: Clarendon, 1965) 77–78.
[26]So also Jeremias, *Theology*, 194–95.
[27]Ibid., 196.

Christian tradition was liturgical prayer, perhaps in conjunction with table fellowship.[28] The contexts into which this prayer has been inserted (Matt 6:5–9a, 14–15; Luke 11:1–2a, 5–13; *Did.* 8.2a, 3) indicate that it came to be used catechetically. The *Ap. Jas.* preserves its fragment of the prayer as a petition of James on behalf of his community. This is in accord with the continued "Christianization" of Jesus' prayer, which has made it into a model prayer of the community (cf. Matt 6:9a // Luke 11:2a). James's request not to be tempted by the Devil (*Ap. Jas.* 4.28–31) gives rise to Jesus' response (4.32–37). The specifics of James's request and Jesus' response are connected by catchwords and synonyms:

ⲡⲓⲣⲁⲍⲉ (to tempt):
4.29 and 35–36
ϯ ⲑⲉϩⲉ (to grant) . . . ϯ (ϩⲙⲁⲧ) (to give [merit]):
4.28 and 32–34
ϩⲛⲉ⸗ (to wish) . . . ⲡ.ⲟⲩⲱϣⲉ (the will):
4.25 and 33
ⲡ.ⲇⲓⲁⲃⲟⲗⲟⲥ (the devil) . . . ⲡ.ⲥⲁⲧⲁⲛⲁⲥ (Satan):
4.30 and 37.

Once again the author of the *Ap. Jas.* has used a portion of a traditional saying to create a dialogue between Jesus and James. Here, too, the tradition has been preserved as a request of a disciple.

[28]See Norman Perrin, *Rediscovering the Teaching of Jesus* (New York: Harper & Row, 1976) 107–8, 151–53; and James Breech, *The Silence of Jesus* (Philadelphia: Fortress, 1983) 51–55.

2.3 THE DIALOGUE IN *AP. JAS.* 5.31–6.11

Ap. Jas. 5.31–6.11:

1) *Exhortation of Jesus: 5.31–35*	
. . . ⲉⲣⲓ ⲕⲁⲧⲁⲫⲣⲟⲛⲓ ϭⲉ ⲙ̄ⲡⲙⲟⲩ |	". . . Scorn death, therefore,
ⲁⲩⲱ ⲛ̄ⲧⲉⲧⲛ̄ϥⲓ ⲣⲁⲟⲩϣ ⲁⲡⲱⲛⲉϩ |	and take concern for life.
ⲁⲣⲓ ⲡⲙⲉⲉⲩⲉ ⲙ̄ⲡⲁⲥⲧⲁⲩⲣⲟⲥ | ⲁⲩⲱ ⲡⲁⲙⲟⲩ	Remember my cross and my death
ⲁⲩⲱ ⲧⲉⲧⲛ̄ⲛⲁ|ⲱⲛ̄ϩ	and you (pl.) will live."
2) *Response of a Disciple:*	
a) Introduction: 5.35–36	
ⲁϩⲓ̈ⲟⲩⲱϣⲃ̄ ⲛ̄ⲇⲉ ⲡⲁ|ϫⲏⲓ̈ ⲛⲉϥ ϫⲉ	And I (James) answered and said to him:
b) Response: 5.36–6.1	
ⲡϫⲁⲉⲓⲥ ⲙ̄|ⲡⲱⲣ· ⲁⲧⲉⲩⲟ ⲁⲣⲁⲛ	"Lord, do not mention to us
ⲙ̄ⲡⲥⲧ(ⲁⲩ)ⲣⲟⲥ | ⲙⲛ̄ ⲡⲙⲟⲩ	the cross and the death,
ⲛⲉⲉⲓ ⲅⲁⲣ ⲥⲉⲟⲩⲏⲟⲩ | ⲙ̄ⲙⲁⲕ	for they are far from you."
3) *Response of Jesus:*	
a) Introduction: 6.1–2	
ⲁϥⲟ̣[ⲩⲱ] ϣ̣ⲃ̄ ⲛ̄ϭⲓ ⲡ̣ϫⲁⲉ̣ⲓ̣ⲥ | ⲡⲁϫⲉϥ ϫⲉ	The Lord answered and said:
b) Response: 6.2–11	
ϩⲁⲙⲏⲛ ϯϫⲟⲩ ⲙ̄ⲙⲁⲥ | ⲛⲏⲧⲛ̄ ϫⲉ	"Truly I say to you (pl.),
ⲙ̣ⲛ̄ ⲗⲁⲁⲩⲉ̣ ⲛ̣ⲁⲟⲩϫⲉ|ⲉⲓ	none will be saved
ⲉⲓⲙⲏⲧⲓ ⲛ̄ⲥⲉⲡⲓⲥ̣ⲧ̣[ⲉⲩⲉ] ⲁ̣ⲡⲁⲥⲧ(ⲁⲩ)ⲣⲟⲥ |	unless they believe in my cross.
ⲛⲉⲛⲧⲁ[ϩ]ⲡⲓⲥⲧⲉⲩⲉ̣ [ⲅⲁ] ⲣ̣[1] ⲁⲡⲁⲥ|ⲧ(ⲁⲩ)ⲣⲟⲥ·	[But] those who have believed in my cross,
ⲧⲱⲟⲩ ⲧⲉ ⲧⲙⲛ̄ⲧ̣ⲉⲣⲟ ⲙ̄ⲡ|{ⲡ}ⲛⲟⲩⲧⲉ	theirs is the Kingdom of God.

[1]On the meaning of ⲅⲁⲣ as "but," cf. BAG, *s.v. γάρ* 4 (152b).

ϣⲱ̣ⲡⲉ ϭⲉ ⲉⲣⲉⲧⲛ̄ϣⲓ|ⲛⲉ	Therefore, become seekers
ⲛ̄ⲥⲁ ⲡⲙⲟⲩ	for death,
ⲛ̄ⲑϩⲉ ⲛⲛⲉⲧⲙⲁ|ⲟⲩⲧ· ⲉⲧϣⲓⲛⲉ	just as the dead who seek
ⲛ̄ⲥⲁ ⲡⲱⲛϩ̄	for life,
ϣⲁϥ|ⲟⲩⲱⲛϩ̄ ⲅⲁⲣ ⲁⲛⲉⲧⲙ̄ⲙⲉⲩ	for that for which they seek
ⲛ̄ϭⲓ ⲡⲉ|ⲧⲟⲩϣⲓⲛⲉ ⲛ̄ⲥⲱϥ· . . .	is revealed to them. . . ."

5.37 ⲁⲧⲉⲩⲟ, ⲁⲧⲉ written over an erased ⲁ̣ⲣⲁⲛ | 6.5 ⲛⲉⲛⲧⲁ[ϩ] Mueller : ⲛⲉⲛⲧⲁ[ⲣ] Emmel | [ⲅⲁ] ⲣ̣ Emmel : [ⲇⲉ] *ed. pr.* | 7 {ⲡ}ⲛⲟⲩⲧⲉ *ed. pr.* (with hesitation)

This passage seems to be a redacted composition. The main indicators of redaction are the following:

a) The noun ⲡ.ⲥⲧⲁⲩⲣⲟⲥ (cross) is found only here (5.33, 37; 6.4, 5–6)[2] in the entire *Ap. Jas.* Its presence in the initial exhortation of Jesus (5.33) interrupts the balanced parallelism between "death" (5.31, 34) and "life" (5.32, 35), a parallelism which is resumed in a final exhortation (6.7–9) only after the I-sayings about Jesus' cross (6.2–7).

b) The response of James (5.36–6.1) is both literarily occasioned by the preceding exhortation (5.33–35) and connected to it and the following response of Jesus (6.2–7) by catchwords ("cross" and "death"):

ⲡ.ⲥⲧⲁⲩⲣⲟⲥ:	5.33 (Jesus) . . . 5.37 (James) . . . 6.4, 5–6 (Jesus)
ⲡ.ⲙⲟⲩ:	5.31, 34 (Jesus) . . . 5.38 (James) . . . 6.8 (Jesus).

The main indicators of the use of tradition are the following:

a) The references to "remembering" and "believing" in Jesus' "cross" are reminiscent of creedal formulas found elsewhere in early Christian literature.

b) The fixed pattern of (1) a teaching of Jesus about his death (5.33–35), (2) a misunderstanding of a disciple (5.35–6.1), and (3) a correction by Jesus (6.1–7) is found in the Synoptics (Mark 8:31–33 // Matt 16:21–23 // Luke 9:22; cf. 9:45; 18:34) and John (6:62, 69–71) in programmatic passages which anticipate the passion and give structure to the narrative.

[2]The verb ⲣ̄ ⲥⲧ̣(ⲁⲩ)ⲣ̣ⲟ̣[ⲩ] occurs only in 5.17.

Identifying the use of creedal formulations in the creation of sayings of Jesus and examining the traditional pattern of Jesus' teaching about the cross will enable us to trace the tradition and redaction in the dialogue in *Ap. Jas.* 5.31–6.11.

Ap.Jas. 6.2–7:

ϩⲁⲙⲏⲛ ϯϫⲟⲩ ⲙ̅ⲙⲁⲥ | ⲛⲏⲧⲛ̅ ϫⲉ	Truly I say to you (pl.),
ⲙ̣ⲛ̅ ⲗⲁⲁⲩⲉ̣ ⲛ̣ⲁⲟⲩϫⲉ|ⲉⲓ	none will be saved
ⲉⲓⲙⲏⲧⲓ ⲛ̅ⲥⲉⲡⲓⲥ̣ⲧ̣[ⲉⲩⲉ] ⲁ̣ⲡⲁⲥⲧ(ⲁⲩ)ⲣⲟⲥ |	unless they believe in my cross.
ⲛⲉⲛⲧⲁ[ϩ]ⲡⲓⲥⲧⲉⲩⲉ̣ [ⲅⲁ]ⲣ̣ ⲁⲡⲁⲥ|ⲧ(ⲁⲩ)ⲣⲟⲥ·	[But] those who have believed in my cross,
ⲧⲱⲟⲩ ⲧⲉ ⲧⲙⲛ̅ⲧ̣ⲉⲣⲟ ⲙ̅ⲡ|{ⲡ}ⲛⲟⲩⲧⲉ	theirs is the Kingdom of God.

The explicit first person statements about believing "in my cross" indicate that this is a product of the early church. The repetition of the phrase "believe in my cross" and the parallelism between "being saved" and receiving "the Kingdom of God" suggest that this is a double saying, formulated as a unit. The first portion of this saying (6.2–4) has the character of a prophetic warning; the second (6.5–7) contains a promise of salvation. The use of the Amen-formula serves to ratify this pronouncement with a solemn oath.

Redactional elements:

The most important feature of redaction in this passage is the use of creedal formulas as models from which to construct these sayings in the name of the Lord. This entire passage is a secondary formulation from an early Christian creed. It is striking that the *Ap. Jas.* formulated this I-saying with reference only to the cross, not to Jesus' vindication in his resurrection and/or exaltation and ascension.[3]

[3]Cf. Rom 4:25; 1 Cor 15:3–5; and see Helmut Koester, "The Structure and Criteria of Early Christian Beliefs," in *Trajectories*, 225.

Formal parallels:

Examples of the incorporation of creedal formulas interpreting Jesus' death into sayings in the Synoptic tradition are rare. The saying in Mark 10:45 par. reflects a secondary stage in the development of the tradition which used the title "Son of Man" to interpret Jesus' death as a "ransom for many."[4] Interpretations of Jesus' death as a sacrifice are found in creedal formulations in connection with the Christian meal in the Synoptic (Matt 26:28; cf. Mark 14:24) and pre-Pauline (1 Cor 11:24, 25) traditions. A saying of the risen Lord in the longer ending of Mark (16:16) indicates how creeds could be used to formulate secondary "dominical" sayings. But whereas these examples do use the language of early Christian proclamation and liturgy, none offers an exact parallel with the Amen-saying in *Ap. Jas.* 6.2–7. For formal parallels to the use of sayings traditions in the composition of the dialogue in *Ap. Jas.* 5.31–6.11, one needs rather to examine the tradition underlying the dialogue as a whole.

The dialogue in *Ap. Jas.* 5.31–6.11 seems to be a variant of the celebrated tradition of Jesus' first "prediction of the passion" in the Synoptic Gospels (Mark 8:31–33 // Matt 16:21–23 // Luke 9:22). The following diagram will permit a comparison of the respective texts:

1) teaching about the passion:
   Mark 8:31 par. // *Ap. Jas.* 5.33–35
2) misunderstanding of a disciple:
   Mark 8:32 par. // *Ap. Jas.* 5.35–6.1
3) correction by Jesus:
   Mark 8:33 par. // *Ap. Jas.* 6.1–7.

Redaction criticism has demonstrated the centrality of this section for the structure and theology of Mark's Gospel.[5] Mark 8:31–33 is the first of three predictions of the passion that Mark has taken from the tradition and attributed to Jesus (cf. Mark 9:31–32 par.; 10:32–34 par.). It is a feature of Mark's own redaction that these predictions have been

[4]See the discussion in Wilhelm Bousset, *Kyrios Christos* (Nashville/New York: Abingdon, 1970) 39; Bultmann, *History*, 143–44; Hahn, *Hoheitstitel*, 57–59; H. E. Tödt, *The Son of Man in the Synoptic Tradition* (Philadelphia: Westminster, 1965) 135–38, 202–11; and Kee, *Community*, 47–48.

[5]See, e.g., the redaction-critical analysis of Norman Perrin and Dennis C. Duling, *The New Testament: An Introduction* (2d ed.; New York: Harcourt Brace Jovanovich, 1982) 239–40, 248–51; and the literary-critical analysis of Norman R. Petersen, *Literary Criticism for New Testament Critics* (Philadelphia: Fortress, 1978) 60–68.

arranged in such a way as to constitute the heart of the central section of his Gospel (8:27–10:45). The first prediction of the passion also marks the turning point of the Gospel, in which, for the first time, Jesus is said to speak "openly" (8:32a).[6] Although Matthew and Luke incorporate into their narratives all three of Mark's passion predictions,[7] they do not use them in a material way to structure their Gospels. Neither does the Gospel of John; but the fact that John independently includes three passion predictions (3:14; 8:28; 12:32–34) in his narrative indicates that they have been taken from the tradition.

Mark 8:27–9:1 is thus the redactional turning point in the Gospel. It includes:

8:27–30: the first "confession" of Jesus' identity by a disciple
8:31–33: the first passion prediction unit, comprising:
1) an *ex eventu* teaching of Jesus about the passion (vs 31),
2) a misunderstanding of a disciple (vs 32), and
3) a correction by Jesus (vs 33)
8:34–9:1: Jesus' instruction about discipleship.[8]

This entire section is form-critically composite:[9]
Mark 8:27–30: The legend[10] of the confession of Peter is introduced with the typical question and answer format of a school debate. The fact that Jesus is depicted as taking the initiative with his own question indicates that this format is a secondary literary device (cf. Mark 12:35).[11] This same format is used in Mark 6:14–16 par. and John 1:19–23 to introduce the question of the identity and activity

[6]Cf. John 16:25, 29; and see James M. Robinson, "Gnosticism and the New Testament," in Barbara Aland, ed., *Gnosis: Festschrift für Hans Jonas* (Göttingen: Vandenhoeck & Ruprecht, 1978) 132–43.

[7]Matt 16:21–22; 17:22–23; 20:17–19; Luke 9:22, 44–45; 18:31–34 (cf. 24:6–8). See the discussion of the passion predictions in Luke in Paul Schubert, "The Structure and Significance of Luke 24," in Walther Eltester, ed., *Neutestamentliche Studien für Rudolf Bultmann* (BZNW 21; Berlin: Töpelmann, 1954) 165–86.

[8]Perrin and Duling (*New Testament*, 248–49) do not separate the dual rebukes of a disciple and Jesus, but instead include Jesus' teaching about discipleship in their analysis of the passion-prediction unit.

[9]See the comprehensive discussions, with complete bibliographies, in Bultmann, *History*, 257–59; Hahn, *Hoheitstitel*, 226–30; and Erich Dinkler, "Peter's Confession and the 'Satan' Saying: The Problem of Jesus' Messiahship," in James M. Robinson, ed., *The Future of Our Religious Past: Essays in Honour of Rudolf Bultmann* (New York: Harper & Row, 1971) 169–202.

[10]So Bultmann, *History*, 257–58; and Dibelius, *Tradition*, 115.

[11]Bultmann, above n. 10.

of John the Baptist. The fact that John 6:60–69 also preserves the tradition of the confession of Peter, again in question and answer form, demonstrates that this legend was transmitted outside the Synoptic Gospels.[12] Its occurrence in *Gos. Thom.* 13: 34.30–35.14 substantiates that this tradition—here with Thomas's being given special status—circulated freely and independently of all four gospels of the NT.

Mark 8:31–33: The tradition of Jesus' first of three *ex eventu* predictions of the passion has been reworked in accordance with Marcan redaction. This is particularly clear in Mark's polemical emphasis on the "suffering" Son of Man (8:31).[13] Moreover, the rebukes of Peter and Jesus (8:32–33 par.), which Mark intentionally inserts directly after this first passion prediction, serve both to emphasize his christology of suffering and to reiterate the motif of secrecy[14] that is so central to the entire Gospel. Accordingly, Mark links up the confession and the rebukes with the catchword ἐπιτιμᾶν (vss 30, 32, 33), a term which Mark uses elsewhere in setting forth his specific understanding of the nature of Jesus' messiahship (cf. 1:25; 3:12).

Mark 8:34–9:1: By appending Jesus' subsequent teaching about discipleship, Mark seeks to demonstrate that, just as Jesus' true messiahship is present in his suffering, so his disciples are to follow him on the road to the passion. These verses are also originally discrete, as an analysis of their frequent parallels throughout various branches of the sayings tradition demonstrates:[15]

[12]See the discussion of the parallels between Mark 8:27–33 par. and John 6:60–71 in Brown, *John (i–xii)*, 301–2; and Dodd, *Historical Tradition*, 219–21. Cf. also John 21:15–19.

[13]See Hahn, *Hoheitstitel*, 46–53; and H. E. Tödt, *The Son of Man in the Synoptic Tradition* (Philadelphia: Westminster, 1965) 141–221. John also knows of and uses the tradition of a threefold prediction of the passion (3:14; 8:28; 12:32–34), but employs his own distinctive vocabulary of the Son of Man's "being lifted up" (ὑψοῦν).

[14]See William Wrede, *The Messianic Secret* (Cambridge/London: Clarke, 1971); the critique of Wrede in Kee, *Community*, 95–96, 167–75; Robinson, "Gnosticism and the New Testament," 132–43; and Frank Kermode, *The Genesis of Secrecy: On the Interpretation of Narrative* (Cambridge/London: Harvard University Press, 1979) 139–40.

[15]See Bultmann, *History*, 82–83.

1) Mark 8:34 // Matt 16:24 // Luke 9:23 // Q (Matt 10:38 // Luke 14:27) // *Gos. Thom.* 55b: 42.27–29 // John 12:26
2) Mark 8:35 // Matt 16:25 // Luke 9:24 // Q (Matt 10:39 // Luke 17:33) // John 12:25
3) Mark 8:36 // Matt 16:26a // Luke 9:25 // *Gos. Thom.* 67: 45.19–20 // *2 Clem.* 6.2—cf. Ign. *Rom.* 6.1; Just. *1 Apol.* 15.12; Clem. Al. *Strom.* 6.14.112.3
4) Mark 8:37 // Matt 16:26b
5) Mark 8:38 // Matt 16:27 // Luke 9:26 // Q (Matt 10:33 // Luke 12:9)—cf. Ps 61:13; *2 Clem.* 11.6; Pol. *Phil.* 5.2; 2 Tim 2:12; *Herm. Sim.* 6.3.6a
6) Mark 9:1 // Matt 16:28 // Luke 9:27—cf. 1 Thess 4:15–17; John 8:51, 52; 21:22, 23; Mark 13:30–31 par.; *Gos. Thom.* 1: 32.12–14.

This last saying (9:1) has been secondarily attached with the typically Marcan redactional introductory formula (καὶ ἔλεγεν αὐτοῖς).[16]

The Gospel of John also knows of the tradition of the confession of Peter in conjunction with a reference to Jesus' death (6:66–69, 70–71). Here, Jesus' death is not introduced with one of John's three passion predictions, but with the first reference to Judas's betrayal (cf. 13:2, 17–30; Mark 14:18 par.). It is possible that the description of Judas as a διάβολος (John 6:70) represents a reworking of the pre-Marcan tradition which applied the term "Satan" to Peter.[17] If so, then two of the three elements of the pattern of Jesus' teaching about the passion and rebuke(s) of a disciple are present in John's independent formulation.[18]

The fact that John preserves throughout his Gospel traditions which Matthew has inserted (Matt 16:17–19) between his reproduction of Mark's text of the confession of Peter (Mark 8:29 // Matt 16:16) and Jesus' command to silence (Mark 8:30 // Matt 16:20) may suggest that Matthew has collected independent Petrine traditions and inserted them into the context of Peter's confession.[19] It is noteworthy that, in the

[16]Cf. Mark 2:27; 4:2, 11, 21, 24; 6:4, 10; 7:9; 8:21; 9:31; 11:17. This phrase characteristically links a saying or saying fragment with a context to which it was not previously connected. In Mark 3:23 and 7:14, προσκαλεσάμενος plus an object is inserted between καί and ἔλεγεν αὐτοῖς. See the discussion of Mark's distinctive vocabulary in his introductory and connecting formulas in Kee, *Community*, 51–53.

[17]See Brown, *John (i–xii)*, 301.

[18]Only the disciple's rebuke of Jesus (cf. Mark 8:32 par.) is missing.

[19]See Brown, *John (i–xii)*, 302. Against Bultmann, *History*, 138–41, 257–59, 408–9, 431–32; John P. Meier, *The Vision of Matthew* (New York: Paulist, 1979) 110; and George W. E. Nickelsburg, "Enoch, Levi, and Peter: Recipients of Revelation in Upper

scene of Peter's rebuke of Jesus (Mark 8:32 // Matt 16:22), Matthew does not truncate Peter's response as Mark does (Mark 8:32: ἤρξατο ἐπιτιμᾶν αὐτῷ), but recreates a dialogue between Jesus and Peter. Such a creation of direct speech is typical of the development of the sayings tradition.[20] Nevertheless, the objection of Peter in Matt 16:22 is a doublet of the tradition: ἵλεώς σοι, κύριε· οὐ μὴ ἔσται σοι τοῦτο. The first phrase is a Septuagintism (ἵλεώς σοι = חלילה + the dative), meaning "be it far from. . . ."[21] The second simply duplicates the meaning of the first (= μὴ γένοιτό σοι). The fact that the *Ap. Jas.* preserves a variant of this first phrase in a comment attributed to James (5.38–6.1: ⲚⲈⲈⲒ ⲄⲀⲢ ⲤⲈⲞⲨⲎⲞⲨ ⲘⲘⲀⲔ) suggests that it was familiar with the tradition, but in a non-Matthean form.

Sitz im Leben and Formal history:

The dialogue in *Ap. Jas.* 5.31–6.11 is a secondary product of the early church. The attribution of statements about Jesus' death on the cross to Jesus himself indicates clearly its post-resurrection provenance.[22] The use of the fixed pattern of a teaching of Jesus about his death (*Ap. Jas.* 5.33–35), a misunderstanding of a disciple (5.35–6.1), and a correction by Jesus (6.1–7) demonstrates that the *Ap. Jas.* is dependent on tradition for its formulation of this dialogue. Like the Synoptics and John, the *Ap. Jas.* has creedal formulas used to construct secondary sayings about the passion. But whereas the Synoptics and John include the tradition as part of a narrative, the *Ap. Jas.* has preserved it as part of a dialogue between Jesus and James. In all

Galilee," *JBL* 100 (1981) 590–600. They all take Matt 16:17–19 to be a pre-Matthean unity which presents what may be the original conclusion to the confession in Mark 8:27–29 // Matt 16:13–16. For an extensive discussion of this problem, see the bibliographic references in their copious notes.

[20]Matthew, e.g., creates such direct comments and adds them to his Marcan source in Matt 26:1–2 (contrast Mark 14:1); Matt 18:1 (contrast Mark 9:33–34); Matt 17:9 (contrast Mark 9:9); and Matt 26:27 (contrast Mark 14:23). See further examples in Bultmann, *History*, 312–13.

[21]See esp. BDF § 128(5). Cf. the Vulgate of Matt 16:22: *absit a te.* For a different reading, cf. Bauer (BAG, *s.v.* ἵλεως [376a]) who takes (the homonym) ἵλεως to be the Greek word for "merciful," and translates ἵλεώς σοι (i.e., εἴη ὁ θεός) as "may God be gracious to you, God forbid."

[22]The post-Easter origin of Mark 8:27–9:1 par. is widely held in the literature, and can hardly be disputed. See, e.g., Bultmann, *History*, 259; Meier, *Vision*, 107 n. 104, and the literature cited there; and Brown, *John (xiii–xxi)*, 1088–89. This is supported by the Easter story in John 21:15–19.

cases, the original liturgical *Sitz im Leben* of the creed has been superseded by its inclusion within a literary context. Mark and John employ the tradition of Jesus' teaching about the passion as *vaticinia ex eventu*, serving to introduce the nature of Jesus' messiahship as that of a secret, suffering Son of Man (so Mark), whose death on the cross is nothing other than his final exaltation (so John), in opposition to those christologies which sought to demonstrate more directly Jesus' power and divine status by means of miracles. The use of the tradition in the dialogue in the *Ap. Jas.* focuses the teaching about Jesus' death on the life of the community (cf. 5.31–32, 33–35; 6.7–11). The insertion of the Amen-saying (6.2–7) within the frame of the two exhortations of Jesus shows that this saying is no longer used for creedal recitation, but for community parenesis.

3

"REMEMBERING" THE WORDS OF JESUS

The opening scene of the *Ap. Jas.* describes a situation in which scribal activity was taking place:

"Now the twelve disciples [were] sitting all together at [the same time], and remembering (ⲉⲩⲉⲓⲣⲉ ⲙ̄ⲡⲙⲉⲉⲩⲉ) what the Savior had said (ⲛ̄ⲛⲉⲛⲧⲁϩⲁⲡⲥⲱⲧⲏⲣ ϫⲟⲟⲩ) to each one of them, whether secretly or openly (ⲉⲓⲧⲉ ⲙ̄ⲡⲉⲧⲑⲏⲡ ⲉⲓⲧⲉ ⲙ̄ⲡⲉⲧⲟⲩⲁⲛϩ̄ ⲁⲃⲁⲗ), they were setting it down (ⲉⲩⲣ̄ ⲧⲁⲥ̣ⲥ̣ⲉ̣ ⲙ̣̄ⲙⲁⲩ) in books. [And] I was writing what was in [my book] . . ."(2.7–16).

This scene portrays a situation in which "the literary production of sayings of Jesus was still being vigorously pursued"; it reflects "a time in which written texts with 'scriptural' authority were not yet normative."[1] The reference to "remembering" provides the critical clue to the date and character of this tradition, since this term was employed in the early church to describe the process of creating, collecting, and transmitting sayings of Jesus. *Ap. Jas.* 2.7–16 intimates that it understood "remembering" as critical production and reproduction. An examination of the use of this technical term in early Christian literature will help clarify the ways in which sayings traditions that were available to the *Ap. Jas.* were understood and utilized in the composition of this document.

Near the end of the first century, Clement of Rome referred to collections of sayings of Jesus as λόγοι,[2] introducing them with a form of the verb "to remember" (μνημονεύειν):

1 Clem. 13.1–2: μεμνημένοι τῶν λόγων τοῦ κυρίου Ἰησοῦ, οὓς ἐλάλησεν διδάσκων . . . οὕτως γὰρ εἶπεν·

1 Clem. 46.7–8: μνήσθητε τῶν λόγων Ἰησοῦ τοῦ κυρίου ἡμῶν. εἶπεν γάρ·

In the former instance (*1 Clem.* 13.2), seven discrete sayings are linked together into a single sentence. Despite the close parallels with passages in all three Synoptic Gospels,[3] there can be no doubt that these sayings have been transmitted independently of the NT.[4] But whether they were taken "from some written collection of sayings of the Lord no longer known to us," or from an "oral, though firmly formulated, local catechism," cannot be determined.[5] In the latter instance (*1 Clem.* 46.8), a variant of a saying found in two different contexts in Mark as well as in in Q[6] is preserved in a form more original than that in the Synoptics.[7] In both cases, sayings collections comparable to Q are

[1]Cameron, "Apocryphon of James," 56.

[2]See James M. Robinson, "LOGOI SOPHON: On the Gattung of Q," in *Trajectories*, 96–98.

[3]In the order as given in *1 Clement*: Matt 5:7; Mark 11:25; Matt 7:12; Luke 6:38a; Matt 7:2a // Luke 6:37a; and Matt 7:2b // Luke 6:38b. *1 Clement*'s sixth saying is not found in the Synoptics.

[4]Koester, *Überlieferung*, 12–16.

[5]Ibid., 16.

[6]Mark 9:42; 14:21; Luke 17:1–2 // Matt 18:6–7.

[7]Koester, *Überlieferung*, 16–19.

known to Clement and introduced with the formula "remembering the words of the (or: our) Lord Jesus." This same quotation formula is also found in Acts 20:35, where a secular Greek proverb[8] is transmitted as an alleged saying of Jesus, introduced as follows:

Acts 20:35: δεῖ . . . μνημονεύειν τε τῶν λόγων τοῦ κυρίου Ἰησοῦ, ὅτι αὐτὸς εἶπεν·

The coupling of this "apocryphal" saying with the technical term of "remembering" locates this tradition in the oral transmission of sayings attributed to Jesus. "Since a word of the Lord which is not found in the Gospels is cited in Acts 20:35 with the formula [of 'remembering'], this formula must originate from a time in which the words of the Lord were not yet fixed in [the written] Gospels [of the NT]."[9]

3.1 PAPIAS AND ORAL TRADITION

The *locus classicus* of the use of the term "remembering" in conjunction with a discussion of sayings traditions is found in the writings of Papias of Hierapolis (ca. 100–150 CE).[10] Although his five-volume "Exegesis of the Sayings of the Lord" (Λογίων κυριακῶν ἐξήγησις) is now lost, a few fragments have been preserved from antiquity,[11] of

[8]According to Thucydides 2.97.4, this proverb was a rule of the Persian court. See this and other parallels in Haenchen, *Acts*, 594 n. 5; and Hans Conzelmann, *Die Apostelgeschichte* (HNT 7; Tübingen: Mohr-Siebeck, 1963) 119. It is possible that Clement also knew of this proverb as a saying of Jesus, since the citation of it in *1 Clem.* 2.1 is in the context of an exhortation to "pay attention to his (Christ's) words (λόγους) which you (pl.) stored up carefully in your hearts." Although there is no formulaic introduction to this "saying" in *1 Clem.* 2.1, one of the sentences of holy law preserved in the collection in *1 Clem.* 13.2 concerns "giving." Cf. *Did.* 1.5; 4.5, 7; *Herm. Mand.* 2.4; and see Robinson, "LOGOI SOPHON," 97.

[9]Koester, *Überlieferung*, 6.

[10]For the date, see F. Wotke, "Papias," PW 18/3 (1949) 966–67; E. Bammel, "Papias," *RGG* 5 (3d ed.; 1961) 47–48; J. Kürzinger, "Papias," *LThK* 8 (2d ed.; 1963) 34–35; Engelbert Gutwenger, "Papias: Eine chronologische Studie," *ZKTh* 69 (1947) 385–416; Theodor Zahn, *Forschungen zur Geschichte des neutestamentlichen Kanons und der altkirchlichen Literatur* (10 vols.; Leipzig: Deichert/Böhme, 1900) 6. 109–12; and William R. Schoedel, *Polycarp, Martyrdom of Polycarp, Fragments of Papias*, in Robert M. Grant, ed., *The Apostolic Fathers: A New Translation and Commentary*, vol. 5 (London/Camden/Toronto: Nelson, 1967) 91–92.

[11]Conveniently collected in thirteen fragments in F. X. Funk and Karl Bihlmeyer, *Die Apostolischen Väter* (SAQ 2/1/1; 3d ed.; rev. Wilhelm Schneemelcher; Tübingen: Mohr-

which the most important are the quotations annotated in the writings of Irenaeus (*Adv. haer.* 5.33.3–4) and Eusebius (*Hist. eccl.* 3.39.1–17). The purpose of Papias's work is stated explicitly in his own preface, as excerpted by Eusebius:

Papias frg. 2 (apud Eus. Hist. eccl. 3.39.3–4):

> Now I shall not hesitate to set down (συγκατατάξαι) for you (sing.) all that I have learned (ἔμαθον) well from the "elders" (τῶν πρεσβυτέρων)[12] and have remembered (ἐμνημόνευσα) well, together with my interpretations (ταῖς ἑρμηνείαις), vouching for their truth (ἀλήθειαν). For I did not (οὐ) delight in those who say much (τὰ πολλά), as (do) the majority (οἱ πολλοί),[13] but (ἀλλά) in those who teach the truth (τἀληθῆ); nor (οὐδέ) in those who remember (μνημονεύουσιν) the commandments of others (τὰς ἀλλοτρίας ἐντολάς),[14] but (ἀλλά) in those who (remember) the (commandments) given to the faith (τῇ πίστει) by the Lord and deriving from the truth (ἀληθείας) itself.
>
> But if ever one came (ἔλθοι) who had accompanied (παρηκολουθηκώς) the "elders" (τοῖς πρεσβυτέροις), I would inquire into the words (τοὺς λόγους) of the "elders" (τῶν πρεσβυτέρων): (as to)[15] what Andrew or what Peter said (εἶπεν), or what Philip, or what Thomas or James, or what John or Matthew, or any other of the disciples (μαθητῶν) of the Lord (said), and that which Aristion and the "elder" (ὁ πρεσβύτερος) John, disciples (μαθηταί) of the Lord, were saying (λέγουσιν). For I did not (οὐ) presume that what came from books (τῶν

Siebeck, 1970) 133–40.

[12]For a discussion of the translation, the "elders," see Hans von Campenhausen, *Ecclesiastical Authority and Spiritual Power in the Church of the First Three Centuries* (Stanford: Stanford University Press, 1969) 162–63; Vielhauer, *Geschichte*, 763; Koester, *Introduction*, 2. 167; Günther Bornkamm, "πρέσβυς," *TDNT* 6 (1968) 671, 676–77; Rudolf Bultmann, *The Johannine Epistles* (Hermeneia; Philadelphia: Fortress, 1973) 95; Johannes Munck, "Presbyters and Disciples of the Lord in Papias: Exegetic Comments on Eusebius, Ecclesiastical History, III, 39," *HTR* 52 (1959) 223–43; and Theodor Zahn, *Introduction to the New Testament* (3 vols.; Edinburgh: T. & T. Clark, 1909) 2. 452.

[13]Cf. Pol. *Phil.* 2.1; 7.2. For the translation "the majority," see BAG, *s.v.* πολύς I.2.β (688a–b); and Bauer, *Orthodoxy and Heresy*, 73 n. 31, 188.

[14]For the use of ἐντολαί (commandments) in conjunction with sayings traditions, cf. the sentence of holy law in 1 Cor 14:37–38 // *Gos. Thom.* 3b: 32.26–33.1; 1 Cor 7:19; *Acts Phil.* 140 (34); 2 Pet 3:2 // Jude 17; and *2 Clem.* 17.3 (cf. Pol. *Phil.* 2.3). See also Swanson, "Christian Prophetic Speech," 189–92, 201; and Hans von Campenhausen, *The Formation of the Christian Bible* (Philadelphia: Fortress, 1972) 131 n. 110. For the use of ἀλλότριος as the equivalent of "heretical," cf. Ign. *Trall.* 6.1; *Phld.* 3.3.

[15]It will be argued below that what Papias actually says presupposes only third-hand acquaintance with these "apostolic" authorities. See Schoedel, *Fragments*, 98.

βιβλίων) would profit me so much as what came from a living and abiding voice (ζώσης φωνῆς καὶ μενούσης).

It is essential to observe the rhetorical artistry of this preface. Eduard Schwartz has shown that Papias had at his disposal "rhetorical devices" which he arranged "according to ancient conventions."[16] The rhetorical techniques used in this particular fragment include the repetition of words and phrases and the balancing of antitheses:

1) The repetition of words and phrases:
   τῶν πρεσβυτέρων . . . τοῖς πρεσβυτέροις . . .
      τῶν πρεσβυτέρων . . . ὁ πρεσβύτερος
   καλῶς . . . καλῶς
   ἐμνημόνευσα . . . μνημονεύουσιν
   οὐ γάρ . . . οὐ γάρ
   τὰ πολλά . . . οἱ πολλοί
   τῶν τοῦ κυρίου μαθητῶν . . . τοῦ κυρίου μαθηταί

2) The balancing of antitheses:
   οὐ γάρ . . . ἀλλά and οὐδέ . . . ἀλλά
   τοῖς τὰ πολλὰ λέγουσιν and τοῖς τἀληθῆ διδάσκουσιν
   τὰς ἀλλοτρίας ἐντολάς and τὰς παρὰ τοῦ κυρίου δεδομένας
   τί and ἅ
   εἶπεν and λέγουσιν
   τὰ ἐκ τῶν βιβλίων and τὰ παρὰ φωνῆς

By definition, Karlmann Beyschlag observes, such artistry was not composed "in the manner of an historical account" but "according to a well-defined formal scheme."[17] This formal schematization can be clearly seen by comparing Papias's preface with two others from the mid- to late second century, both of which are also preserved only in Eusebius: the prologue of the treatise "Against the Montanists" by the Anonymous[18] (Eus. *Hist. eccl.* 5.16.3–5) and that of the "Extracts from

[16]Schwartz, "Ueber den Tod der Söhne Zebedaei: Ein Beitrag zur Geschichte des Johannesevangeliums," *Abhandlungen der königlichen Gesellschaft der Wissenschaften zu Göttingen, Philologisch-historische Klasse*, NS, 7/5 (Berlin: Weidmann, 1904) 9.

[17]Beyschlag, "Herkunft und Eigenart der Papiasfragmente," *StPatr 4* (TU 79; Berlin: Akademie-Verlag, 1961) 276, with his own reference to Eduard Norden, *Agnostos Theos: Untersuchungen zur Formengeschichte religiöser Rede* (4th ed.; Darmstadt: Wissenschaftliche Buchgesellschaft, 1956) 316 n. 1. E. Bammel refers to Papias's prefatory remarks as "a mere literary scheme" ("Papias," 48).

[18]The provenance of this treatise "Against the Montanists" is also located in or around Hierapolis, where the Montanists were at home. This is confirmed by the fact

the Law and the Prophets" by Melito of Sardis (Eus. *Hist. eccl.* 4.26.13–14). A synoptic comparison reveals that

> the formal relationship of these two proems with the preface of Papias is immediately obvious: all three prologues are composed of two parts; it is in the second part that the circumstances or particulars are specifically mentioned which characterize the author in regard to his work.[19]

In order to facilitate this comparison, these other two prologues are cited below. A paragraph division will indicate the bipartite formal structure; verbal parallels, technical terms, and rhetorical clichés will be given in parentheses in Greek:

The Anonymous "Against the Montanists"
(apud Eus. Hist. eccl. 5.16.3–5):[20]

> For a long and protracted time, my dear Abercius Marcellus, I have been urged (ἐπιταχθείς) by you (sing.) to compose a treatise (συγγράψαι τινὰ λόγον) against the sect (αἵρεσιν) of those called after Miltiades, but until now I was somewhat reluctant, not (οὐκ) from any lack of ability to refute the lie and testify to the truth (ἀληθείᾳ), but (δέ) from timidity and scruples lest I might seem to some to be adding to the writings (ἐπισυγγράφειν) or injunctions (ἐπιδιατάσσεσθαι) of the word of the new covenant of the gospel (τῷ τῆς τοῦ εὐαγγελίου καινῆς διαθήκης λόγῳ), to which no one who has chosen to live according to the gospel itself can add (προσθεῖναι) and from which he cannot take away (ἀφελεῖν).[21]
>
> But when I had just come (γενόμενος) to Ancyra in Galatia and perceived that the church in that place was torn in two by this new movement which is not, as they call it, prophecy (προφητείας) but much rather, as will be shown, false prophecy (ψευδοπροφητείας), I disputed concerning these people themselves and their propositions. . . . Thus the church rejoiced and was strengthened in the

---

that the addressee of this treatise, Abercius Marcellus, himself composed an anti-Montanist inscription as an epitaph, erecting it near the southern gate of the city of Hierapolis. See the text (inscription no. 657) and the discussion in W. M. Ramsay, *The Cities and Bishoprics of Phrygia* (1 vol. in 2 parts; Oxford: Clarendon, 1897) part 2. 709–16, 722–29, 736–37.

[19]Beyschlag, "Papiasfragmente," 277.

[20]*Eusebius: The Ecclesiastical History* (trans. Kirsopp Lake; 2 vols.; LCL; Cambridge: Harvard University Press; London: Heinemann, 1965) 1. 472–75, adapted.

[21]Cf. Deut 4:2; 12:32; and see W. C. van Unnik, "De la règle Μήτε προσθεῖναι μήτε ἀφελεῖν dans l'histoire du canon," in idem, *Sparsa Collecta: The Collected Essays of W. C. van Unnik* (2 vols.; NovTSup 30; Leiden: Brill, 1980) 2. 123–56.

truth (ἀλήθειαν), but our opponents were crushed for the moment and our adversaries were distressed. Therefore the "elders" (τῶν πρεσβυτέρων) of that place asked (ἀξιούντων) me to leave some note (ὑπόμνημά τι) of what had been said against the opponents of the word of the truth (τῷ τῆς ἀληθείας λόγῳ). . . .

Melito "Extracts from the Law and the Prophets" (apud Eus. Hist. eccl. 4.26.13–14):[22]

Melito to Onesimus his brother, greeting.

Since you (sing.) often desired (ἠξίωσας), in your zeal for the true word (τὸν λόγον), to have extracts (ἐκλογάς) from the Law and the Prophets concerning the Saviour, and concerning all our faith (τῆς πίστεως), and, moreover, since you wished to know (μαθεῖν) the accurate facts about the ancient writings (τῶν παλαιῶν βιβλίων), how many they are in number, and what is their order (τάξιν), I have taken pains to do thus, for I know your zeal for the faith (τὴν πίστιν) and interest in the word (τὸν λόγον), and that in your struggle for eternal salvation you esteem these things more highly than all else in your love towards God.

Accordingly when I came (ἀνελθών) to the east and reached (γενόμενος) the place where these things were preached (ἐκηρύχθη) and done (ἐπράχθη), and learnt (μαθών) accurately the books of the Old Testament (τὰ τῆς παλαιᾶς διαθήκης βιβλία), I set down (ὑποτάξας) the facts and sent (ἔπεμψα) them to you.

When Papias recounts the particular circumstances which occasioned his writing, he testifies that at issue was a dispute about the collection, circulation, and interpretation of traditions of sayings of Jesus. Papias states explicitly that he preferred the immediacy of oral traditions from a "living and abiding voice" to the evanescence of written traditions from "books." Although it is not at all clear what particular books are being referred to here, there is no doubt that, for Papias, the transmission of traditions about and from Jesus was best preserved by establishing a protective boundary between the "great mass" of written "forgeries"[23] and the authentic, verifying, living word.

Such an appeal to oral traditions is not in itself exceptional. Basilides, for example, who was a younger contemporary of Papias,[24] is said to have produced his own "Gospel" and then a commentary on it in

[22] *Eusebius: The Ecclesiastical History,* 1. 392–93.

[23] The phrase is Bauer's, *Orthodoxy and Heresy*, 204.

[24] For the date, cf. Clem. Al. *Strom.* 7.17.106.4; and see Johannes Quasten, *Patrology* (3 vols.; Westminster, MD: Newman; Utrecht-Brussels: Spectrum, 1950) 1. 257.

twenty-four "books" (βιβλία [Eus. *Hist. eccl.* 4.7.7]).[25] According to Clement of Alexandria, Basilides allegedly derived his teaching from Glaukias, the "interpreter" (ἑρμηνεύς) of Peter (*Strom.* 7.17.106.4). Hippolytus of Rome, on the other hand, relates that it was Mathias who passed on to Basilides "secret words which he heard from the Savior when he was taught in private" (λόγους ἀποκρύφους, οὓς ἤκουσε παρὰ τοῦ σωτῆρος κατ' ἰδίαν διδαχθείς [*Ref.* 7.20.1]). What is new in Papias is that

> despite all his preference for the oral, [Papias] is obliged to distinguish his information expressly from "different," falsified traditions, and will give credence only to those mediators of tradition who teach and preserve the "truth" of the original commandments, that is to say, who have remained orthodox. The tradition is no longer [*sic*] regarded as an univocal entity, the "genuineness" of which can be assumed without question; and even its exegesis has become matter for dispute.[26]

The fact that Papias expressly seeks to set down his own "interpretations" of the λόγια of Jesus, in conscious opposition to the "heretical majority," means that the tendency of his five-volume "Exegesis" is anti-Gnostic:[27]

[25]See Puech, "Gnostic Gospels and Related Documents," 346–48; and von Campenhausen, *Formation,* 139.

[26]Von Campenhausen, *Formation,* 134.

[27]So Bauer, *Orthodoxy and Heresy,* 184–88, 204–5, 214–15; Vielhauer, *Geschichte,* 762; E. Schwartz, "Ueber den Tod der Söhne Zebedaei: Ein Beitrag zur Geschichte des Johannesevangeliums," *Abhandlungen der königlichen Gesellschaft der Wissenschaften zu Göttingen, Philologisch-historische Klasse,* NS, 7/5 (Berlin: Weidmann, 1904) 11; Martin Dibelius, "Papias," *RGG* 4 (2d ed.; 1930) 892; and Kurt Niederwimmer, "Johannes Markus und die Frage nach dem Verfasser des zweiten Evangeliums," *ZNW* 58 (1967) 186. Against George Kennedy, "Classical and Christian Source Criticism," in William O. Walker, Jr.,ed., *The Relationships Among the Gospels: An Interdisciplinary Dialogue* (Trinity University Monograph Series in Religion 5; San Antonio: Trinity University Press, 1978) 147–52; Munck, "Presbyters and Disciples," 230; and Schoedel (*Fragments,* 100–101), who asserts that Papias's language is conventional and nonpolemical, echoing "Jewish ideas of tradition" such as are found in Philo *Vit. Mos.* 1.4. But whereas Philo does say that he "learned" (μαθών) the story of Moses "both from the sacred books" (βίβλων τῶν ἱερῶν) and "from some of the 'elders' (τινων πρεσβυτέρων) of the nation," he goes on to say that—unlike Papias—he "interwove" (συνύφαινον) what he was "told" (τὰ λεγόμενα) with what he "read" (τοῖς ἀναγινωσκομένοις). The fact that Papias prefers the oral to the written tradition is not at all insignificant, and certainly does not, as Schoedel maintains, "reflect simply rhetorical stock in trade."

> The "Exegesis" of Papias is occasioned not primarily by the interests of the Jesus tradition in general, but by the fact that Christian Gnostics were producing new gospels, claiming those already in existence for themselves, and enlisting an apparently extensive exegetical literature for their own ideas.[28]

Nevertheless, the appeal Papias makes to the authority of oral tradition closely identifies his means of legitimating his own interpretations with that of many Gnostics. Irenaeus's statement that certain Gnostics alleged that the truth "was not delivered by means of written documents, but *viva voce*" (*Adv. haer.* 3.2.1),[29] could be accurately applied to Papias. Both groups appealed to eyewitnesses. But whereas formerly the authority of Jesus alone had been considered sufficient for the transmission of the tradition, it was now deemed necessary to guarantee this authority by establishing the legitimacy of its transmission.[30] Accordingly, Papias was obliged to defend his claim by testing the accuracy of what was said by the trustworthiness of the person(s) who transmitted it. It is in this context that the "elders" (πρεσβύτεροι) are mentioned.

The term πρεσβύτερος (both singular and plural) is not used here as "a title for office-bearers in the local congregation" but as "a term for members of the older generation who are regarded as mediators of the authentic tradition and reliable teachers."[31] When Papias mentions seven of the Lord's "disciples" by name, he contrasts them and *what* they *said* with a certain Aristion and ὁ πρεσβύτερος John and *that which* they *were saying.* The syntax of the sentence requires one to understand that a generational distinction is being made[32] between Aristion

[28]Vielhauer, *Geschichte,* 762.

[29]"Non enim per litteras traditam illam [ueritas] sed per uiuam uocem." Cf. Tertullian *Praescr. haer.* 21 and 25.

[30]See von Campenhausen, *Formation,* 121, 129, 132 n. 119.

[31]Bornkamm, "πρέσβυς," 676. Vielhauer argues similarly: "As authorities . . . he [Papias] mentions the πρεσβύτεροι = the 'elders,' by which he understands not officials of the church (*Amtsträger,* presbyters) but transmitters of the tradition (*Traditionsträger*)" (*Geschichte,* 763).

[32]So Bornkamm, "πρέσβυς," 676–77; Schoedel, *Fragments,* 98; R. M. Grant, *The Earliest Lives of Jesus* (London: SPCK, 1961) 16; and John F. Bligh, "The Prologue of Papias," *TS* 13 (1952) 234–40. Against Zahn, *Introduction,* 2. 452.

and the "elder" John, who were the actual sources[33] of Papias's tradition, and the seven "disciples" mentioned by name. The πρεσβύτεροι, including Papias's own "sponsor"[34] John, seem to be "pupils" of these disciples. This is certainly how Eusebius (*Hist. eccl.* 3.39.2, 7) and Irenaeus (*Adv. haer.* 5.5.1; 5.36.2) understood them, and there is no reason to think their joint testimony is tendentious.[35] At most, then, Papias claimed second-hand acquaintance with the apostles; and if the distinction between the apostle John and the "elder" John is taken seriously, then Papias probably claimed only third-hand acquaintance with the authorities of the first-century, "apostolic" age.[36] The use of the verb ἔρχεσθαι to describe the activity of the "followers" (παρακολουθεῖν) of the πρεσβύτεροι may suggest that the traditions were being transmitted orally by itinerant teachers.[37] There is certainly no notion here of an ecclesiastical office to which appeal of authority is made.[38]

3.2 PAPIAS AND WRITTEN TRADITION

A second excerpt in Eusebius from Papias's "Exegesis of the Sayings of the Lord," in which ὁ πρεσβύτερος is again cited as Papias's informant in the transmission of the tradition, deals with the Gospel of Mark. In this, the first external attestation of the Gospel of Mark by name, Papias responds to certain charges made against Mark and his Gospel,

[33]So Schoedel, *Fragments*, 102; Bammel, "Papias," 48; and Beyschlag, "Papiasfragmente," 278.

[34]The term is Bornkamm's, above n. 31.

[35]So also Bornkamm, "πρέσβυς," 676 n. 164. Against Zahn, *Introduction*, above n. 32; Munck, "Presbyters and Disciples," 236–37; and H. J. Lawlor, "Eusebius on Papias," *Hermathena* 43 (1922) 208–9. The recent analysis of Robert M. Grant ("Papias in Eusebius' Church History," in *Mélanges d'histoire des religions offerts à Henri-Charles Puech* [Paris: Presses Universitaires de France, 1974] 209–13), that Eusebius's account of Papias and his work consists of two parts (the first part: *Hist. eccl.* 3.39.1, 3–4, 9–10, 14–17, without the last sentence—and a later, second part: *Hist. eccl.* 3.39.2, 5–8, 11–13, plus the last sentence of 17), is an important contribution to the evolution of this part of Eusebius's *Historia ecclesiastica*, but does not argue against the observation being made here.

[36]Cf. Luke 1:1–4; and see Schoedel, *Fragments*, 98.

[37]Bornkamm, "πρέσβυς," 677.

[38]So Rudolf Bultmann, *The Johannine Epistles* (Hermeneia; Philadelphia: Fortress, 1973) 95; von Campenhausen, *Ecclesiastical Authority*, 162–63; and Bornkamm, "πρέσβυς," above n. 37.

allegations that Mark was confused, disingenuous, and selective in his presentation of the Jesus tradition. Papias responds as follows:

Papias frg. 2 (apud Eus. Hist. eccl. 3.39.15–16):

> And this the "elder" (John)[39] used to say:
>
> Mark, having been Peter's interpreter (ἑρμηνευτής),[40] wrote accurately—but not in order (τάξει)[41]—all that he remembered (ἐμνημόνευσεν)[42] of the things which were said or done (λεχθέντα ἢ πραχθέντα) by the Lord.[43] For neither had he heard (ἤκουσεν) the Lord nor had he followed (παρηκολούθησεν) him, but later, as I have said, (he followed) Peter, who adapted (ἐποιεῖτο) his teachings to the needs (πρὸς τὰς χρείας) (of his audience)[44] but did not make (ποιούμενος), as it were, an orderly arrangement (σύνταξιν) of the sayings of the Lord (τῶν κυριακῶν λογίων).[45] Thus, Mark

[39]Although the introduction to this fragment of Papias does not actually name the "elder," he is almost certainly to be identified with the aforementioned John. Eusebius (*Hist. eccl.* 3.39.14) would seem to confirm this, since he states that "in the same writing" Papias "transmitted other interpretations of the words of the Lord" (ἄλλας . . . τῶν τοῦ κυρίου λόγων διηγήσεις) by Aristion and "(other) traditions of the 'elder' John" (καὶ τοῦ πρεσβυτέρου Ἰωάννου παραδόσεις).

[40]For the translation "interpreter," see Josef Kürzinger, "Das Papiaszeugnis und die Erstgestalt des Matthäusevangeliums," *BZ*, NS, 4 (1960) 27; and Johannes Behm, "ἑρμηνεύω," *TDNT* 2 (1964) 663 n. 3.

[41]Horace Abram Rigg, Jr. ("Papias on Mark," *NovT* 1 [1956] 161–83) emends the text to τάχει, interpreting the passage to mean that Mark wrote accurately but "not at all hastily—in a slipshod manner" (p. 171). The problems with his suggestion are (1) that he thus overlooks the central importance of the "orderly arrangement" (τάξις, σύνταξις, and συντάσσειν) in Papias's entire discussion, and (2) that he takes the alleged relationship of Mark and Peter to be historically true.

[42]Several interpreters have understood Peter—not Mark—to be the subject of ἐμνημόνευσεν. See Kennedy, "Source Criticism," 147; Lawlor, "Papias," 200; and William R. Farmer, *Jesus and the Gospel* (Philadelphia: Fortress, 1982) 96. But this would require an abrupt change of subject and verb within a single sentence, and seems to be contradicted by Papias's subsequent statement that Μάρκος . . . ἀπεμνημόνευσεν.

[43]Zahn (*Introduction*, 2. 453–54) argues that only this first sentence constitutes "the statement of the presbyter John." The rest, he says, is from Papias himself (as indicated by Papias's ὡς ἔφην). Although this interpretation is possible, it seems difficult to distinguish "Papias" from his "source" at any point in this brief fragment.

[44]Following the suggested translation of Kennedy, "Source Criticism," 147; so also BAG, *s.v.* χρεία 2 (885a); Burnett Hillman Streeter, *The Four Gospels: A Study of Origins* (New York: Macmillan, 1925) 17; and Farmer, *Jesus*, 96. For the alternative translation, that Peter "presented his teachings in *chria*-form," see R. O. P. Taylor, *The Groundwork of the Gospels* (Oxford: Blackwell, 1946) 29–30, 75–90; followed by Schoedel, *Fragments*, 106–7; and Grant, *Earliest Lives*, 17.

[45]For the translation of λόγια in Papias, see BAG, *s.v.* λόγιον (476b); Robinson, "LOGOI SOPHON," 71–113; Vielhauer, *Geschichte*, 261–62, 759–62; Lawlor, "Papias," 189–204; T. W. Manson, "The Life of Jesus: A Survey of the Available

> did not err in writing some things (ἔνια) in this way as he remembered (ἀπεμνημόνευσεν) them. For he was concerned (ἐποιήσατο πρόνοιαν) about one thing: to omit (παραλιπεῖν) nothing of the things he had heard (ἤκουσεν) nor to falsify (ψεύσασθαι) anything in them. . . .[46] Matthew, conversely (οὖν),[47] did make an orderly arrangement (συνετάξατο) of the (Lord's) sayings (τὰ λόγια) in the "Hebrew language" (Ἑβραΐδι διαλέκτῳ)[48] —and each interpreted (ἡρμήνευσεν)[49] them as he was able.

It is crucial to observe that the Gospel of Mark is under attack from other, unnamed quarters, and that Papias's response constitutes a defense of the accuracy and authenticity of this Gospel.[50] Papias isolates two particular charges and endeavors to answer them as one. The charges are (1) that Mark did not write his Gospel "in order," and (2) that his Gospel is suspect because he was not an eyewitness, not having known Jesus personally. The apology Papias makes, especially concerning this second allegation, centers on the alleged relationship of Mark and Peter. In order to defend Mark's testimony as authentic, Papias was obliged to make the claim that the Gospel of Mark comprised the full and final account of the "remembrances" of Peter. Accordingly,

---

Material. (4) The Gospel According to St. Matthew," *BJRL* 29 (1945/46) 392–428; F. X. Funk and Karl Bihlmeyer, *Die Apostolischen Väter* (SAQ 2/1/1; 3d ed.; rev. Wilhelm Schneemelcher; Tübingen: Mohr-Siebeck, 1970) xlv; and R. Gryson, "A propos du témoignage de Papias sur Matthieu: Le sens du mot ΛΟΓΙΟΝ chez les pères du second siècle," *EThL* 41 (1965) 530–47.

[46]Here Eusebius inserts his own interpretive comment: *ταῦτα μὲν οὖν ἱστόρηται τῷ Παπίᾳ περὶ τοῦ Μάρκου. περὶ δὲ τοῦ Ματθαίου ταῦτ' εἴρηται.*

[47]For the adversative οὖν, cf. BAG, *s.v.* οὖν 4 (593a). Some might be tempted to translate οὖν inferentially, taking Papias's comment about Matthew to mean that "since Mark did not make an orderly composition, Matthew therefore did." But it will be shown in the discussion below (pp. 108–12) that Papias neither knew of nor addressed the "Synoptic problem."

[48]For the meaning of the "Hebrew language," see Poul Nepper-Christensen, *Das Matthäusevangelium: Ein judenchristliches Evangelium?* (Acta theologica Danica 1; Aarhus: Aarhus University Press, 1958) 37–135; Kürzinger, "Papiaszeugnis," 30–36; Wayne A. Meeks, "Hypomnēmata from an Untamed Sceptic: A Response to George Kennedy," in *Relationships Among the Gospels*, 163–66; and Johannes Munck, "Die Traditionen über das Matthäusevangelium bei Papias," in *Neotestamentica et Patristica: Eine Freundesgabe, Herrn Professor Dr. Oscar Cullmann zu seinem 60. Geburtstag überreicht* (NovTSup 6; Leiden: Brill, 1962) 249–60.

[49]See Kürzinger, "Papiaszeugnis," 26–29; and Meeks, "Hypomnēmata," 165.

[50]So also Reginald H. Fuller, "Classics and the Gospels: The Seminar," in *Relationships Among the Gospels*, 180. Against Schoedel, *Fragments*, 108; and A. F. Walls, "Papias and Oral Tradition," *VC* 21 (1967) 137–40.

the objective of Papias was to place Mark securely under the indisputable authority of the apostle Peter.[51]

Papias's mentioning of Mark, identified as the interpreter of Peter, locates the source of authority with a disciple of Jesus in a debate over sayings of Jesus. Once again, the technical term of "remembering" is used to describe the process of collecting, composing, and transmitting traditions of and from Jesus. To the charge that Mark did not compose his Gospel "in order,"[52] Papias replies that Peter himself did not make an "orderly arrangement" of the Lord's sayings. Thus, Mark is not to be blamed for the manner in which he presented his traditions in writing. Mark's concern was rather for accuracy; he took pains to transmit faithfully what he had heard from Peter as he "remembered" it.

The mode of argumentation used to protect Mark's Gospel from attack is paralleled in a contemporaneous discussion about "how to write history" by Lucian of Samosata.[53] After lampooning all manner of self-styled "Thucydideses, Herodotuses, and Xenophons," Lucian states that the genuine historian must be discreet and discriminating, knowing how to be selective about what to choose and what to avoid:

Luc. Hist. conscr. 6:[54]

> I mean how to begin, how to arrange his material (*τάξιν ἥντινα τοῖς ἔργοις ἐφαρμοστέον*), the proper proportions for each part, what to leave out, what to develop, what it is better to handle cursorily, and how to put the facts into words (*ἑρμηνεῦσαι*) and fit them together (*συναρμόσαι*).

[51]So also Vielhauer, *Geschichte*, 260.

[52]Precisely what is meant by "not in order" is a matter of considerable debate. Koester (*Introduction*, 2. 167) interprets this as "not in the (correct) sequence." Streeter (*Four Gospels*, 17 n. 1) understands it to mean not in "chronological" order. Kürzinger translates: "not in a literary composition" ("Papiaszeugnis," 35); Lawlor ("Papias," 200) translates similarly. Terence Y. Mullins ("Papias on Mark's Gospel," *VC* 14 [1960] 218–19) understands this not as a defense of Mark's alleged lack of order, but of Mark's "incomplete" presentation of the tradition. James Moffatt (*An Introduction to the Literature of the New Testament* [2d ed.; Edinburgh: T. & T. Clark, 1912] 188–89) argues that the meaning is not historical or chronological order, but a lack of "artistic arrangement" and "orderliness"; so also Grant, *Earliest Lives*, 18. F. H. Colson similarly interprets *οὐ τάξει* to mean not in "rhetorical order, that ordering which will produce a satisfactory and readable work" ("Τάξει in Papias," *JTS* 14 [1913] 63).

[53]For the date (ca. 120–180 CE), see Walter Manoel Edwards and Robert Browning, "Lucian," in *Oxford Classical Dictionary* (2d ed.; Oxford: Clarendon, 1970) 621.

[54]*Lucian* (trans. K. Kilburn; 8 vols.; LCL; London: Heinemann; Cambridge: Harvard University Press, 1959) 6. 8–9.

Once the appropriate material has been selected, its arrangement should be a matter of literary art:

Luc. Hist. conscr. 47–48:[55]

> As to the facts (πράγματα) themselves, he (i.e., the historian) should not assemble (συνακτέον) them at random, but only after much laborious and painstaking investigation. He should for preference be an eyewitness (ἐφορῶντα), but, if not, listen to those who tell (τοῖς ἐξηγουμένοις) the more impartial story, those whom one would suppose least likely to subtract (ἀφαιρήσειν) from the facts or add (προσθήσειν) to them out of favour or malice. When this happens let him show shrewdness and skill in putting together the more credible story. When he has collected (ἀθροίσῃ) all or most of the facts let him first make them into a series of notes (ὑπόμνημά τι), a body of material as yet with no beauty or continuity. Then, after arranging them into order (ἐπιθεὶς τὴν τάξιν), let him give it beauty and enhance it with the charms of expression, figure, and rhythm.

The situation depicted by Lucian is closely related to that which is presupposed by Papias in his discussion of Mark. Lucian insists that historians either be eyewitnesses or get their story from the most reliable witness(es), that they be selective and arrange their materials as adeptly as possible, and that they be skillful in elucidating them. Papias insists that Mark, as a follower and interpreter of Peter, received his traditions firsthand from a disciple of the Lord, and that his scrupulous recording of all that he remembered constituted an accurate and able explication.[56] Moreover, it is just at the point of defending Mark's absence of literary order—despite all Mark's care for accuracy in writing down the teachings of Peter—that the Gospel of Matthew is mentioned. As the text now stands, the reference to Matthew contrasts the compositional technique of Mark, who did not arrange his materials in an orderly manner, with that of Matthew, who did. It also distinguishes their respective roles in the history of the transmission of the tradition.

The numerous attempts to understand this fragment of Papias have foundered on a misreading of the text, a sort of scholarly Scylla and Charybdis which has persisted in plaguing most interpreters, leading

[55] Ibid., 6. 60–61. Cf. Quint. *Inst. orat.* 7.Pref.3; and Dion. Hal. *De Thuc.* 10.

[56] Whereas Lucian asserts that the historian is to be selective, Papias maintains that Mark did not add to, subtract from, or tamper with his source, but recorded "all (ὅσα) that he remembered." The statement that Mark wrote "some things" (ἔνια) does not indicate that there were "others" which were omitted; ἔνια simply refers to those things that are found in the Gospel of Mark.

them astray into asking the wrong questions or focusing on something other than Papias's main point(s). On the one hand, there are those who take Papias's testimony about the alleged relationship of Mark and Peter at face value, uncritically assuming it to be historically true. On the other hand, there are those who focus their attention on inferences drawn from Papias's terse remarks about Matthew, the λόγια, and the "Hebrew language." In each case, an unquestioned acceptance of Papias and his tradition or a conjectural reconstruction of Matthew's and Mark's use of sources has dominated the discussion and burdened the interpretation. In both cases, the main thrust of Papias's apology in this fragment seems to have been overlooked: a defense of the accuracy and authenticity of Mark's Gospel text.

In order to make my reading of Papias more clear, it will be useful to sketch briefly two major points of interpretation with which I am in disagreement. This will locate my position within the vast range of the scholarly discussion, bring it into relief, and help define the situation which Papias characterizes as one of "remembering."

1) *Mark and Peter:*

Mark's activity as the ἑρμηνευτής of Peter is frequently taken to be that of "translating" (rather than "expounding"). This is generally interpreted to mean that Mark translated Peter's Aramaic (or Hebrew) sermons into Greek. This is said to have been done in one or more of the following ways:

a) Mark made use of Peter's *chriae* (χρεῖαι), lessons which Peter drew up "with a view to supplying maxims and anecdotes to be learnt in order to be quoted."[57] Accordingly, "what Mark reproduced in his writing was not a version of his own, summarizing his general recollections of Peter's conversation or speeches, but the considered statements of Peter himself."[58]
b) Mark made use of *notes* (ὑπομνήματα) which he took while listening to Peter's sermons. These were then translated into Greek and put into "narrative order" in Mark's Gospel.[59]

[57]R. O. P. Taylor, *The Groundwork of the Gospels* (Oxford: Blackwell, 1946) 30.

[58]Ibid., 29. See also Schoedel, *Fragments*, 106–7.

[59]Kennedy, "Source Criticism," 148. See also Birger Gerhardsson, *Memory and Manuscript: Oral Tradition and Written Transmission in Rabbinic Judaism and Early Christianity* (ASNU 22; Uppsala: Almquist & Wiksells; Lund: Gleerup; Copenhagen: Munksgaard, 1961) 195–96, 201–2; and the critique of Gerhardsson by Morton Smith, "A Comparison of Early Christian and Early Rabbinic Tradition," *JBL* 82 (1963) 169–76.

c) Mark "first translated what Peter had written and then, later, wrote down all that he remembered of what Peter had said about Jesus' actions and words." Consequently, "Peter's translated material forms the bulk of Mark's writing and Mark's own additions from memory constitute a minute portion."[60]

d) Mark functioned in the capacity of a rabbinic translator (*methurgeman*), who regularly translated "biblical texts and sermons orally into the vernacular."[61] According to this view, "in its treatment of Mark, the fragment of Papias exhibits everywhere rabbinic terminology and formulaic language, and therefore requires a definitive *interpretatio semitica.*"[62]

The fundamental problem with all these interpretations of Papias is that they fail to explain adequately the origins and developments of Mark's Gospel text. Instead of concentrating first and foremost on an analysis of Mark's own compositional history, based on its collections of oral and written sources that were produced and preserved in the life of the worshiping Marcan community, these interpretations start with the testimony of Papias and then attempt to explain Mark on that basis. Such methodological imprecision fails to do justice to both Mark and Papias, truncating both texts and both traditions.

The origin of Papias's tradition that Mark was a disciple of Peter seems to be based on an extrapolation from the pseudepigraphical statement in 1 Peter 5:13 (in which "Peter" speaks of "Mark, my son"). Eusebius relates that Papias knew and used 1 Peter (*Hist. eccl.* 3.39.17),[63] and he reports that Clement and Origen also based their understanding of the alleged relationship of Peter and Mark on this same verse (2.15.2; 6.25.5, respectively). Despite Mark's use of Jesus

[60]Terence Y. Mullins, "Papias on Mark's Gospel," *VC* 14 (1960) 222. According to this view, "the charge against Mark" was "that he had added material of his own to the translation he had made of Peter's written reminiscences and that he should not have done so" (p. 223).

[61]Ethelbert Stauffer, "Der Methurgeman des Petrus," in J. Blinzler, O. Kuss, and F. Mussner, eds., *Neutestamentliche Aufsätze: Festschrift für Prof. Josef Schmid zum 70. Geburtstag* (Regensburg: Pustet, 1963) 292.

[62]Ibid., 286. See the critique by W. C. van Unnik, "Zur Papias-Notiz über Markus (Eusebius H. E. III 39, 15)," in idem, *Sparsa Collecta: The Collected Essays of W. C. van Unnik* (2 vols.; NovTSup 29; Leiden: Brill, 1973) 1. 70–71.

[63]According to Robert M. Grant's analysis ("Papias in Eusebius' Church History," in *Mélanges d'histoire des religions offerts à Henri-Charles Puech* [Paris: Presses Universitaires de France, 1974] 209–13) of the compositional history of *Hist. eccl.* 3.39, the reference to 1 Peter dates from the same time and situation of composition in which Eusebius quoted the fragment of Papias.

traditions in which the authority of Peter is clearly expressed,[64] the claim that Mark was a disciple and "interpreter" of Peter is historically spurious. It is rather a "learned deduction"[65] from a passage of scripture, a "literary fiction" whose occasion "may be sought in the exposed position in which 'orthodoxy' in Asia Minor or an orthodox bishop of Asia Minor in the second century was found over against heretical movements."[66]

Just as Papias was obliged to appeal to the *πρεσβύτεροι* to verify the accuracy of the oral tradition by the trustworthiness of those who mediated it, so also he was obliged to defend the written Gospel of Mark by associating it with the credentials of the apostle Peter. This attempt to legitimate a text and certify its authority by recourse to a chain of apostolic tradition is also held in common with the Gnostics.[67] One can see this most clearly in Ptolemy's *Epistula ad Floram* (*apud* Epiph. *Pan.* 33.3.1–33.7.10), in which the Valentinian Ptolemy expresses the hope that the "catholic" Flora will "become worthy (*ἀξιουμένη*) of the apostolic tradition (*τῆς ἀποστολικῆς παραδόσεως*) which we also have received (*καὶ ἡμεῖς παρειλήφαμεν*) by way of succession (διαδοχῆς), together with the confirmation (*μετὰ καὶ τοῦ κανονίσαι*)[68] of all our words (*τοὺς λόγους*) by the teaching of our Savior (*τῇ τοῦ σωτῆρος ἡμῶν διδασκαλίᾳ*)" (Epiph. *Pan.* 33.7.9).[69]

Since Gnostics no less than Papias could and did trace their heritage to individual apostolic authorities, the ultimate argument in the debate rested on the cogency of one's interpretations.[70] For, at this early date, there was no universally recognized creed, canon of Scripture, or ecclesiastical office to which appeal of authority could be made. Accordingly, even Irenaeus, who later became known for his zealous attempts to demonstrate the apostolic succession of the "orthodox" (*Adv. haer.* 3.3.1), was obliged to state at the outset of his work that

[64]See most recently Koester, *Introduction*, 2. 167.

[65]Meeks, "Hypomnēmata," 169.

[66]Kurt Niederwimmer, "Johannes Markus und die Frage nach dem Verfasser des zweiten Evangeliums," *ZNW* 58 (1967) 185–86.

[67]See von Campenhausen, *Ecclesiastical Authority*, 158; and Rudolf Bultmann, *Theology of the New Testament* (2 vols.; London: SCM, 1955) 2. 139.

[68]For the translation "the confirmation," see that of Gilles Quispel: "In this case also, we shall confirm (*nous confirmerons*) our understandings by the words of our Savior" (*Ptolémée: Lettre à Flora* [SC 24; 2d ed.; Paris: Editions du Cerf, 1966] 73). Note that von Campenhausen (*Formation*, 86 n. 131) has corrected his initial rendering of *κανονίσαι* (originally mistranslated as a reference to "the canonical collection of Jesus' words" [*Ecclesiastical Authority*, above n. 67]) to agree with Quispel's translation.

[69]Cf. Iren. *Adv. haer.* 3.3.1; and Clem. Al. *Strom.* 6.7.61.3.

[70]So Bauer, *Orthodoxy and Heresy*, 184.

certain Gnostic "heretics" were "dealing recklessly with the sayings of the Lord (τὰ λόγια τοῦ κυρίου), becoming evil interpreters (ἐξηγηταί) of the things which have been well spoken" (*Adv. haer.* 1.Pref.). Correct interpretation, therefore, was the warp and woof of Papias's own five-volume "Exegesis." It was also the objective Papias claims for Mark, and, he says, the achievement of both Matthew and Mark.

2) *Matthew, the λόγια, and the "Hebrew language*":

Papias's statement that Ματθαῖος μὲν οὖν Ἑβραΐδι διαλέκτῳ τὰ λόγια συνετάξατο (Eus. *Hist. eccl.* 3.39.16) has been almost universally understood to mean that "Matthew collected (or: composed) the sayings in (the) Hebrew language."[71] Scholarly consensus has presumed that the emphasis of this sentence is to be placed on the accusative (τὰ λόγια) and the dative (Ἑβραΐδι διαλέκτῳ). Since what Papias says does not seem to describe adequately the Gospel of Matthew, his statement has generally been interpreted in one of two ways:

a) Papias is not referring to the Gospel of Matthew as we have it, since Matthew was composed in Greek, on the basis of written Greek sources, shaped on the generic pattern of the Gospel of Mark. Consequently, the "collection of sayings" written in a Semitic language under the authority of Matthew is best understood as a reference to (a Semitic version of) the Synoptic Sayings Source Q.[72]
b) The term λόγια is not restricted solely to sayings (collections), but can refer to both sayings and stories, that is, to the entire "Gospel" of Matthew.[73] This, it is argued, is how Papias himself understood the term, since he has just equated Peter and Mark's σύνταξις τῶν κυριακῶν λογίων with τὰ ὑπὸ τοῦ κυρίου ἢ λεχθέντα ἢ πραχθέντα.[74]

[71]Koester, *Introduction*, 2. 172; Robinson, "LOGOI SOPHON," 74; Schoedel, *Fragments*, 109–10; Kennedy, "Source Criticism," 147; Vielhauer, *Geschichte*, 261; Lawlor, "Papias," 201; Manson, "Life of Jesus," 393; Bruno de Solages, "Le témoignage de Papias," *BLE* 71 (1970) 11; and Theodor Zahn, "Papias von Hierapolis, seine geschichtliche Stellung, sein Werk und sein Zeugniss über die Evangelien," *ThStK* 39 (1866) 691.

[72]See esp. Koester, *Introduction*, above n. 71; and Manson, "Life of Jesus," 392–428.

[73]Schoedel, *Fragments*, 109; Dibelius, *Tradition*, 233 n. 2; Vielhauer, *Geschichte*, 759; Lawlor, "Papias," 192–93; Meeks, "Hypomnēmata," 169; and R. Gryson, "A propos du témoignage de Papias sur Matthieu: Le sens du mot ΛΟΓΙΟΝ chez les pères du second siècle," *EThL* 41 (1965) 547.

[74]It should be noted that, even granting the position of the majority of scholars who take the λόγια to refer to both sayings and stories, the primary concern here and elsewhere in Papias's five-volume "Exegesis" is with the sayings tradition. See von Campenhausen, *Formation*, 131 n. 110; and Schoedel, *Fragments*, 97. See also the discussion

The fundamental problem with both of these interpretations of Papias is that they fail to explain why the Gospel of Matthew is mentioned at all. The tendency of most scholars has been to amass evidence for and against the various possible renderings of λόγια and Ἑβραΐς διάλεκτος.[75] But what has been generally overlooked is that Papias's intention throughout this fragment is to defend the Gospel of Mark from attack. Whether Papias intended to contrast "Mark, who did not make a literary composition, with Matthew, who did,"[76] is not completely clear. The extant fragment certainly contrasts Matthew and Mark, but that may be the work of Eusebius. We know that Eusebius inserted his own interpretive comment between quotations of Papias's remarks about Mark and Matthew (*Hist. eccl.* 3.39.16: ταῦτα μὲν οὖν ἱστόρηται τῷ Παπίᾳ περὶ τοῦ Μάρκου. περὶ δὲ τοῦ Ματθαίου ταῦτ' εἴρηται). It is possible that this insertion has obscured the comparison that Papias himself was trying to make, creating the impression that a seemingly independent statement was made about Matthew. But we do not know the extent of Eusebius's abridgment of Papias, nor whether Eusebius's own comment interrupted Papias's continuous remarks.[77] Given the fact that Papias's concern in this entire section (*Hist. eccl.* 3.39.3–4, 15–16) is to guarantee the authority of the tradition by establishing the legitimacy of its transmission, one should assess Papias's discussion of Matthew and Mark by asking the question of his understanding of their role in the formation of the sayings-of-Jesus tradition.

It is important to observe that Papias consistently makes a distinction between different generations or stages in the transmission of the tradition. In each case, Papias draws attention to the historical trajectory of transmission, from the disciples of Jesus to those who received the tradition transmitted by them. The mode of transmission (oral or written) is also distinguished in each case. This may be seen graphically as follows:

---

of the textual and stylistic variants of λόγος and λόγιον in Robinson, "LOGOI SOPHON," 74–75 nn. 10, 11. Note that a few of the manuscripts of *Hist. eccl.* 3.39.15 read κυριακῶν λόγων rather than κυριακῶν λογίων; see the critical text of Eduard Schwartz, *Eusebius Werke 2/1: Die Kirchengeschichte* (GCS; Leipzig: Hinrichs, 1903) 290, line 26.

[75]E.g., Manson, "Life of Jesus," above n. 72.

[76]This is the position of Meeks, "Hypomnēmata," 165.

[77]Against Meeks, above n. 76.

3.39.4:

seven μαθηταί:
Andrew, Peter, Philip, Thomas,
James, John, Matthew

↓ ORAL

two πρεσβύτεροι:
Aristion, John

↓ ORAL

Papias

↓ WRITTEN

3.39.15:	*3.39.16:*
Peter	Matthew
↓ ORAL	↓ WRITTEN
Mark	ἕκαστος
↓ WRITTEN	↓ WRITTEN

Since Peter and Matthew were mentioned among the seven μαθηταί of the Lord (3.39.4), they are understood to belong to the first generation of the transmission of the tradition. The clear implication of the statements about Mark is that, though he neither heard nor followed the Lord, he had received the tradition orally from Peter, and so was a reliable, authoritative witness. As the text now stands (as excerpted by Eusebius), the reference to Matthew serves in part to contrast the literary technique of Mark, whose written composition was not "in order," with that of Matthew, whose was. But in terms of Papias's understanding of the history of the tradition, the reference to Matthew is designed to locate Matthew's testimony at the earliest stage of transmission. By stating that Matthew "composed" (συνετάξατο) the λόγια "in the Hebrew language,"[78] Papias means that it was not in Greek, but in what was thought to be the language of Jesus himself.[79] The import of

[78]See the discussion of the "Hebrew language" in Joseph A. Fitzmyer, "The Languages of Palestine in the First Century A.D.," in idem, *A Wandering Aramean: Collected Aramaic Essays* (SBLMS 25; Missoula: Scholars, 1979) 43; and Meeks, "Hypomnēmata," 164 n. 10, 165.

[79]Kürzinger ("Papiaszeugnis," 32–35) and Bammel ("Papias," 48) unconvincingly interpret this to mean that Matthew composed the λόγια "according to a Hebrew manner

this statement is on the proximity of Matthew's written words with the original sayings of Jesus. The emphasis is thus not on an alleged Semitic Gospel of Matthew,[80] nor on its putative translation into Greek,[81] but on the earliness of the tradition and the reliability of its testimony.

The identity of "each" (ἕκαστος) who "interpreted" (ἡρμήνευσεν) the tradition as he saw fit is not known. The suggestion that this refers to "each Evangelist" (i.e., Matthew and Mark)[82] is plausible, but depends on the conjecture that Papias's remarks were continuous, and that his statement about Matthew was not an independent one but followed directly upon a discussion about Mark that Eusebius has excerpted. But since every other reference to individuals in this fragment of Papias makes mention of their place in the transmission of the tradition, it seems best to take Papias's comment about "each" to refer to each interpreter of Matthew. The account of the "composition of Matthew" and the "interpretation of each" is a fragment of a longer excerpt in Papias, of which Eusebius has preserved only a sentence. Just as Mark "did not err" in writing down what he received from Peter "as he remembered" it (ὡς ἀπεμνημόνευσεν), so each who interpreted the λόγια of Matthew is approved by the fact that he did so "as he was able" (ὡς ἦν δυνατός). The emphasis of Papias's remark about Matthew is, therefore, not on the elusive Ἑβραΐδι διαλέκτῳ,[83] but on Matthew's alleged role in the history of the written stage of transmission of the tradition (συνετάξατο). The apologetic statement that "each interpreted" (ἡρμήνευσεν . . . ἕκαστος) that tradition as best he could is also designed to emphasize its written mode of transmission. This would seem to be confirmed by the passages in Lucian (*Hist. conscr.* 6, 47–48), which speak of the historians' "putting

---

of presentation (*Darstellungsweise*)."

[80]Note the similar, indiscriminate statements made by various early church writers about an alleged translation of a "Jewish-Christian Gospel" from the "Hebrew language": Hegesippus (*apud* Eus. *Hist. eccl.* 4.22.8); Eus. *Theoph.* 4.22; and Jerome *Epist. ad Hedyb.* 120.8; *Comm. in Isa.* 4 (on Isa 11:2).

[81]Note that Papias never claims to have seen a Semitic Matthew. Only Jerome (above n. 80) makes such a claim—and Poul Nepper-Christensen (*Das Matthäusevangelium: Ein judenchristliches Evangelium?* [Acta theologica Danica 1; Aarhus: Aarhus University Press, 1958] 64–75) and Alfred Schmidtke (*Neue Fragmente und Untersuchungen zu den judenchristlichen Evangelien* [TU 37/1; Leipzig: Hinrichs, 1911] 67) have shown that claim to be specious. For the tradition that the Gospel of Matthew is somehow related to "the language spoken by the Jews," most early church writers have simply followed the lead of Papias. Cf. Eus. *Hist. eccl.* 3.24.6; 5.8.2; 5.10.3; 6.25.4.

[82]Kürzinger, "Papiaszeugnis," 29; followed by Meeks, "Hypomnēmata," 165.

[83]So Meeks, "Hypomnēmata," 165–66.

facts into words" (ἑρμηνεῦσαι) in presenting or expounding their materials. Neither Mark, the ἑρμηνευτής of Peter, nor the unnamed interpreter(s) of Matthew is presented as a "translator";[84] each is rather understood as an "expositor," an exegete.

In every instance, Papias's discussion of the stages of the tradition goes back to the earliest followers of Jesus. The reliability of the tradition, whether handed down orally or in written form, is guaranteed by authoritative "remembrances." Papias's preference for oral tradition is confirmed by the fact that he understands his own testimony to go directly back to the μαθηταί of the Lord, unencumbered by the mediation of books.[85] Attempts to understand this fragment without observing its emphasis on the various stages of transmission, with its apologetic attention to the mode of transmission, overlook the primary purposes of Papias.

3.3 ASSIMILATION OF THE SAYINGS TRADITION

Our analysis of the fragments of Papias has shown that Papias used the term "remembering" technically with reference both to the composition of written Gospel texts (Mark and Matthew) and to sayings traditions transmitted orally by itinerant Christian teachers (the "living and abiding voice"). This latter usage confirms the conclusion drawn from our observation of the use of the term "remembering" in *1 Clement* and the book of Acts: the formulaic employment of this term to introduce collections of sayings of Jesus is a practice which began with the relatively free production of sayings traditions and which continued, despite the existence of written gospels, without restriction to the gospels of the NT. The fact that Papias's opponents also practiced the "remembrance" of traditions which differed in a number of respects from

[84]Against Schoedel, *Fragments*, 107; Theodor Zahn, "Papias von Hierapolis, seine geschichtliche Stellung, sein Werk und sein Zeugniss über die Evangelien," *ThStK* 39 (1866) 694–95; and Kennedy, "Source Criticism," 150.

[85]Note that, despite Papias's defense of the Gospel of Mark, his comments about Mark (and, most likely, Matthew as well) are still disparaging. See Streeter, *Four Gospels*, 19. Against A. F. Walls, "Papias and Oral Tradition," *VC* 21 (1967) 137–40. Nevertheless, we cannot deduce from this that Papias himself condemned the Gospels of Mark and Matthew—at least not explicitly. Although Papias clearly prefers the witness of oral tradition to that gathered from books, even he participates in the interpretive activity of "orderly composition" in books (*Hist. eccl.* 3.39.3: συγκατατάξαι).

his own, moreover, meant that Papias was obliged to appeal to certain individual authorities as the guarantors of his tradition. This was the case for written texts no less than for oral traditions. Accordingly, Papias's mentioning of Mark, identified as the interpreter of Peter, locates the source of authority with a disciple of Jesus in a debate over sayings of Jesus.

The practice of using the technical term of "remembering" to refer to collections of sayings of Jesus came to an end shortly after the time of Papias. In Polycarp's "second" *Letter to the Philippians* (*Phil.* 1–12),[86] which most likely dates from the middle of the second century,[87] independent sayings traditions were adapted to conform to the Gospels of Matthew and Luke. These sayings are also introduced with the term "remembering":

Pol. Phil. 2.3: μνημονεύοντες δὲ ὧν εἶπεν ὁ κύριος διδάσκων·

Here, Polycarp quotes portions of the catechism in *1 Clem.* 13.2, but harmonizes these sayings to make them agree with the readings in Matt 7:1 and Luke 6:38.[88] This is done in support of the fight against the "heretics."[89] "Whoever perverts the words of the Lord (ὃς ἂν μεθοδεύῃ τὰ λόγια τοῦ κυρίου) to suit his own desires," Polycarp warns, "is the firstborn of Satan" (*Phil.* 7.1; cf. 2.1). Accordingly, in urging Christians to "forsake the foolishness of the majority (τῶν πολλῶν) and their false teachings (ψευδοδιδασκαλίας) and return to the word (τὸν λόγον) which was delivered (παραδοθέντα) to us from the beginning" (*Phil.* 7.2), Polycarp quotes as a word of the Lord (καθὼς εἶπεν ὁ κύριος) the saying in Mark 14:38b // Matt 26:41b: "the spirit is willing, but the flesh is weak." Thus, despite Polycarp's freedom to adapt sayings collections to the needs of his situation, his tendency to bring such collections into conformity with the written gospels of his church attests to a wishful thinking which sought to restrict such

[86]See esp. the analysis of P. N. Harrison, *Polycarp's Two Epistles to the Philippians* (Cambridge: Cambridge University Press, 1936).

[87]For this date, see Koester, *Überlieferung*, 121–23; and von Campenhausen, *Formation*, 178 n. 157. Harrison (*Polycarp's Two Epistles*, 315) prefers to date this "second" letter ca. 135 CE; Vielhauer (*Geschichte*, 562–63) is noncommittal.

[88]See the discussion in Koester, *Überlieferung*, 115–18.

[89]So also Bauer, *Orthodoxy and Heresy*, 72–73; Robinson, "LOGOI SOPHON," 98; and Koester, *Introduction*, 2. 307.

freedom on account of the alleged "misuse of the sayings tradition by gnosticizing heretics."[90]

The tendency to bring the sayings tradition into conformity with the written gospels of the NT, as part of a coordinated anti-Gnostic polemic, is also in evidence in 2 Peter, the latest writing to be included in the NT.[91] 2 Peter reproduces virtually the entire text of Jude, but with several significant alterations. One is particularly important for our purposes. Jude, written near the end of the first century,[92] referred to its authorities quite matter-of-factly, introducing one of their oral apocalyptic sayings (Jude 18) with the term "remembering":

Jude 17: μνήσθητε τῶν ῥημάτων τῶν προειρημένων ὑπὸ τῶν ἀποστόλων τοῦ κυρίου ἡμῶν Ἰησοῦ Χριστοῦ, ὅτι ἔλεγον ὑμῖν·

This is clearly a variant of the introductory sayings formula found in *1 Clement* and Acts.[93] But when 2 Peter reproduces this verse, the indicators of an oral provenance are gone, and Jude's traditional authorities have been made into figures of the distant past: the "holy prophets" of the pre-Christian era and "your apostles" of bygone days:

2 Pet 3:2: . . . μνησθῆναι τῶν προειρημένων ῥημάτων ὑπὸ τῶν ἁγίων προφητῶν καὶ τῆς τῶν ἀποστόλων ὑμῶν ἐντολῆς τοῦ κυρίου καὶ σωτῆρος. . . .

Here, though the term "remembering" is retained from 2 Peter's source, the appeal for authority seems to be polemically based on written documents[94] of past heroes, not on oral traditions from a "living and abiding voice."

The replacement of independent sayings collections with written gospels is clearly visible in the writings of the church apologist Justin (ca. 150–165 CE).[95] He is, in fact, the first Christian writer to use the term

[90]Robinson, "LOGOI SOPHON," above n. 89.

[91]According to Vielhauer, "As a date of composition, one can accept the middle or second half of the second century" (*Geschichte*, 599).

[92]For the date, see Koester, *Introduction*, 2. 246; and Vielhauer, *Geschichte*, 594.

[93]Robinson ("LOGOI SOPHON," 96 nn. 50, 53) observes that the reading of ῥῆμα instead of λόγος is not significant. Luke also uses ῥῆμα in conjunction with the verb "to remember" in Luke 22:61; 24:8; and Acts 11:16.

[94]So Koester, *Introduction*, 2. 296.

[95]For the date of Justin's writings, see Johannes Quasten, *Patrology* (3 vols.; Westminster, MD: Newman; Utrecht-Brussels: Spectrum, 1950) 1. 199; and Koester, *Introduction*, 2. 342.

εὐαγγέλιον to refer to a written gospel text (*1 Apol.* 66.3; *Dial.* 100.1). In calling these gospels the "Memoirs (ἀπομνημονεύματα) of the Apostles" (*1 Apol.* 67.3; *Dial.* 103.6, 8; 104.1; 105.1, 6; 106.1, 4; 107.1), and in associating them with the writings of the OT (*1 Apol.* 67.3; *Dial.* 119.6), Justin testifies to the fact that "it was a regular practice to read" the gospels "in public worship alongside the writings of the prophets."[96] When Justin would refer to Jesus' sayings as λόγοι (e.g., *Dial.* 76.5; 100.3), this was to place them on a par with OT Scripture, whose texts he also introduced as λόγοι (e.g., *Dial.* 31.2; 62.3; 65.3; 79.3; 109.1).[97]

Consequently, it is not surprising that only vestiges of the early Christian practice of introducing sayings traditions with the technical term "remembering" survive in Justin. What he calls the "Memoirs of the Apostles"[98] are actually the Gospels of Matthew and Luke (and, perhaps, Mark). Although he knew of a few sayings transmitted independently of the NT,[99] Justin's "primary interest" in gospel literature "was the systematic work of creating a harmonized text of the gospels that would agree as closely as possible with the words of the prophecies from the Old Testament."[100] This is clear even when the

[96]Von Campenhausen, *Formation*, 167–68. The "prophets," of course, encompass the entire OT (pp. 168 n. 95, 257 n. 257).

[97]Whereas written gospels are quoted as authoritative texts by Justin, the contemporaneous citation of "the gospel" in *2 Clem.* 8.5 (λέγει γὰρ ὁ κύριος ἐν τῷ εὐαγγελίῳ) refers to sayings given under the authority of the Lord, not the authority of the text. The author of *2 Clement* does not use the Gospels of Matthew and Luke directly, but presupposes a harmonizing collection of sayings that was composed on the basis of Matthew and Luke. See Koester, *Überlieferung*, 11–12, 65, 110–11; and idem, *Introduction*, 2. 235.

[98]Richard Heard ("The ΑΠΟΜΝΗΜΟΝΕΥΜΑΤΑ in Papias, Justin, and Irenaeus," *NTS* 1 [1954/55] 122–29) has argued that Justin used documents that had no titles, and so adopted Papias's phrases to describe the "'Memoirs' of the Apostles," which he then referred to as "Gospels" (*1 Apol.* 66.3). See the discussion of "gospels" and "memoirs" in Johannes Weiss, *Das älteste Evangelium* (Göttingen: Vandenhoeck & Ruprecht, 1903) 6–11; Grant, *Earliest Lives*, 20, 119–20; Nils Alstrup Dahl, "ANAMNESIS: Memory and Commemoration in Early Christianity," in idem, *Jesus in the Memory of the Early Church* (Minneapolis: Augsburg, 1976) 26–28; and Karl Ludwig Schmidt, "Die Stellung der Evangelien in der allgemeinen Literaturgeschichte,' in Hans Schmidt, ed., ΕΥΧΑΡΙΣΤΗΡΙΟΝ: *Studien zur Religion und Literatur des Alten und Neuen Testaments, Hermann Gunkel zum 60. Geburtstage, dem 23. Mai 1922 dargebracht* (2 vols.; FRLANT, NS, 19; Göttingen: Vandenhoeck & Ruprecht, 1923) 2. 50–134.

[99]E.g., *1 Apol.* 61.4 // John 3:3a, 5b // Matt 18:3 par. It has already been demonstrated (above, pp. 66–68) that Justin's source of this saying was the liturgy of the church, not the Gospel of John. Note also that Justin does not employ the term "remembering" to introduce this saying, but uses instead the formula καὶ γὰρ ὁ Χριστὸς εἶπεν.

[100]Koester, *Introduction*, 2. 342–43. The sayings in *1 Apol.* 16.9–12 (cf. *Dial.* 76.5) that

rare occurrence of the term "remembering" is preserved. In one instance, after quoting a chain of scriptural passages to which sayings of Jesus are linked (*Dial.* 17.2, 3–4), Justin states that his purpose was to "bring to remembrance (ἐπιμνησθείς) brief words (λόγια) of his (Jesus') in line with the prophetic (words)" of the OT (*Dial.* 18.1). Here, the term λόγια seems to be used as the equivalent of "pericope."[101] Similarly, when introducing a more extensive, catechetical collection of sayings of Jesus in *1 Apol.* 15–17,[102] Justin prefaces the collection with the statement that his intention was "to bring to remembrance (ἐπιμνησθῆναι) some of the teachings (διδαγμάτων) of Christ himself" (*1 Apol.* 14.4). In both these cases, the verb ἐπιμιμνήσκεσθαι is now used to mean "to quote" or "to (re)cite." Justin's own usage thus bears witness to the fact that the original meaning of this term as it had been used in the church has come to an end. Sayings collections deriving from the oral tradition became pressed into the service of the written gospels of the NT. "With the final discontinuation of the oral transmission of Jesus' sayings, the *Sitz im Leben*" of the genre *Logoi Sophon* was gone.[103] By the time of Irenaeus (ca. 190 CE), and the pressures of his so-called fourfold gospel canon (*Adv. haer.* 3.11.8),[104] the words of Jesus were "remembered" no more.

3.4 THE GOSPEL OF JOHN AND THEOLOGICAL REFLECTION

The Gospel of John also uses the technical term of "remembering" with reference to individual sayings of Jesus. In John 15:20, a saying (λόγος) is typically introduced with the verb μνημονεύειν:

John 15:20a: μνημονεύετε τοῦ λόγου οὗ ἐγὼ εἶπον ὑμῖν·

---

have parallels in *2 Clem.* 4.2, 5 and *Gos. Naz.* frg. 6 (according to the "Zion Gospel" Edition) also show that Justin was using a Gospel harmony based on Matthew and Luke. See Koester, *Überlieferung*, 79–94.

[101]See Robinson, "LOGOI SOPHON," 99–100 with n. 63. Note also the designation of certain OT passages as "brief *logoi*" in *Dial.* 65.3; 109.1.

[102]See A. J. Bellinzoni, *The Sayings of Jesus in the Writings of Justin Martyr* (NovTSup 17; Leiden: Brill, 1967) 49–100.

[103]Robinson, "LOGOI SOPHON," 102–3. See also Werner H. Kelber, *The Oral and the Written Gospel* (Philadelphia: Fortress, 1983) 200–201, 203.

[104]See the treatment of Irenaeus in von Campenhausen, *Formation*, 182–209.

The saying which follows (15:20b) refers back to an Amen-saying already spoken by Jesus (13:16a), and found (without the introductory "amen" and the formula of "remembering") independently in Q (Matt 10:24 // Luke 6:40). What is distinctive here is that Jesus himself is portrayed as speaking, enjoining his disciples to remember his own words, as part of an extended collection of "farewell discourses" after the supper. This saying was probably inserted by the Evangelist into a series of parallel sayings that express the fact that the Revealer and the Johannine community are to share the same destiny (15:18, 19a, 20cd).[105] Accordingly, the Jesus of the farewell discourses discloses how he and the disciples are to suffer; how he is to be glorified; and how, after his glorification, the disciples' "remembrance" of his words will sustain them in tribulation (16:4a) and, with the help of the Paraclete, maintain them in an ongoing revelation (14:26).

John also employs the term "remembering" when commenting upon certain stories in his Gospel narrative. The first two instances are found in the interpretation of the story of the cleansing of the temple (2:13–19, 20–22). The initial occurrence (2:17) interrupts the scene;[106] its insertion interprets Jesus' commands (2:16) in the hindsight of Scripture (Ps 68:10 [LXX]), with the meaning that "Jesus' zeal will lead him to his death."[107] The second occurrence (2:22) is added to the story, explicitly interpreting Jesus' apocalyptic saying (2:19) from the perspective of the resurrection. Both occurrences are clearly redactional, the work of either the Evangelist or the final Editor, for whom "remembering" denotes "theological reflection."[108] In every instance, even when commenting upon the narrative tradition, John uses the term "remembering" to refer to sayings, not stories.

The apocalyptic saying (2:19) which concludes this story, and which serves as the focal point for the disciples' post-resurrection reflection (2:22), has an enormously complex tradition history.[109] This saying seems to be based on a familiar Jewish-apocalyptic prediction, well known before 70 CE, that a new and glorious temple would arise in the messianic age (e.g., *1 Enoch* 90.28–29; cf. Tob 13:16; 14:5). When this saying came to be applied to the Jesus tradition, it was initially

[105]Bultmann, *John*, 548 with n. 3.

[106]Ibid., 124. Against Rudolf Schnackenburg, *The Gospel according to St John* (3 vols.; HTCNT; New York: Herder and Herder, 1968) 1. 348.

[107]Bultmann, *John*, 124. So also Schnackenburg, *John*, 1. 347; and Brown, *John (i–xii)*, 124.

[108]MacRae, *Invitation to John*, 52.

[109]See esp. the discussion in Bultmann, *History*, 120–21, 401; idem, *John*, 126 n. 1; and the literature cited there.

understood as a simple, still anonymous threat of the destruction of the Jerusalem temple (Mark 13:2 par.; cf. Luke 19:41–44; Acts 6:14). In some Christian circles, however, this threat was attributed to Jesus himself, and was combined with a prophecy of the rebuilding of the temple in three days (Mark 14:58 // Matt 26:61; Mark 15:29 // Matt 27:40; cf. Matt 12:40). Mark is clearly embarrassed by the fact that certain Christians attributed this "prediction " to Jesus. In referring to these persons as "false witnesses," Mark seeks to put distance between his tradition and theirs, and thus testifies to the fact that his opponents were also locating the authority of their message in sayings of Jesus and stories about him.[110] John's version of this saying is distinctive in that it (1) combines the tradition of the threat of the temple's destruction with the prophetic reference to the rebuilding of it in three days, and (2) portrays Jesus himself as speaking.[111] The use of the ambiguous ἐγερῶ (2:19) with reference to the "rebuilding" is a deliberate Johannine double-entendre, secondarily imported from a post-resurrection situation (2:21, 22),[112] and characteristically employed as part of John's motif of misunderstanding (2:20).[113] In stating (vs 22) that only after the resurrection did the disciples "remember" (ἐμνήσθησαν) what Jesus said, the author of the Gospel of John presents himself in the role of the Paraclete and his readers in the role of the disciples, and makes it explicit that only after the resurrection (ἠγέρθη ἐκ νεκρῶν), and in the light of Scripture (τῇ γραφῇ), could gospel texts be written.

The last instance of the term "remembering" in John's narrative is found in the interpretation of the story of Jesus' entry into Jerusalem (12:12–13, 14–15, 16). This constitutes an exact parallel with the redactional use of this term in 2:17, 22. In both passages the motif of prophecy is a secondary "remembrance" (2:17 = Ps 68:10 [LXX]; 12:15 = Zech 9:9), and Jesus' "glorification" (12:16) in the latter is synonymous with his "resurrection" (2:22) in the former. Once again, the Gospel of John testifies that Jesus was explicable only after the resurrection. Consequently, John's use of the technical term of "remembering" to distinguish between the incomprehensible ministry

[110]See Dieter Lührmann, "Biographie des Gerechten als Evangelium: Vorstellungen zu einem Markus-Kommentar," *Wort und Dienst*, NS, 14 (1977) 46; Norman R. Petersen, *Literary Criticism for New Testament Critics* (Philadelphia: Fortress, 1978) 79–80; and Theodore J. Weeden, "The Heresy that Necessitated Mark's Gospel," *ZNW* 59 (1968) 145–58.

[111]Bultmann, *John*, 126 n. 1.

[112]Note that all other instances of this saying preserve the original οἰκοδομεῖν: Mark 14:58 // Matt 26:61; Mark 15:29 // Matt 27:40; and *Gos. Thom.* 71: 45.35 (ⲕⲱⲧϥ).

[113]See Bultmann, *John*, 126 nn. 1–2, 127 n. 1.

of the earthly Jesus and the post-resurrection period of understanding the work and words of Jesus must be seen as a key hermeneutical principle in the production and composition of his written Gospel text.

3.5 COMPOSITION OF THE *APOCRYPHON OF JAMES*

Whereas John's Gospel bears witness to the fact that only after the resurrection could Jesus traditions be understood, John still seeks to validate the sayings of Jesus prior to his death as a source of authority and basis of revelation. This is achieved by constructing the farewell discourses of Jesus, locating the hermeneutical turning point of the Gospel in Jesus' life prior to the passion. What had formerly been spoken "in parables" is perceived, in anticipation of the cross and resurrection, as having become "open" (16:25, 29; cf. Mark 4:34; 8:32):[114]

> ταῦτα ἐν παροιμίαις λελάληκα ὑμῖν·
> ἔρχεται ὥρα ὅτε οὐκέτι ἐν παροιμίαις λαλήσω ὑμῖν,
> ἀλλὰ παρρησίᾳ περὶ τοῦ πατρὸς ἀπαγγελῶ ὑμῖν. . . .
> λέγουσιν οἱ μαθηταὶ αὐτοῦ·
> ἴδε νῦν ἐν παρρησίᾳ λαλεῖς,
> καὶ παροιμίαν οὐδεμίαν λέγεις. (16:25, 29)

As a result, Jesus' exaltation on the cross, which is understood as the consummation of his work of revelation, is brought into conformity with his manifestation as the revealing word. Continuity between the sayings of the earthly Jesus and the risen Lord is provided by those guiding "remembrances" (16:13; 14:26) bestowed on the community by the Paraclete. As Jesus "goes to the Father, so will his return as the Paraclete guarantee the lasting presence of revelation in the

[114]In a series of articles, James M. Robinson has demonstrated that this hermeneutical shift is a fundamental compositional clue to the creation of the canonical "gospel" genre. See his "On the *Gattung* of Mark (and John)," in *Jesus and Man's Hope*, 1. 99–129; idem, "LOGOI SOPHON," 71–113; idem, "Gnosticism and the New Testament," 125–43; and idem, "Jesus: From Easter to Valentinus (or to the Apostles' Creed)," *JBL* 101 (1982) 5–37. See also Robert W. Funk, "The Parables: A Fragmentary Agenda," in *Jesus and Man's Hope*, 2. 294–98.

community."[115] This notion of continuity is carried out to its logical conclusion by the Gospel of Luke, which explicitly equates the sayings of the risen Lord with the "remembered" words of Jesus' public ministry (cf. Luke 24:6, 8, 25–27, 32, 44–45). As such, the "resurrected Christ only repeats what Jesus had said prior to Easter."[116]

The *Ap. Jas.* also recognizes the cross and resurrection as the decisive moment of interpretation. Consequently, sayings of the earthly Jesus are acknowledged as valid only when properly understood after, and in light of, the resurrection. Continuity with the tradition is provided by the private revelation of the risen Lord to James and Peter, which identifies Jesus' teaching after the resurrection with what he had said "many times" prior to it (*Ap. Jas.* 8.30–33; 13.36–14.4).[117] Here, too, the technical reference to speaking formerly "in parables" and now "openly" is used to locate the hermeneutical disclosure of Jesus' words as "riddles" whose interpretation is finally being "resolved":[118]

Ap. Jas. 7.1–6:

> I first spoke with you (pl.) in parables (ϩⲛ̄ ϩⲙ̄ⲡⲁⲣⲁⲃⲟⲗⲏ),
> and you did not understand (ⲛⲉⲣⲉⲧⲛ̄ⲣ ⲛⲟⲉⲓ ⲉⲛ).
> Now, in turn, I speak with you openly ([ϩ] ⲛ̣̄ ⲟⲩⲱⲛϩ̄ ⲁⲃⲁⲗ),
> and you do not perceive (ⲛ̄ⲧⲉ̣ⲧ̣ⲛ̄ⲣ ⲁⲓⲥⲑⲁⲛⲉ ⲉⲛ).

Unlike the gospels of the NT, however, the *Ap. Jas.* does not attempt to produce a "life" of Jesus in which to situate the event of interpretation, but chooses instead to maintain a post-resurrection setting in giving its account of the "remembered" words of Jesus:

Ap. Jas. 12.31–13.1:

> As long as I am with you (pl.), give heed to me and obey me. But when I am to depart from you, remember me (ⲉⲣⲓ ⲡⲁⲙⲉⲉⲩⲉ). And remember me (ⲉⲣⲓ ⲡⲁⲙⲉⲉⲩⲉ) because I was with you without your knowing me (ⲙ̄ⲡⲉⲧⲛ̄ⲥⲟⲩⲱⲛⲧ). Blessed are those who have known me (ⲛⲉⲛⲧⲁϩⲥⲟⲩⲱⲛⲧ̄). Woe to those who have heard (ⲛ̄ⲛⲉⲉⲓ ⲛ̄ⲧⲁϩⲥⲱⲧⲙ̄) and have not believed (ⲙⲡⲟⲩⲣ̄ ⲡⲓⲥⲧⲉⲩⲉ)! Blessed are those who have not seen (ⲛⲉⲧⲉ ⲙ̄ⲡⲟⲩⲛⲉⲩ) [but] have [had faith] (ⲁⲩ̣[ⲛⲁϩⲧⲉ]).

[115]Koester, *Introduction*, 2. 191.

[116]Robinson, "Easter to Valentinus," 37. See Paul Schubert, "The Structure and Significance of Luke 24," in Walther Eltester, ed., *Neutestamentliche Studien für Rudolf Bultmann* (BZNW 21; Berlin: Töpelmann, 1954) 165–86.

[117]Cf. *Ep. Pet. Phil.* 135.3–8; and *Apoc. Pet.* (NHC 7, 3) 72.9–26.

[118]See esp. Robinson, "Gnosticism and the New Testament," 132–43.

The sayings traditions in the *Ap. Jas.* are thus inserted into an account of a post-resurrection appearance of Jesus (2.7–39), and, in turn, embedded within the frame of a letter (1.1–2.7; cf. 16.12–30). The proem of this "letter" is highly stylized, exhibiting the same rhetorical features that were observed in the fragments of Papias: a bipartite formal structure, the repetition of words and phrases, and the balancing of antitheses. Its schematization can be clearly seen in the citation below; words and phrases which indicate the rhetorical workmanship will be given in parentheses in Coptic. This will serve to highlight its similarities with the prologues of Papias (Eus. *Hist. eccl.* 3.39.3–4), the anti-Montanist Anonymous (Eus. *Hist. eccl.* 5.16.3–5), and Melito of Sardis (Eus. *Hist. eccl.* 4.26.13–14):

Ap. Jas. 1.8–2.7:

Since you (sing.) asked (ⲁⲕⲣ̄ ⲁⲝⲓⲟⲩ) me to send (ⲁⲧⲣⲁⲧⲛ̄ⲛⲁⲩ) you a secret book (ⲛ̄ⲟⲩⲁⲡⲟⲕⲣⲩⲫⲟ[ⲛ]) <which> was revealed (ⲉⲁⲩϭⲁⲗⲡ̄<ϥ> ⲁⲃⲁⲗ) to me and Peter by the Lord, I could neither refuse you nor (ⲟⲩⲧⲉ) speak (directly) to you, but (ⲇⲉ) [I have written] it ([ⲁϩⲓⲥⲁ]ϩϥ̄) in Hebrew letters (ϩⲛ̄ ϩⲉⲛⲥϩⲉⲉⲓ ⲙⲙⲛ̣̄ⲧϩⲉⲃⲣⲁⲓⲟⲥ) and have sent it (ⲁϩⲓ̈ⲧⲛ̄ⲛⲁⲟⲩϥ) to you—and to you alone. But inasmuch as you are a minister of the salvation (ⲙ̄ⲡⲟⲩϫⲉⲉⲓ̈) of the saints, endeavor earnestly and take care not to recount (ⲁⲧⲙ̄ϫⲟⲩ) this book (ⲙ̄ⲡⲓϫⲱⲙⲉ) to many (ⲁϩⲁϩ)—this which the Savior did not desire [to] recount ([ⲁ]ϫⲟⲟϥ) to all of us, his twelve disciples (ⲙ̄ⲙⲁⲑⲏⲧⲏⲥ). But blessed are those who will be saved (ⲛⲉⲧⲛⲁⲟⲩϫⲉⲉⲓ) through faith (ⲧⲡⲓⲥⲧⲓⲥ) in this discourse (ⲙ̄ⲡⲓⲗⲟⲅⲟⲥ).

Now I sent (ⲁϩⲓ̈ⲧⲛ̄ⲛⲁⲩ) you ten months ago another secret book (ⲛ̄ⲕⲉⲁⲡⲟⲕⲣⲩⲫⲟⲛ) which the Savior revealed (ⲉⲁϥϭⲁⲗⲡϥ̄ ⲁⲃⲁⲗ) to me. But that one you are to regard in this manner, as revealed (ⲛ̄ⲧⲁϩⲟⲩϭⲁⲗⲡϥ̄) to me, James. And this one, [. . . revealed ([ⲛ]ⲧⲁϩⲟ̣[ⲩ]ϭ̣ⲁⲗⲡ̣[ϥ]) . . .] those who [. . .], therefore, and seek [. . .] thus also [. . .] salvation ([ⲟⲩ]ϫⲉⲉⲓ) and [. . .].

Like the prologue of Papias, this letter frame serves to preface the body of "remembered" discourse and dialogue in the *Ap. Jas.* Both proems are written in the first person singular, appeal to individual disciples as special recipients of the revelation and authoritative witnesses of the tradition, and distinguish between oral and written stages of its transmission. The fact that the *Ap. Jas.* is alleged to have been written "in Hebrew," when it is manifestly an originally Greek document, is intended to locate this text in the earliest stages of the tradition. In this respect, the *Ap. Jas.* is to be compared with Papias's statement that the Gospel of Matthew was composed "in Hebrew." In both cases, this reference is meant to guarantee the authority and secure the reliability of their respective gospel texts.

It is immediately following this proem, in the scene which opens the account of Jesus' post-resurrection appearance (2.7–39), that the *Ap. Jas.* describes the situation in which scribal activity was taking place. In this scene (2.7–16), the technical term of "remembering" (ⲉⲩⲉⲓⲣⲉ ⲙ̄ⲡⲙⲉⲉⲩⲉ) is used in a programmatic way to introduce those sayings which compose the body of discourse and dialogue in the *Ap. Jas.* The hermeneutical moment of "remembering what the Savior had said . . . , whether secretly or openly" (ⲉⲓⲧⲉ ⲙ̄ⲡⲉⲧⲑⲏⲡ ⲉⲓⲧⲉ ⲙ̄ⲡⲉⲧⲟⲩⲁⲛϩ̄ ⲁⲃⲁⲗ [2.10–14]), is disclosed when "the Savior appeared (ⲁϥⲟⲩⲱⲛϩ̣̄ ⲁ̣ⲃ̣[ⲁⲗ]), . . . five hundred and fifty days after he arose from the dead" (2.17–21). The manifestation of the "openness" (ⲟⲩⲱⲛϩ̄ ⲁⲃⲁⲗ [2.13–14; 7.5]) of Jesus' teaching, therefore, is simultaneous with the "appearing" (ⲟⲩⲱⲛϩ̄ ⲁⲃⲁⲗ [2.17]) of the risen Lord. This suggests that the "parables" of the past are perceived to be yielding their "resolution" in and as a result of Jesus' resurrection. Accordingly, the term "remembering" is understood here as the introduction to a collection of "secret sayings"[119] of Jesus, and is used to refer to the composition of these sayings in "secret books," of which the *Ap. Jas.* is one.

The use of the technical term of "remembering" the words of Jesus, therefore, is an important clue both to the identification of the sources of the traditions in the *Ap. Jas.* and to the date and nature of its composition. Our analysis has shown that this term was regularly employed in the early church to introduce collections of sayings of Jesus, both oral and written, that date from a time in which sayings traditions were not yet restricted to the written gospels of the NT. The evidence of the use of this term to refer to the composition of written documents, moreover, likewise dates from this same time, that is, from the end of the first century to the middle of the second. The testimony of Papias demonstrates that appeals of authority were made to certain individual figures of the past in order to guarantee the transmission and legitimate

[119]Cf. Mark 4:2–34; *Gos. Thom.* 1: 32.12–14; and see Robinson, "LOGOI SOPHON," 92–95. Cf. vestiges of this tradition in *Gos. Mary* 10.4–6: ϫⲱ ⲛⲁⲛ ⲛ̄ⲛ̄ϣⲁϫⲉ ⲙ̄ⲡⲥⲱ(ⲧⲏ)ⲣ ⲉⲧⲉⲉⲓⲣⲉ ⲙⲡⲉⲩⲙⲉⲉⲩⲉ ⲛⲁϊ ⲉⲧⲉⲥⲟⲟⲩⲛ ⲙ̄ⲙⲟⲟⲩ ⲛ̄ⲛⲁⲛⲟⲛ ⲁⲛ ⲟⲩⲇⲉ ⲙⲡⲛ̄ⲥⲟⲧⲙ̀ⲟ̓ⲩ ("tell us the words of the Savior which you [fem. sing.] remember, which you know [but] we do not, nor have we heard them"); and *1 Apoc. Jas.* 30.7–8: ⲁⲣⲓ ⲡⲙⲉⲉⲩⲉ ⲛ̄ⲛⲉⲛⲧⲁϊϫⲟⲟⲩ ("remember the things which I have said").

the interpretation of such sayings traditions. The *Ap. Jas.*'s appeal to James (and, to a lesser degree, Peter) locates the source of authority with a disciple of Jesus in a debate over sayings of Jesus.

By the time of Irenaeus, near the end of the second century, the process of bringing independent sayings traditions into conformity with the NT "scriptures" was well under way. It is likely, then, that the collection and composition of the sayings traditions in the *Ap. Jas.* date from a time prior to Irenaeus. The *Ap. Jas.*'s programmatic employment of "remembering"—a term which Irenaeus does not use technically[120]—to describe its critical process of producing and reproducing sayings of Jesus suggests that this took place between the end of the first and middle of the second century. Attempts to date the *Ap. Jas.* early in the third century, in response to "a developing orthodox consensus about tradition, creed and canonical scripture such as is reflected in Irenaeus's *Adversus haereses,*"[121] would seem to be misguided. In fact, precisely the opposite historical reconstruction is far more likely to be the case: the *Ap. Jas.* is to be judged among the predecessors of Irenaeus.

Irenaeus is clearly writing to counter the claims of authority made by certain Gnostic "heretics"; in his defense of the four gospels of the NT, Irenaeus (*Adv. haer.* 3.11.9) explicitly attacks such writings as the noncanonical *Gospel of Truth.* The alleged parallels between the *Ap. Jas.* and Irenaeus suggest not that the *Ap. Jas.* was written in a context in which "the four gospel canon seems to be a given,"[122] but rather that Irenaeus was attempting to make a critique of the well-attested tradition, both within and without the NT, that the authority of the sayings tradition is not reducible to a single written word. The *Ap. Jas.*'s freedom in the use of sayings, the role given to James and Peter as

[120]The Latin equivalent of μνημονεύειν (= *meminisse*) is used in Irenaeus to mean "to quote" or "to (re)cite" a passage from a written Gospel text: *Adv. haer.* 2.22.3; 4.10.1; and 5.21.2 (quoting John 2:23; 5:39–40; and Luke 4:6–7, respectively); cf. *commemoratus est* in 4.2.3 (quoting John 5:46–47). Cf. Just. *1 Apol.* 14.4; and see Grant, *Earliest Lives,* 120. Against Johannes Weiss, *Das älteste Evangelium* (Göttingen: Vandenhoeck & Ruprecht, 1903) 8 n. 1. Note that Irenaeus does not engage in the critical process of "remembering" the words of Jesus. Neither do his successors. In terms of the history of the genre of sayings collections, the activity of production and reproduction (i.e., creating, collecting, composing, and transmitting the tradition) of sayings of Jesus was not cultivated in the third century. Sayings collections deriving from the oral tradition had indeed become pressed into the service of the written gospels of the NT.

[121]As asserted by Pheme Perkins, "Johannine Traditions in *Ap. Jas.* (NHC I, *2*)," *JBL* 101 (1982) 403.

[122]As Perkins ("Johannine Traditions", 413) maintains. The very fact that Irenaeus has to argue so vigorously for his position shows that it was not a "given."

authority figures in the transmission of the tradition, and the use of the technical term of "remembering" strongly suggest that the composition of this noncanonical gospel dates from the first half of the second century, when "the memory of Jesus was alive in the traditions of worshiping communities which produced and preserved sayings in Jesus' name."[123]

[123]Cameron, "Introduction," in *Other Gospels*, 15.

CONCLUSION

With the recent discovery and publication of the *Ap. Jas.* from Nag Hammadi, the spectrum of early Christian literature about Jesus has been significantly expanded. The use of sayings traditions in the composition of this document affords us the opportunity to raise anew the question of the forms and genres in which Jesus traditions were transmitted. The *Ap. Jas.* states explicitly that it is providing a written record of those sayings which Jesus revealed privately to James and Peter. Only some of these sayings are also found in the NT. The *Ap. Jas.* is thus a source of as well as witness to the development of sayings traditions. This monograph has endeavored to analyze the *Ap. Jas.* form-critically in order to clarify the ways in which sayings of Jesus were used and transformed in early Christian communities: how they were produced, collected, edited, and used to compose discourses and dialogues. In this concluding chapter I shall summarize my arguments and assess their implications for our understanding of the origins and developments of gospel literature.

Beginning inductively with a formal analysis of select portions of the text, the first main chapter sought to isolate and examine originally discrete sayings which were used to construct a discourse of Jesus in the second half of the *Ap. Jas.* Three formal traditions are representative of the discourse portion of the text: similes, prophecies, and wisdom sayings. Since it is widely held that similes and parables are among the most distinctive forms of the sayings-of-Jesus tradition, the three similes in the *Ap. Jas.* were considered first. Each is form-critically discrete, secondarily allegorized, and previously unattested.

The simile of the Ear of Grain (12.22–27) is formally and materially comparable with other agricultural similes and parables that derive from the earliest stages of the Jesus tradition. Since it displays no source-critical or redaction-critical dependence on the NT or other early Christian literature, and betrays no influence of the language of the early church, it is to be judged as an independent, primary source of the sayings-of-Jesus tradition. The simile of the Grain of Wheat (8.16–23), on the other hand, has been so completely revised to correspond to the catalogue of characteristics of the Word, to which it is attached, that its original form and meaning are virtually irrecoverable. There is little reason to think that this simile derives from the earliest stages of the Jesus tradition. It seems rather to provide material evidence for the early Christian practice of producing similes, parables, and allegories in Jesus' name.

The simile of the Date-Palm Shoot (7.24–28) is by far the most difficult of the three, with a complex formal and textual history within an established tradition of plant-lore. The date-palm evokes the figure of a proverbial, prolific plant which can thrive yet strangely wither, mysteriously perish yet be immortal. The conflicting images of infertility and abundance intimate that the Date-Palm Shoot is a fragment of one or more similes that has been expanded internally. As originally conceived, the situation in the simile was utterly negative; it emphasized the premature loss of fruit, on account of the temporary infertility of the tree. The application, on the other hand, describes precisely the opposite situation: a rich harvest. The simile itself is form-critically isolable and could be very old. The present edition of the text, however, is clearly the work of a later generation, which seems to have understood the tradition allegorically and employed it self-critically. In all three similes, the similarities of language and style in the secondary frames which introduce and conclude each simile suggest that these frames have been composed by the same circle, which seems to be closely related to the final stages of editing the entire *Ap. Jas.*

The second section of this chapter dealt with the formal analysis of a prophecy of judgment (9.24–10.6). This prophecy is part of a long and rich tradition in Judaism and early Christianity that regarded pronouncements of the prophets as divinely commissioned announcements of God's threats and reproaches. Previously unattested, this saying bears witness to the practice of producing prophetic sayings in the name of the Lord. The statements that the accused failed "to speak" and sinned against the "spirit" indicate that the spirit was understood as the spirit of prophecy, and that possession of the spirit was thought to empower one to prophesy. The implication of its legal and liturgical provenance is that participation in the Kingdom requires prophetic certification, which is understood to be properly localized in the James community. Parallels with those Christian prophetic sayings of the Jesus tradition that have been embedded in the letters of Paul and the

Synoptic Sayings Source Q suggest an early date for the production and circulation of this utterance in the name of the Lord.

The final section of this chapter dealt with the pericope (12.31–13.1)that contains the closest parallel in the *Ap. Jas.* with any saying found in the NT. This passage is a mixed form, a combination of a fragmentary wisdom speech and a collection of prophetic sayings that have been molded into a discourse of a departing revealer. Neither portion of this composite piece has an original connection with Jesus. The fragment of the farewell speech of Wisdom may reflect a version of an early tradition that Wisdom had been totally rejected, had found no habitation on earth. The woe and blessing which conclude this passage make no reference to the "I" of the speaker, but concern a prophetic response to faith in the revealed word. Comparison with the macarism that climaxes the Gospel of John demonstrates that the *Ap. Jas.* is not dependent on the NT for its tradition, but preserves this saying independently of John, in a less-redacted form, as part of a collection of sayings which are used to construct a discourse of Jesus.

The second main chapter sought to isolate and examine the use of sayings to compose dialogues of Jesus in the first half of the *Ap. Jas.* Form-critical analysis enabled us to identify elements of tradition and redaction, demonstrating that originally discrete sayings were used to compose three of these dialogues. In the dialogue in *Ap. Jas.* 2.21–35, questions and comments of the disciples have been constructed out of sayings that were formulated as answers of Jesus. This dialogue is based on two traditional sayings which are quoted and reformulated to construct a dialogue. The first saying (2.24–25), which speaks of going to the place from which one has come, has its *Sitz im Leben* in esoteric teaching within a wisdom-school tradition. The second saying (2.29–33) is a prophetic pronouncement which originally spoke of entering the Kingdom at the Lord's bidding. The editor's addition of the positive causal qualification of the protasis has transformed the original meaning of this saying to state, instead, that one can enter the Kingdom only if one is full. Through the repetition of the catchwords "go," "come," and "bid," a dialogue has been constructed: the questions and comments of the disciples are corrected by redacted sayings of Jesus. One traditional saying thus functions to interpret another. Jesus' call of James and Peter constitutes an invitation to esoteric instruction. With this scene, the frame of the post-resurrection appearance of Jesus is brought to a conclusion. The dialogue in *Ap. Jas.* 2.21–35 thus sets the stage for Jesus' private revelation to James and Peter, which makes up the body of the text.

The dialogue in *Ap. Jas.* 4.22–37 is also constructed out of two traditional sayings. In both instances, these have been attributed to James; it is Jesus' response which is the editorial product. The first (4.25–28) is a fragment of a saying found in the triple tradition in the Synoptic Gospels. This saying seems to have been formulated as a general rule of the community, perhaps among itinerant Christian prophets. The second (4.28–31) is a fragment of the final two petitions of the longer version of the Lord's prayer. The *Ap. Jas.*'s reference to the "wicked devil" shows that it contains a portion of the tradition that is not found in the Gospel of Luke. In presenting this saying as a petition of James on behalf of his community, the *Ap. Jas.* continues the "Christianization" of the tradition, which has made Jesus' prayer into a model prayer of the community.

The dialogue in *Ap. Jas.* 5.31–6.11 illustrates how creedal formulas have been used to create sayings of Jesus. The Amen-saying in *Ap. Jas.* 6.2–7, with its reference to believing in Jesus' cross, is clearly a product of the early church. It is striking that this creed refers only to the cross, not to Jesus' vindication in his resurrection and/or exaltation and ascension. Evidence of tradition in the composition of this dialogue is furnished by the *Ap. Jas.*'s utilization of the fixed pattern of a teaching of Jesus about his death, a misunderstanding of a disciple, and a correction by Jesus. This is a variant of the tradition of Jesus' predictions of the passion, which is incorporated in programmatic passages in the Synoptics and John to anticipate the passion and give structure to their narratives. In the *Ap. Jas.*, this tradition is used to create a dialogue between Jesus and James. The insertion of the Amen-saying within the frame of two exhortations of Jesus shows that the tradition is no longer used for creedal recitation, but for community parenesis.

The third main chapter sought to examine the *Ap. Jas.*'s reference to "remembering" the words of Jesus. This term was employed technically in the early church to describe the process of creating, collecting, and transmitting sayings of Jesus. The use of "remembering" in *1 Clement* and the book of Acts demonstrates that the formulaic employment of this term to introduce collections of sayings of Jesus is a practice which began with the relatively free production of sayings traditions and which continued, despite the existence of written gospels, without restriction to the gospels of the NT. The extant fragments of Papias attest to the use of this term to describe the transmission and interpretation of both oral and written sayings traditions. Whereas formerly the authority of Jesus alone had been considered sufficient for the transmission of the tradition, it was now deemed necessary to guarantee this authority by establishing the legitimacy of its transmission. Accordingly, Papias was obliged to defend the genuineness of his own "remembrances" of the sayings of Jesus by testing the accuracy of what was said by the trustworthiness of the person(s) who transmitted it.

When seeking to defend the Gospel of Mark from attack, Papias centers his apology on the alleged relationship of Mark and Peter. The Gospel of Mark is purported to comprise the full and final account of the "remembrances" of Peter. Papias's mentioning of Mark, identified as the interpreter of Peter, locates the source of authority with a disciple of Jesus in a debate over sayings of Jesus. Once again, the technical term of "remembering" is used to describe the process of collecting, composing, and transmitting traditions of and from Jesus. The fragmentary excerpt about Matthew serves to contrast the compositional technique of Mark, who did not make an orderly arrangement of his materials, with that of Matthew, who did. It also distinguishes their respective roles in the history of the transmission of the tradition.

John's use of the technical term of "remembering" to distinguish between the incomprehensible ministry of the earthly Jesus and the post-resurrection period of understanding the work and words of Jesus must be seen as a key hermeneutical principle in the production and composition of his written Gospel text. Like John, the *Ap. Jas.* also recognizes the cross and resurrection as the decisive moment of interpretation. Unlike John and the other gospels of the NT, however, the *Ap. Jas.* does not attempt to produce a "life" of Jesus in which to situate the event of interpretation, but chooses instead to maintain a post-resurrection setting in giving an account of its "remembered" words of Jesus. The opening scene of the *Ap. Jas.* describes a situation in which scribal activity was taking place. In this scene, the technical term of "remembering" is used in a programmatic way to introduce those sayings which compose the body of discourse and dialogue in the *Ap. Jas.* The hermeneutical moment of "remembering" what the Savior had said is disclosed when the Savior appeared; the manifestation of the "openness" of Jesus' teaching, therefore, is simultaneous with the "appearing" of the risen Lord. Accordingly, the term "remembering" is understood here as the introduction to a collection of "secret sayings" of Jesus, and is used to refer to the composition of these sayings in "secret books," of which the *Ap. Jas.* is one.

The practice of using the technical term of "remembering" to refer to collections of sayings of Jesus came to an end shortly after the time of Papias. With the final discontinuation of the oral transmission of Jesus' sayings, the *Sitz im Leben* of the genre *Logoi Sophon* was gone.

By the time of Irenaeus, and the pressures of his so-called fourfold gospel canon, the words of Jesus were "remembered" no more. It is likely, therefore, that the collection and composition of the sayings traditions in the *Ap. Jas.* date from a time prior to Irenaeus. The *Ap. Jas.*'s freedom in the use of sayings, the role given to James and Peter as authority figures in the transmission of the tradition, and the use of the technical term of "remembering" strongly suggest that the composition of this noncanonical gospel dates from the first half of the second century, when the memory of Jesus was alive in the traditions of worshiping communities which produced and preserved sayings in Jesus' name.

This investigation of the sayings traditions in the *Ap. Jas.* suggests that the *Ap. Jas.* is based on independent sayings collections that were contemporary with other early Christian writings which presented sayings of Jesus. The *Ap. Jas.*'s explicit statement that it is providing a written record of (some of) Jesus' sayings must be taken seriously. By isolating traditional sayings intertwined in the *Ap. Jas.*'s account of Jesus' revelation to James and Peter, one can identify its use of sources and delineate the history of the transmission of its traditions. Including this document in the group of texts acknowledged as primary sources of the sayings-of-Jesus tradition will enable us to come to a more precise understanding of the historical developments of gospel literature. Analysis of the *Ap. Jas.*'s use of sayings to compose discourses and dialogues of Jesus has particularly important consequences for our understanding of the compositional history of writings such as the Gospel of John, since it is clear that John has also incorporated originally discrete sayings into the production of elaborate dialogues of Jesus in the first half of the Gospel as well as his extended farewell discourse in the second half.

It is curious that, though the *Ap. Jas.* states that the special revelation of Jesus was given to James and Peter alone, inasmuch as Jesus did not wish to reveal it to all of the twelve disciples, the content of this revelation is generally not arcane. However, the juxtaposition of public and private teaching seems to be inherent within all written traditions about Jesus. It has been suggested that the hermeneutical presupposition of traditions of the sayings of Jesus is the motif of secrecy. The *Gospel of Thomas* states this explicitly. The Gospel of Mark intimates this in its use of the term "parable" as a "riddle" in need of interpretation. By "parable" Mark refers not just to individual similes of Jesus; the entire teaching ministry of Jesus is subsumed under this notion. The Gospel of John, moreover, distinguishes between the incomprehensible ministry of the earthly Jesus and the post-resurrection period of understanding the work and words of Jesus. This functions literarily in John's twofold division of his Gospel into the public and private ministry of Jesus.

This monograph has shown that the *Ap. Jas.* comprises a private revelation of Jesus, composed largely of sayings, which has been secondarily inserted into a post-resurrection account and embedded within the frame of a letter. Continuity with the tradition is provided by the revelation of the risen Lord to James and Peter, which identifies Jesus' teaching after the resurrection with what he had said many times prior to it. Here, too, the technical reference to speaking formerly "in parables" and now "openly" is used to locate the hermeneutical disclosure of Jesus' words as "riddles" whose interpretation is finally being "resolved." The *Ap. Jas.* is, therefore, an important source of as well as witness to the origins and developments of sayings traditions. The historical clue to its place in this development is the use of the technical term of "remembering" the words of Jesus. The hermeneutical clue is the motif of secrecy. The literary clue is the use of "parables" in the composition of discourses and dialogues. The *Ap. Jas.* asserts its role in the sayings tradition as critical production and reproduction. Recognizing the importance of this document in the spectrum of early Christian literature means that the Synoptic Gospels of the NT can no longer be regarded as unique or sufficient for understanding the trajectory of the Jesus tradition. The "Synoptic problem" must now be seen as a gospels problem.

SELECT BIBLIOGRAPHY OF TEXTS CITED

Adriaen, M.
S. Hieronymi presbyteri opera I/2: Commentariorum in Esaiam libri I–XI (CChr 73; Turnhout: Brepols, 1963).

Allberry, C. R. C.
A Manichaean Psalm-Book, Part II (Stuttgart: Kohlhammer, 1938).

Attridge, Harold W.
Nag Hammadi Codex I (The Jung Codex) (NHS; Leiden: Brill, forthcoming).

Bensly, Robert L.
The Fourth Book of Ezra (Texts and Studies 3/2; Cambridge: Cambridge University Press, 1895; Liechtenstein: Kraus, 1967).

Blanc, Cécile
Origène: Commentaire sur Saint Jean, vol. 2 (SC 157; Paris: Editions du Cerf, 1970).

Buffière, Félix
Anthologie grecque, vol. 12 (13 vols.; Paris: Société d'Edition "Les Belles Lettres," 1970).

Cameron, Ron, and Dewey, Arthur J.
The Cologne Mani Codex (P. Colon. inv. nr. 4780) "Concerning the Origin of his Body" (SBLTT 15; Missoula: Scholars, 1979).

Charles, R. H.
The Ascension of Isaiah (London: Black, 1900).

Charlesworth, James Hamilton
The Odes of Solomon: The Syriac Texts (SBLTT 13; Missoula: Scholars, 1977).

Idem
Old Testament Pseudepigrapha, vol. 1: *Apocalyptic Literature and Testaments* (Garden City: Doubleday, 1983).

Cohn, Leopold, and Wendland, Paul
Philonis Alexandrini opera quae supersunt (7 vols.; Berlin: Reimer, 1896–1930).

Conybeare, F. C.; Harris, J. Rendel; and Lewis, Agnes Smith
The Story of Aḥiḳar (2d ed.; Cambridge: Cambridge University Press, 1913).

Crouzel, Henri, and Simonetti, Manlio
Origène: Traité des principes, vol. 1 (SC 252; Paris: Editions du Cerf, 1978).

De Jonge, M.
The Testaments of the Twelve Patriarchs (PVTG; Leiden: Brill, 1978).

Epstein, I.
The Babylonian Talmud: Seder Neziḳin (London: Soncino, 1935).

Idem
*The Babylonian Talmud: Seder Zera*ʿim (London: Soncino, 1948).

Ernout, A.
Pline l'ancien: Histoire naturelle, vol. 13 (37 vols.; Paris: Société d'Edition "Les Belles Lettres," 1956).

Evans, Ernest
Tertullian: Adversus Marcionem (2 vols.; Oxford Early Christian Texts; Oxford: Clarendon, 1972).

Idem
Tertullian's Treatise on the Resurrection (London: SPCK, 1960).

The Facsimile Edition of the Nag Hammadi Codices: Codices I–XIII (Leiden: Brill, 1972–77).

Freedman, H., and Simon, Maurice
Midrash Rabbah I: Genesis, vol. 1 (10 vols.; London: Soncino, 1939).

Funk, F. X., and Bihlmeyer, Karl
Die Apostolischen Väter (SAQ 2/1/1; 3d ed.; rev. Wilhelm Schneemelcher; Tübingen: Mohr-Siebeck, 1970).

Girod, Robert
Origène: Commentaire sur l'Evangile selon Matthieu, vol. 1 (SC 162; Paris: Editions du Cerf, 1970).

Goodspeed, Edgar J.
Die ältesten Apologeten (Göttingen: Vandenhoeck & Ruprecht, 1914).

Grant, Robert M.
Theophilus of Antioch: Ad Autolycum (Oxford Early Christian Texts; Oxford: Clarendon, 1970).

Hall, Stuart George
Melito of Sardis: On Pascha and Fragments (Oxford Early Christian Texts; Oxford: Clarendon, 1979).

Harnack, Adolf von
Marcion: Das Evangelium vom fremden Gott (TU 45; 2d ed.; Leipzig: Hinrichs, 1924).

Hartel, Wilhelm
S. Thasci Caecili Cypriani opera omnia, 3/1 (CSEL; Vienna: Geroldi, 1868).

Harvey, W. Wigan
Sancti Irenaei episcopi Lugdunensis libros quinque adversus haereses (2 vols.; Cambridge: Typus academicus, 1857).

Hilberg, Isidore
Sancti Eusebii Hieronymi epistulae, Part II (CSEL 55; Vienna: Tempsky; Leipzig: Freytag, 1912).

Holl, Karl
Epiphanius (Ancoratus und Panarion), vols. 1–2 (3 vols.; GCS; Leipzig: Hinrichs, 1915–22).

[Horner, G.]
The Coptic Version of the New Testament in the Southern Dialect, otherwise called Sahidic and Thebaic (7 vols.; Oxford: Clarendon, 1911–24).

Hude, Karl
Herodoti historiae (2 vols.; Scriptorum classicorum bibliotheca oxoniensis; 3d ed.; Oxford: Clarendon, 1926).

Idem
Xenophontis commentarii (Bibliotheca scriptorum graecorum et romanorum teubneriana; 1934; reprint, Stuttgart: Teubner, 1969).

Jeremias, Joachim
Unknown Sayings of Jesus (2d ed.; London: SPCK, 1964).

Johnson, J. de M.; Martin, Victor; and Hunt, Arthur S.
Catalogue of the Greek Papyri in the John Rylands Library, Manchester (2 vols.; Manchester: Manchester University Press, 1915).

Joly, Robert
Hermas: Le Pasteur (SC 53; 2d ed.; Paris: Editions du Cerf, 1968).

Jones, Henry Stuart, and Powell, John Enoch
Thucydidis historiae, vol. 1 (2 vols.; Scriptorum classicorum bibliotheca oxoniensis; Oxford: Clarendon, 1942).

Kayser, C. L.
Flavii Philostrati opera (2 vols.; Bibliotheca scriptorum graecorum et romanorum teubneriana; Leipzig: Teubner, 1870–71; reprint, Hildesheim: Olms, 1964).

Knibb, Michael A.
The Ethiopic Book of Enoch (2 vols.; Oxford: Clarendon, 1978).

Krause, Martin, and Labib, Pahor
Die drei Versionen des Apokryphon des Johannes im koptischen Museum zu Alt-Kairo (Wiesbaden: Harrassowitz, 1962).

Labriolle, Pierre de
Tertullien: De praescriptione haereticorum (Textes et documents; Paris: Picard, 1907).

Layton, Bentley
The Gnostic Treatise on Resurrection from Nag Hammadi (HDR 12; Missoula: Scholars, 1979).

Idem
"The Hypostasis of the Archons," *HTR* 67 (1974) 351–425.

Idem
"The Hypostasis of the Archons (Conclusion)," *HTR* 69 (1976) 31–101.

Idem
Nag Hammadi Codex II: CG II, 2–II, 7 together with XIII, 2, Brit. Lib. Or.4926(1), and P. Oxy. 1, 654, 655* (NHS; Leiden: Brill, forthcoming).

Lefort, L. Th.
S. Pachomii vita bohairice scripta (CSCO 89/7; Louvain: Durbecq, 1953).

Lipsius, Richard Adelbert, and Bonnet, Maximilian
Acta apostolorum apocrypha (2 vols. in 3 parts; Leipzig: Mendelssohn, 1891–1903; reprint, Hildesheim: Olms, 1959).

Long, H. S.
Diogenis Laertii vitae philosophorum (2 vols.; Scriptorum classicorum bibliotheca oxoniensis; Oxford: Clarendon, 1964).

MacLeod, M. D.
Luciani opera, vols. 1 and 3 (4 vols.; Scriptorum classicorum bibliotheca oxoniensis; Oxford: Clarendon, 1972–80).

Malinine, Michel; Puech, Henri-Charles; Quispel, Gilles; Till, Walter; Kasser, Rodolphe; Wilson, R. McL.; and Zandee, Jan
Epistula Iacobi Apocrypha (Zurich/Stuttgart: Rascher, 1968).

Mara, M. G.
Evangile de Pierre (SC 201; Paris: Editions du Cerf, 1973).
Mayeda, Goro
Das Leben-Jesu-Fragment Papyrus Egerton 2 und seine Stellung in der urchristlichen Literaturgeschichte (Bern: Haupt, 1946).
Ménard, Jacques-E.
"L'Evangile selon Philippe" (Th.D. diss., University of Strasbourg, 1967).
Meyer, Marvin W.
The Letter of Peter to Philip (SBLDS 53; Chico: Scholars, 1981).
Migne, J.-P.
Didymi Alexandrini opera omnia, vol. 1 (PG 39; Paris: Migne, 1863).
Idem
Eusebii Pamphili, Caesareae Palaestinae episcopi, opera omnia quae exstant, vol. 6 (PG 24; Paris: Migne, 1857).
Idem
Sancti Eusebii Hieronymi Stridonensis presbyteri opera omnia, vol. 2 (PL 23; Paris: Garnier, 1883).
Nauck, August
Porphyrii philosophi platonici opuscula selecta (Bibliotheca scriptorum graecorum et romanorum teubneriana; Leipzig: Teubner, 1886).
Omar, Sayed
Das Archiv des Soterichos (P. Soterichos) (Papyrologica Coloniensia 8; Opladen: Westdeutscher Verlag, 1979).
Parrott, Douglas M.
Nag Hammadi Codices V,2–5 and VI with Papyrus Berolinensis 8502, 1 and 4 (NHS 11; Leiden: Brill, 1979).
Quispel, Gilles
Ptolémée: Lettre à Flora (SC 24; 2d ed.; Paris: Editions du Cerf, 1966).
Rehm, Bernhard
Die Pseudoklementinen I: Homilien (GCS; 2d ed.; rev. Franz Paschke; Berlin: Akademie-Verlag, 1969).
Idem
Die Pseudoklementinen II: Rekognitionen in Rufins Übersetzung (GCS; Berlin: Akademie-Verlag, 1965).
Resch, Alfred
Agrapha: Aussercanonische Schriftfragmente (TU 30/3–4; 2d ed.; Leipzig: Hinrichs, 1906).

Idem
Aussercanonische Paralleltexte zu den Evangelien (TU 10/3; Leipzig: Hinrichs, 1895).

Richardson, Ernest Cushing
Hieronymus: Liber de viris inlustribus (TU 14; Leipzig: Hinrichs, 1896).

Rivaud, Albert
Platon: Oeuvres complètes, vol. 10 (14 vols.; Paris: Société d'Edition "Les Belles Lettres," 1925).

Rousseau, Adelin, and Doutreleau, Louis
Irénée de Lyon: Contre les Hérésies, 3/2 (SC 211; Paris: Editions du Cerf, 1974).

Sanders, J. A.
The Psalms Scroll of Qumrân Cave 11 (DJD 4; Oxford: Clarendon, 1965).

Schmidt, Carl
The Books of Jeu and the Untitled Text in the Bruce Codex (NHS 13; trans. Violet MacDermot; Leiden: Brill, 1978).

Idem
Gespräche Jesu mit seinen Jüngern nach der Auferstehung (TU 43; Leipzig: Hinrichs, 1919; reprint, Hildesheim: Olms, 1967).

Idem
Pistis Sophia (NHS 9; trans. Violet MacDermot; Leiden: Brill, 1978).

Schmidtke, Alfred
Neue Fragmente und Untersuchungen zu den judenchristlichen Evangelien (TU 37/1; Leipzig: Hinrichs, 1911).

Schwartz, Eduard
Eusebius Werke: Die Kirchengeschichte (2 vols.; GCS; Leipzig: Hinrichs, 1903–8).

Seyfarth, Wolfgang
Ammiani Marcellini rerum gestarum libri qui supersunt, vol. 1 (2 vols.; Bibliotheca scriptorum graecorum et romanorum teubneriana; Leipzig: Teubner, 1978).

Smith, Morton
Clement of Alexandria and a Secret Gospel of Mark (Cambridge: Harvard University Press, 1973).

Stählin, Otto
Clemens Alexandrinus (2 vols.; GCS; Leipzig: Hinrichs, 1905–6).

Idem

Clemens Alexandrinus, vol. 3 (GCS; 2d ed. Ludwig Früchtel; Berlin: Akademie-Verlag, 1970).

Strycker, Emile de

La Forme la plus ancienne du Protévangile de Jacques (Subsidia hagiographica 33; Brussels: Société des Bollandistes, 1961).

Till, Walter C.

Die gnostischen Schriften des koptischen Papyrus Berolinensis 8502 (TU 60; 2d ed. Hans-Martin Schenke; Berlin: Akademie-Verlag, 1972).

Tischendorf, Constantin

Evangelia apocrypha (Editio altera; Leipzig: Mendelssohn, 1876).

Turner, John D.

The Book of Thomas the Contender from Codex II of the Cairo Gnostic Library from Nag Hammadi (CG II, 7) (SBLDS 23; Missoula: Scholars, 1975).

Usener, Hermann, and Radermacher, Ludwig

Dionysii Halicarnasei quae exstant, 5/1 (Bibliotheca scriptorum graecorum et romanorum teubneriana; Stuttgart: Teubner, 1965).

Vitelli, G.

Papiri greci e latini, volume primo (n.ⁱ 1–112) (3 vols.; Pubblicazioni della Società italiana; Florence: Ariani, 1912).

Waszink, J. H.

Quinti Septimi Florentis Tertulliani de anima (Amsterdam: Meulenhoff, 1947).

Wendland, Paul

Hippolytus Werke 3: Refutatio omnium haeresium (GCS; Leipzig: Hinrichs, 1916).

West, M. L.

Hesiod: Works and Days (Oxford: Clarendon, 1978).

Wimmer, Friedrich

Theophrasti Eresii opera quae supersunt omnia, vol. 1 (3 vols.; Leipzig: Teubner, 1854).

Winterbottom, M.

M. Fabi Quintiliani institutionis oratoriae libri duodecim, vol. 2 (Scriptorum classicorum bibliotheca oxoniensis; Oxford: Clarendon, 1970).

INDICES

The following list includes passages and authors material to the discussion.

1) PASSAGES

a) Old Testament and Apocrypha

b) Old Testament Pseudepigrapha and other Jewish Literature

c) New Testament

d) Early Christian Literature and the Ancient Church

e) Greek and Latin Authors

2) MODERN AUTHORS